Contributions to the History of Education

III

Pioneers of Modern Education

Pioneers of Modern Education

1600—1700

by

JOHN WILLIAM ADAMSON,

Professor of Education in the University of London

CAMBRIDGE:
at the University Press
1921

CAMBRIDGE UNIVERSITY PRESS
Cambridge, New York, Melbourne, Madrid, Cape Town,
Singapore, São Paulo, Delhi, Mexico City

Cambridge University Press
The Edinburgh Building, Cambridge CB2 8RU, UK

Published in the United States of America by Cambridge University Press, New York

www.cambridge.org
Information on this title: www.cambridge.org/9781107622272

First printed 1905
Second impression 1921
First published 1921
First paperback edition 2013

A catalogue record for this publication is available from the British Library

ISBN 978-1-107-62227-2 Paperback

PREFACE.

TO the objection that the current century is the twentieth, a writer who craves attention to a book on seventeenth-century education may very fairly reply that in his field at least there is no such incongruity between the two periods as the objection would insinuate. He might, it is true, either allege the general truth that the study of "origins" is often most fruitful in practical results, or he might base himself upon the particular assertion that the two centuries share in a peculiar manner. certain great tendencies of thought and action. But his best defence lies in pointing to the relationship, direct and unmistakeable, between the theory and practice of the modern school-room and the changes which were suggested or actually brought about by men who laboured in the earlier time. Not a few of the conceptions, small as well as great, which we are apt to consider characteristic of our own, or of the generation or two immediately senior to us, are but re-statements of principles and devices which took their earliest modern shape in that same seventeenth century.

For example, the wide recognition of Education as a social force, and the consequent expediency of state-provided systems of instruction, universal and compulsory, are commonly set down as nineteenth-century convictions. The attempt to include within the ordinary school-curriculum those branches of study which have been more especially advanced by scientific research is often spoken of as inspired solely by the progress which the Experimental Sciences have recently achieved; and, similarly, the spirit of an age pre-eminently commercial is credited with the introduction of modern languages into the same curriculum. Again, from different quarters comes the demand for a closer association between the tasks of the school-room and the every-day life outside its walls, that there may no longer exist "la disconvenance entre l'école et la vie" against which Taine protested. Amongst teachers themselves there is to-day an evident desire to attack the problems of method from a base more or less scientific, and, particularly, through a more discriminating study of the mental powers of children. With these reforms it is usual to connect the names of Rousseau, Pestalozzi, Froebel, Herbart and others who flourished during the eighteenth and nineteenth centuries; it is one purpose of this book to show how great was the share of the seventeenth century in formulating these and the like fundamental ideas of the pedagogy of our time.

The main theme is the introduction of "modern studies" into the school-course and the breaking-down of the monopoly vested, by force of circumstance and not always with express intention, in the ancient languages. Many causes, not all scholastic, conspired to overthrow that monopoly in the end; the following pages endeavour to set out the three most influential causes of the more directly scholastic kind which came into play during the period under consideration. The most potent was undoubtedly the "New Philosophy," to use the co-temporary phrase designating the beginnings of modern inductive science. Even more immediately operative was the desire for a type of instruction especially suitable to the courtier, the soldier, the diplomatist and the man of affairs, a desire which called into being the "Academies," schools, or colleges, French in origin, but by no means confined to French soil. The third influence in modernizing the studies of the school-room has not attained that general recognition which its importance deserves. During the last twenty years of the seventeenth century, movements in favour of popular education on the large scale took place in France, in Germany and in England; chiefly religious and moral in origin, they also reveal signs of the commercial and industrial motives which usually, in part, actuate proposals for educational change. The three movements attained different measures of success; but they made popular instruction possible at a later time and founded the traditional curriculum of the elementary school, while contributing to establish new studies in schools of a higher grade.

Of course, it is not asserted that the conception of State school-systems, etc., began *ab ovo* with Comenius and his contemporaries. The *Republic* of Plato alone is a sufficient confutation of such a thesis, were there no sign remaining of the world-wide educational activity of the Church. Moreover, while Plato was forgotten, or ignored, and Churchmen often took too restricted a view of what was educationally necessary, men contemporary, or almost so, with Comenius, anticipated him not only in the design of a popular organization of schools, but even in some of his projected reforms in both the matter and manner of instruction. Martin Luther, John Knox, Richard Mulcaster are names which readily occur to the mind. But the educational schemes of Luther and of Knox were not effectively realised in their own life-time, and Mulcaster, even to his fellow-countrymen, remained but a voice, and one not always listened to with pleasure.

Compared with these men, Comenius had two supreme advantages. He reached a much wider audience than did either Knox or Mulcaster, and, above all, he wrote in days when the educational system was ripe for reform and circumstances had begun to make reform possible. The publication of the *Advancement of Learning* and the *Novum Organum* gave a cogency to his pleas which had been wanting in the sixteenth century. The man's genius and character co-operated with

a 5

the state of affairs to make him in a very real sense the founder of modern pedagogy.

While much of the story gathers about the thought and activity of Comenius, there were also educational pioneers in England now forgotten, or, if not forgotten, remembered by reason of achievements in other fields. To these, and especially to Samuel Hartlib, a name which should be honoured by all friends of Education, some of the following chapters are devoted ; it is hoped that excerpts from their writings, no longer generally accessible, will not unduly tax the reader's patience. They speak a language expressing modes of thought nearer akin to our own than those natural to a Pestalozzi, a Froebel, or a Herbart ; and, expression apart, the characteristic "practicality" of these followers of Bacon ought to commend them to the national idiosyncrasy.

The book, however, aims at a wider survey than a purely English one ; and in the foreign section the writer has tried to indicate the great services (too seldom even named in text-books of educational history) which were rendered to the world by St Jean-Baptiste de la Salle. As a foil to the ideals of education or of instruction presented by the innovators, the actual practice of the seventeenth-century school-room, reformed and unreformed, is described on the authority of those who knew it at first hand. It is hoped that a full index, bibliography and tables of contents and of "dates" will increase the usefulness of the book to students of the history of Education.

August 1, 1905.

CONTENTS.

TABLE OF DATES

1617 The Fruchtbringende Gesellschaft *f.* by Ludwig of Anhalt-Köthen, Moritz of Hesse and others.
   Methodus Institutionis nova quadruplex of Rhenius and others.
1618 Outbreak of the Thirty Years' War.
   Ratke at Anhalt-Köthen.
   Collegium Mauritianum reconstituted.
   English translation of Napier's *Descriptio* (1614).
1619 Kepler's *Harmonice Mundi*: third Law announced.
   Harvey makes known his theory of the circulation of the blood.
1620 Bacon's *Novum Organum.*
   Drebbel's Thermometer.
   Simon Stevin *d.*
1621 Snell discovers the law of refraction of light.
1623 Bacon's *De Augmentis Scientiarum.*
1625 Nicole (*d.* 1695) *b.*
1626 Bacon *d.*
1627 Bacon's *New Atlantis* published.
1628–32 Comenius's *Didactica Magna.*
   Hartlib comes to London from Elbing.
   Harvey's *Exercitatio Anatomica de Motu Cordis.*
1630 Dury leaves Elbing.
   Deaths: Harvey, Kepler.
1631 Comenius's *Janua Linguarum Reserata.*
1632 Locke *b.* (*d.* 1704).
   Galileo before the Inquisition.
1635 Ratke *d.*
   Spener *b.*
   The *Académie Française f.*
   Boston (New England) Latin School, proposed foundation of.
1636 Harvard founds his college for the clergy.
1637 Descartes' *Discourse on Method.*
   Hartlib prints *Conatuum Comenianorum Praeludia*=Pro-dromus of 1639.
1638 Port-Royal education begins under Singlin and Lancelot.
   The Oratorian Académie Royale de Juilly *f.*
   Comenius publishes the *Conatuum Pansophicorum Diluci-datio* and begins a Latin version of the Great Didactic.

1638 Busby provisionally appointed at Westminster (*v.* 1640).

1639 Horrocks observes the transit of Venus.

1640 Ernest, Duke of Saxe-Gotha.

Richelieu founds an Academy at Richelieu.

The Earl of Arundel (in the House of Lords) moots the institution of an academy.

Busby appointed Head Master of Westminster: holds office till death in 1695. (See 1638.)

1641 Hartlib and Dury: *Briefe Relation*, etc.

House of Commons resolves to employ Church property for "the Advancement of Learning and Piety" (June 15). Comenius in London (Sep. 22 to June, 1642).

Hartlib: *Macaria*.

Andreas Reyher at the Gotha Gymnasium.

Salem Town's meeting decides to erect a Common School.

1642 Comenius and Hartlib: *A Reformation of Schooles*.

Duke Ernest and Reyher: *Schulmethodus*, followed by school-books.

The Seminary of St Sulpice *f.* by Olier.

Galileo *d.*

1643 Torricelli invents the Barometer.

1644 Charles at Oxford: Parliament orders the reform of Cambridge. Siege of York (April).

Milton: *Of Education* (June 5).

Marston Moor (July 2).

Evelyn in France.

1645 Meetings begin at Gresham College: whence Royal Society *f.*, 1662.

1646 The "Little Schools" of Port-Royal fully organized in Paris.

Dury: *Exercitation of Schooling*.

1647 Hartlib: *Considerations*, etc.

1648 Peace of Westphalia.

Petty: *The Advice of W. P.*, etc.

Hartlib: *A Continuation of Mr J. A. Comenius' School Endeavours*.

Cromwell suppresses the Welsh insurrection.

Death of the Jesuit, Calasanzio, founder of the Scuole Pie.

Nova Solyma.

1666 Démia begins a public school-system and trains teachers at Lyons (1666–79).

1667 Paris Observatory *f.*

1670 The Sisters of the Holy Child Jesus, a Rheims congregation, *f.*

1671 Comenius *d.* (*b.* 1592).
Westminster vestry teaches parish children.
Nicole: *Treatise on the Education of a Prince.*

1672 Thos. Gouge in S. Wales.

1673 Reyher *d.* at Gotha.

1675 Duke Ernest *d.*
Greenwich Observatory *f.*

1676 Francke at the Gotha Gymnasium.

1679 Nyel goes to Rheims.
Port-Royal girls' school dispersed.

1680 Dury *d.* (*b.* 1596).

1683 Foubert's Academy, London.

1684 Foundation of the Institute of the Brothers of the Christian Schools: Seminary, or training college, opened at Rheims.

1686 Madame de Maintenon founds Saint Cyr.

1687 Newton: *Principia.*
Fénelon: *Sur l'éducation de filles.*
Deaths: Petty, Nyel.

1688 De la Salle and the Institute go to Paris.
Thomasius lectures at Leipzig in *German.*

1689 Francke and Spener at Dresden.

1690 Locke: *Essay concerning Human Understanding.*
The Institute has 1000 pupils in four Parisian schools.

1691 Francke, Professor of Greek and Oriental Languages at Halle.

1693 Locke: *Some Thoughts concerning Education.*

1694 The Friedrich University of Halle *f.*
Francke opens the Poor School, Bürger-schule and Pädagogium.
Mary Astell: *Serious Proposal to the Ladies.*

1695 De la Salle: *La Conduite des Écoles* (about this time).
Francke's Orphanage.

1696 Seminarium Praeceptorum at Halle.

CHAPTER I.

THE NEW PHILOSOPHY.

THE closing years of the sixteenth century saw the completion (1599) by the Company of Jesus of their *Ratio Studiorum*, which, reaching its final shape after the laborious corrections dictated by fifteen years' experience, proved its framers to be without question the most efficient school-masters of their time. What the average school of the early seventeenth century was like a later chapter will show; for the very best exponents of their type of education we must turn to the Jesuit colleges. Their striking success was not the consequence of the formulation of new principles, nor of the employment of novel methods. On the contrary, the Society accepted the principles and methods which were generally held by their contemporaries; the schools of the Order differed from other schools in the superlative efficiency with which the current educational doctrines were applied to practice.

We must not, then, look to the Jesuit school-room if we would observe the genesis of those ideas of reform in education which are our subject; nor, indeed, shall we find it in any school-room. Reform and change are aspects of the actual thought of the moment; by the nature of the case, schools tend to busy themselves rather with what is regarded as permanent, that is, with the approved, established thought of the past, whether immediate or remote. To be a little

A. 1

"behind the times" makes for the stability of the school as for that of other institutions which go deep into social life.

We shall therefore, in the end, get closer to our subject and attain a better-proportioned view of it, if, turning for a moment from schools and ideas respecting education, we look out over a wider prospect, that intellectual life of the time from which school-reforms, as all other readjustments, were to spring.

In the early seventeenth century Scholasticism still maintained a precarious hold over the official life of the Church and of the Universities, and through these an even weaker grasp upon the schools. But with respect to the intellectual life and tendencies of the time as a whole, Scholasticism was a spent force. Whereas during the Middle Ages the disposition had been to see all Truth in a definite Theology, or in the system of thought which passed for Aristotle's, from the sixteenth century onwards contempt of the Schoolmen and of authority in things intellectual generally had become characteristic of an increasing number of men. The contempt was not always enlightened, and, therefore, was sometimes undeserved, for the newer men often flagrantly sinned, when judging their predecessors, by ignoring those very rules of enquiry and of verification which they so vehemently insisted upon in the field of their own particular studies. For them, Scholasticism chiefly meant an uncritical acceptance of principles enunciated by a few great thinkers, chief of whom was Aristotle, by which name was understood, not the preeminent philosopher revealed by more intelligent study to later times, but a partly fictitious personage, to whom much was attributed for which the real Aristotle was not responsible. The earlier revolt against authority in the religious sphere had now become an intellectual revolt in general; and, whether it is Ramus writing a new logic, or Campanella meditating a new philosophy, or Bruno fiercely inveighing against all establishments, religious, philosophic, or scientific, the note of revolt is common to all. It is true that the official guardians of orthodoxy burned Bruno, and gave Galileo no small trouble; but retaliation of this kind was an episode only in the struggle, not a decisive battle. Men had acquired new views of Truth, and they were securing command over new avenues of approach to her, so that, as William Harvey said, "They were not so bound to their instructress, Antiquity, that they must leave their friend, Truth, in the lurch, and desert her in the sight of all men."

What this new mode of regarding Truth promised to effect may be inferred from even an incomplete enumeration of discoveries made by its assistance before the expiration of the first quarter of the seventeenth century. In 1601 died Tycho Brahe, Professor of Astronomy *and Astrology* at Prague, whose observations were embodied in a series of tables, lunar, planetary and solar, which rendered very material service to subsequent enquirers. He was succeeded by his assistant, John Kepler, who in 1609 made known the first two laws of Planetary Motion called by his name, and ten years later published the third law. The conceptions expressed in these three laws and in the thesis of Copernicus (enunciated in 1543) revolutionised Astronomy and laid the foundations of the science as it is now pursued. Galileo, too, by his brilliant advocacy of the Copernican astronomy, had become a fellow-labourer with Kepler, while he had also established the science of Mechanics and extended the range of Pure Mathematics.

Simon Stevin of Bruges, who died in 1620, made contributions to the study of fortification and of such branches of applied mathematics as Mechanics and Hydrostatics. In 1586 he had published a booklet of some seven pages in Dutch, called "The Tenth, easily showing how all calculations in every-day affairs may be done in whole numbers, not broken into fractions." If this is not, as has been declared, "the invention of the decimal system," the book certainly brought that system into the range of ordinary lay knowledge and use.

It is interesting to note that the author confidently anticipated the adoption of a decimal coinage, weights, and measures. In 1614 Napier published his *Description of Logarithms*, thus making known a discovery of incalculable importance in almost every part of mathematical science.

These great steps of progress in mathematics and the sciences more especially allied to mathematics are matched by cotemporary discoveries in the natural and physical sciences. For example, the final year of the sixteenth century saw the birth of the science of Magnetism in the publication of William Gilbert's treatise "On the Magnet, Magnetic Bodies, and that Great Magnet, the Earth." The transition from ancient to modern science is signified by the invention of the microscope in 1608, of the telescope before 1610, and, in 1620, of a thermometer by Drebbel, an invention anticipated by Galileo in the air-thermometer. Galileo, indeed, was associated with the earliest forms of all three instruments; the exact date of the invention of the telescope and the name of its inventor are not matters on which authorities agree, but in 1610 the invention was certainly known to Galileo, who, constructing an improved instrument, discovered in that year the satellites of Jupiter, and later the rings of Saturn.

Again, the studies in Anatomy which Vesalius had commenced in the first half of the preceding century received their crown prior to 1628 in the discovery of the circulation of the blood by William Harvey. Before practising in London Harvey had been a student in the University of Padua, the scene of the much earlier professorial labours of Vesalius, whose intellectual heir he may, therefore, be deemed. Vesalius had been a persistent advocate and exponent of the method of observation and experiment, and as insistent a foe to the tradition which preferred the authority of Galen, the Aristotle of Medicine. His attitude was that of Galileo, Kepler, Gilbert, Harvey and the rest whose successes are so notable in the history of science during the seventeenth century. These men are prominent in that history; but many of their contemporaries' names are less well remembered whose contributions to knowledge belong to the common inheritance of the civilised world. There is, for example, Harriot, Sir Walter Raleigh's companion in America, who made maps illustrating the explorations in Virginia, who shares with Galileo the credit of discovering the satellites of Jupiter and the Sun-spots, and who made one of the most important contributions to the theory of algebraic equations. Mercator, the cartographer, was an elder contemporary of Harriot, who stands midway between him and van Helmont, the Flemish mystic, chemist, and physiologist, to whom we owe the term "gas." The word appeared in 1624; three years earlier the Dutchman Snell discovered the law of refraction of light.

The series is continued in the second quarter of the seventeenth century in the mathematical studies of Descartes, Fermat, and others, in the names of Horrocks, who first observed the transit of Venus in 1639, of Torricelli, who invented the barometer in 1643, of Pascal, who on the Puy de Dôme confirmed Torricelli's observations. More particularly germane to our subject are those meetings which, begun at Gresham College in 1645 and continued at Oxford, led to the foundation of the Royal Society in 1662; amongst the devotees of the New Philosophy who attended these scientific discussions in the earlier days were Boyle, Hooke, Wallis, Wilkins, Seth Ward, and William Petty. The close of the half-century was marked by the invention of the air-pump by Guericke of Magdeburg, and the construction of a second instrument by Boyle.

Even the foregoing meagre catalogue, incomplete as it is, suffices to show, by the number of scientific students mentioned, and their wide distribution over the countries of Europe, that during the period under consideration there was both a fairly general repudiation of the tradition which relied upon authority and a very considerable advance in many directions in the knowledge of natural forces and conditions.

His intellectual eminence notwithstanding, the share of Francis Bacon in this comparative wealth of scientific enquiry, discovery, and invention, was small. Possible charges of employing a merely carping criticism, or of a want of modesty in dealing with a name unquestionably great, must here be deprecated. Of Bacon's general position as thinker and writer it would be an altogether superfluous temerity to speak; the point was settled long ago. There is, however, a community of ideas between him and the educational reformer, Comenius, sufficiently great to justify the assertion that the latter must be regarded as the pupil of the English philosopher; in other words, Bacon has had a profound, albeit indirect, influence upon the history of education by way of Comenius. This community of ideas is, perhaps, most discernible in those matters of fact and of scientific method in which Bacon was most astray; as one would expect to find, if the relationship of the two men were that here assumed. The presentment of Bacon's scientific labours immediately following is, therefore, admittedly not complete, and its standpoint is determined by the particular exposition in view.

In the first place, Bacon's actual concrete achievements in science were and, in the circumstances, could only have been small, or even trifling. The great book (or, perhaps one ought to say, the great library) which he planned he did not complete; the span of even a long and untroubled life would probably not suffice to complete it. But we have the *Advancement of Learning* (1605), with its expansion, eighteen years later, in the *De Augmentis*, and the proudly named *Novum Organum* of 1620. These, with many smaller books and tractates, reveal to us the essentials, and more, of Bacon's science and philosophy. They show, too, that their author was, first and foremost, a rhetorician endowed with a most glowing imagination. Seizing the master-ideas of the time.

and recognising their ultimate possibilities as by a prophetic insight, his rhetorical powers made it easy for him to bring these ideas and visions clearly and convincingly before the minds of ordinary men. To do these things successfully argues no small claim to greatness; but the greatness is that of the fervid orator and prophet rather than that of the man of science. Many were then reaching conclusions or perfecting discoveries which men of a later time grew to consider especially Baconian; it was Bacon's function to give a voice to these thoughts, and an interpretation to these deeds, which they would otherwise have lacked outside the small republic of learned men. His enthusiasm for Natural Science, his tireless industry in her cause, his exceptional powers of imagination and of expression made him the poet, the prophet, and the journalist of the New Philosophy.

Yet he failed to interpret accurately either the methods or the aims of cotemporary students of science. So long as he remains in the region of general expressions he reflects the views of these investigators faithfully enough, as when in the opening lines of *Novum Organum* he insists that the true method of physical science must be one of experiment and observation: or again, when he asserts, in one form or another, the characteristic thought, that the aim of physical science is the improvement of man's material condition, "the relief of man's estate." Here, for example, is a passage from the first book of the *Advancement of Learning*; Bacon is speaking of the errors which have retarded science. "But the greatest error of all the rest, is the mistaking or misplacing of the last or farthest end of knowledge: for men have entered into a desire of learning and knowledge, sometimes upon a natural curiosity, and inquisitive appetite; sometimes to entertain their minds with variety and delight; sometimes for ornament and reputation; and sometimes to enable them to victory of wit and contradiction; and most times for lucre and profession; and seldom sincerely to give a true account of their gift of reason, to the benefit and use of men : as if there were sought in knowledge a couch, whereupon to rest a searching and restless spirit ; or a terrace, for a wandering and variable mind to walk up and down with a fair prospect ; or a tower of state, for a proud mind to raise itself upon ; or a fort or commanding ground, for strife and contention ; or a shop, for profit or sale ; and not a rich storehouse, for the glory of the Creator, and the relief of man's estate."

But when these generalities, so admirably set forth, require to be brought down to the particular, there is revealed the gulf between the gorgeous rhetorician and the drab working men of science.

Except in the most general sense, the method of Bacon, and the historical or actual processes employed by scientific men are not the same. " The method of Bacon," indeed, is a phrase wanting in any very precise meaning, since he has nowhere made a clear and compact statement of its nature. But, taking that meaning of the phrase which is fairly conveyed by the *Novum Organum* and such indications of method as are scattered about the *De Augmentis*, two things may be said of the Baconian method as so inferred. First, it was intended to be of so mechanical a nature, that men of the most mediocre powers should be, in employing it, on a level with the most distinguished. " For our method of discovering the sciences merely levels men's wits, and leaves but little to their superiority, since it achieves everything by the most certain rules and demonstrations " (*Nov. Org.* I. Aph. cxxii.)—a conception which was afterwards to haunt the minds of educational innovators for many a day with strange consequences. Secondly, the strict Baconian method is unworkable, or at least was never employed with much success. He himself discovered nothing by its help ; and the discoveries made by his contemporaries and successors have been made by ignoring it. That he misconceived the nature of modern scientific method appears in the nineteenth aphorism of the first book of the *Novum*

Organum: in which he contrasts his own method with that of Scholasticism: "There are, and can be but two ways of investigating and discovering truth. The one hurries on rapidly from the senses and particulars to the most general axioms, and from them, as principles and their supposed indisputable truth, derives and discovers the intermediate axioms. This is the way now in use. [The reference, of course, is to established custom, not to the doings of the pioneers.] The other constructs its axioms from the senses and particulars, by ascending continually and gradually, till it finally arrives at the most general axioms, which is the true but unattempted way." Subsequent history favours the belief that it is also the impossible way.

The truth seems to be that Bacon was very partially informed as to the doings of his scientific contemporaries. For example: Kepler had dedicated a most important book[1], containing the statement of the third of his Planetary Laws, to James I, at a time when Bacon was Lord Chancellor and Baron Verulam, yet the latter makes no mention of Kepler. In 1623 Bacon inserted this passage in the *De Augmentis*, the enlarged and Latin form of the *Advancement*: "In Arithmetic, there is still wanting a sufficient variety of short and commodious methods of calculation, especially with regard to progressions, whose use in physics is very considerable." There is not a hint here of the vastly important "short and commodious methods of calculation" which had been made possible since Napier invented logarithms in 1614, an English translation of the Latin book of that year having been published *in London* in 1618. Contrast the behaviour of the rhetorician with that of Kepler, who warmly congratulated Napier and introduced the use of logarithms into Germany; or of Briggs, the Savilian professor at Oxford, who performed a journey to Merchiston especially to make the acquaintance of the great mathematician whose discovery he made accessible to learned Europe, though the

[1] *Harmonice Mundi* (Augsburg, 1618–19).

news did not reach Bacon. Again, Bacon failed to grasp the importance of some first-rate scientific theories of which he *had* heard, his failure being due either to imperfect information, or to that sense of his own importance which made him describe himself as one who "perhaps ought to be an architect of philosophy and the sciences" (*De Aug.* VII. cp. 1). The architect, of course, could not interest himself much in the doings of masons, or even of clerks of the works. From whatever cause, Bacon permitted himself to write about "the extravagant idea of the diurnal motion of the earth, an opinion which I am convinced is most false" (*De Aug.* III. cp. 4). Similarly he undervalued the studies of Gilbert in magnetism, ranking them with the futilities of the alchemist. Gilbert's name appears several times in the *Novum Organum* in passages which illustrate another of Bacon's limitations. He despised the labours of the specialist; "men," said he, "waste all their time on probing some solitary matter, as Gilbert on the magnet, and the alchemists on gold" (*N. O.* Bk. I. Aph. lxx.). He writes elsewhere, "If anyone attempt to give himself up to things, and to discover something new, yet he will only propose and destine for his object the investigation and discovery of some one invention, and nothing more; as the nature of the magnet, the tides, the heavenly system, and the like, which appear involved in some degree of mystery, and have hitherto been treated with but little success. Now it is the greatest proof of want of skill, to investigate the nature of any object in itself alone; for that same nature, which seems concealed and hidden in some instances, is manifest and almost palpable in others, and excites wonder in the former, while it hardly attracts attention in the latter" (*N. O.* Bk. I. Aph. lxxxviii.). Certainly, there can be no philosophising worth the name, apart from the widely extended view of things which is only to be gained from the summits; but before the heights are scaled there is much humdrum work to be done on the lower levels. That work belongs to the specialist, whom Bacon contemns as a waster of time. The fact is evidence that he had no great grasp of the idea of method as it was conceived by some of his own contemporaries and as it has been applied in the actual progress of scientific discovery. More than that, his boast that he took "all knowledge for his province," and his desire to establish chiefly "the most general axioms," lead us to suspect that he·had not himself so completely emerged from the schools whose "unprofitable subtilty" he was ever ready to proclaim.

That Bacon ignored the labours of contemporaries, or undervalued them, was not singular in an age when Galileo appeared to care nothing for Kepler, and when Harvey failed to see the importance of the discoveries made by foreign anatomists. These things were so, in part from personal causes, and in part from lack of information, owing to the barriers erected in the republic of letters by the religious divisions of the sixteenth century. But, in Bacon's case, at least, there is the further fact that he was ill-equipped for discovery in Physical Science. The second book of the *Novum Organum*, which is mainly concerned with experiment, furnishes illustrations of the author's shortcomings in this respect. His assertion that Heat is Motion seems to have been a brilliant guess, expressed without realising very much of what was implied, but also implying that which is not. He says: "From the instances taken collectively, as well as singly, the nature whose limit is heat appears to be motion. This is chiefly exhibited in flame, which is in constant motion, and in warm or boiling liquids, which are likewise in constant motion. It is also shown by the excitement or increase of heat by motion, as by bellows or draughts...It is also shown by the extinction of fire and heat upon any strong pressure, which restrains and puts a stop to motion[1]." Earlier in the book he had declared that iron, when heated, did *not* expand

---

[1] "The First Vintage of the Form of Heat." (*N. O.* Bk. II. xx.)

(xviii. 10), and that air is a better conductor of heat than are metals (xii.).

In Bacon's mind there was a curious combination of the man of science and the man of the pre-scientific ages, a combination which Comenius faithfully reflects, though, indeed, it also existed, and naturally so, in many enquirers of their time. The *naïve* attitude of the Schoolmen appears in the statement that "wood and metal are not equally cold" (*N. O.* II. xiii.), and in such passages as these which follow. "The irritation of surrounding cold increases heat, as may be seen in fires during a sharp frost. We think that this is owing not merely to the confinement and compression of the heat (which forms a sort of union) but also by the exasperation of it, as when the air or a stick are violently compressed or bent, they recoil, not only to the point they first occupied, but still further back. Let an accurate experiment, therefore, be made with a stick, or something of the kind, put into the flame, in order to see whether it be not sooner burnt at the sides than in the middle of it" (*ibid.*). Again, comparing "the effects of fire with those of time," he says, "Time dries, consumes, undermines, and reduces to ashes as well as fire, and perhaps to a much finer degree; but as its motion is very slow, and attacks very minute particles, no heat is perceived" (*N. O.* II. xx.). Neither is Bacon wanting in credulity. Thus he believes the story that ashes remain undisturbed for a year on the windless summit of Mount Olympus, and that the tops of extremely lofty mountains are free from snow owing to their altitude (*N. O.* II. xii.). Such beliefs and such a way of regarding natural forces are serious hindrances to the would-be physicist; yet, ill-equipped as he was, he anticipated the direction, and sometimes the results, of enquiries carried out long after his death. Thus Newton's decomposition of white light is foreshadowed in Bacon's reference to prisms, and in his statement that colour is but a modification of light (*op. cit.* II. xxii.). So, too, he made a noteworthy approach to a theory of the tides (xxxvi.) and urged the employment of clocks, moved by weights and springs, and placed at varying altitudes, in order to determine the nature of weight (*ibid.*).

Nevertheless, it does not seem extreme to assert that had Bacon never penned a line the progress of physical science would have been what it has been. There is a tragic irony about one of the clauses of his last testament, which directed that an endowment of £200 was to be provided for advancing the study of the Natural Sciences at Oxford and Cambridge; but the intention was never carried out, as there were "no effects."

Bacon's greatest services in this field of knowledge were of the indirect kind. By the brilliance of his rhetoric, by his intellectual daring, by his inextinguishable optimism, he caught the attention of thoughtful, intelligent men, and concentrated for them in his books the influences which favoured the study of science in his day. For such men he became a personification of that New Philosophy, which able men of science, lacking his powers of imagination or of expression, were then actually constructing. In his quality of prophet, coryphaeus, or journalist (for he was all these in turn), he fired the imagination of many, and moved not a few to thought and action.

Influence of this kind is nowhere more clearly marked than in the subsequent history of educational opinion. Comenius was meditating his reforms in the years when Bacon's books were appearing, and largely through him the English writer was to affect the thought and practice of all Europe in the particular direction of method and educational administration.

Yet Bacon himself said little that can be expressly referred to schools or schoolmasters. A page of the *Advancement of Learning* (Bk. II.) on "pedantical knowledge" became in the *De Augmentis* a half-chapter on Pedagogy (Bk. VI. cp. 4). In the enlarged form, a well-deserved compliment is paid to the Jesuits, the most efficient corporation of schoolmasters then at work, a compliment which is remarkable as coming from

one whose ideal of culture was almost the contradictory of
theirs. The half-chapter in the *De Augmentis* begins: "As
for Pedagogy, it were the shortest way to refer it to the Jesuits,
who, in point of usefulness, have herein excelled...We highly
approve the education of youth in colleges, and not wholly
in private houses or schools [*i.e.* day-schools]. For in colleges
there is not only a greater emulation of the youth among
their equals, but the teachers have a venerable aspect and
gravity, which greatly conduces towards insinuating a modest
behaviour, and the forming of tender minds from the first,
according to such examples; and besides these there are many
other advantages of a collegiate education."   Possibly the
writer had the Jesuit colleges in mind in this reference to
the boarding-school and the value of emulation; elsewhere,
he speaks of the "Colleges of Jesuits abroad, in regard of
whose diligence in fashioning the morals and cultivating the
minds of youth, I may say, as Agesilaus said to his enemy
Pharnabasus, 'Seeing that you are what you are, would that
you were on our side'" (*De Aug.* I. 1). In this half-chapter
on Pedagogy, Bacon deprecates superficiality in the matter
of study, and narrowness and pedantry in its methods. He
goes on to plead that education shall be modified in accordance with the powers and limitations of the pupil: "the suiting
of the studies to the genius is of singular use; which masters
should duly attend to, that the parent may thence consider
what kind of life the child is fittest for. And further, it must
be carefully observed, not only that everyone makes much
greater progress in those things whereto he is naturally inclined, but also, that there are certain remedies in a proper
choice of studies for particular indispositions of mind. For example, inattention and a volatility of genius may be remedied
by mathematics, wherein, if the mind wander ever so little,
the whole demonstration must be begun anew"—a thought
repeated in the Essay, "Of Studies." The teacher is reminded
of the danger which lurks in exercises injudiciously appointed,
the writer agreeing with Cicero that "faults as well as faculties

are generally exercised in exercises, whence a bad habit is sometimes acquired and insinuated together with a good one." A teacher may adopt one of two orders of instruction: "the one beginning with the easier, leads gradually on to more difficult things; and the other, commanding and imposing such as are harder at first, so that when these are obtained, the easier may be more agreeably despatched." He favours an intermixture of both orders, putting the matter in the fashion of a familiar analogy which is characteristic of him— "For it is one method to begin swimming with bladders, and another to begin dancing with loaded shoes." The section on Pedagogy closes with a commendation of the practice of training boys in the dramatic art, "a discipline" which "the Jesuits judiciously retain." The practice "strengthens the memory, regulates the tone of the voice, and the efficacy of pronunciation; gracefully composes the countenance and the gesture, procures a becoming degree of assurance; and, lastly, accustoms youth to the eye of men."

To the chapter of the *De Augmentis* just considered may be added the second chapter of the same sixth book, which is a disquisition on Method[1]. The writer is not thinking of the schoolboy, but of the defects in the mode of scientific enquiry. The "methods of instruction and of discovery," "the logical method," and the "psychological method" are all noticed as one might find them in a present-day treatise on teaching. Bacon notes it as a defect that the method of discovery is too seldom employed, the dogmatic method too frequently usurping its place; and, further, the question whether the logical or the psychological method (the terms, of course, are not Bacon's) is to be adopted on a given occasion, is to be determined by "the informations and anticipations of the science to be delivered that are before infused and impressed upon the mind of the learner"—that is, the choice of method must be decided by what the Herbartians call the "apperception-mass" of the pupil.

Bacon's comments on the state of particular branches of

[1] Cp. *Adv. of Learning*, II. xvii—xix.

learning in his day also have an indirect reference to the school-room. In the *Advancement* he complains of the neglect of history, of modern languages, of politics, and of general literature, for none of which is there collegiate foundation or endowment. He goes on to say that States must be prepared to expend large sums on instruments and apparatus, if knowledge is to minister to the wants of the age, and the curriculum set up in days long since fled must be changed. On this last head he protests that Logic and Rhetoric are studies fitter for graduates than for the children who usually study them.

These few passages from the *De Augmentis* scarcely constitute an educational theory, of which, indeed, Bacon was not especially writing. It is the trend of his thought as a whole, the attempt, as he himself puts it, "towards restoring or cultivating a just and legitimate familiarity betwixt the mind and things," which was powerfully to affect the history of educational opinion and practice. To the mere multiplication of schools he was opposed. When, in 1611, he endeavoured to procure the setting aside of Thomas Sutton's will, which founded the Charterhouse as Hospital and School, he declared that of schools the country already had enough. Writing to King James about the terms of Sutton's will, he said: "Concerning the advancement of learning, I do subscribe to the opinion of one of the wisest and greatest men of your kingdom, that, for grammar schools, there are already too many, and therefore, no providence to add where there is excess. For the great number of schools which are in your Highness's realm, doth cause a want, and likewise an overthrow; both of them inconvenient, and one of them dangerous; for by means thereof, they find want in the country and towns, both of servants for husbandry, and apprentices for trade; and on the other side, there being more scholars bred than the State can prefer and employ, and the active part of that life not bearing a proportion to the preparative, it must need fall out that many persons will be bred unfit for other vocations, and unprofitable for that in which they were bred up, which fill the realm full of indigent, idle and wanton people, who are but *materia rerum novarum*"—touch-wood for revolutionists. Bacon proposes, as an amendment to Sutton's will, that the money be spent at the Universities on readerships in the arts and professions—"Therefore I could wish that in both the Universities the lectures, as well of the three professions, Divinity, Law, and Physick, as of the three heads of Science, Philosophy, Arts of Speech, and the Mathematicks, were raised to £100 a-piece."

The source of Bacon's influence, as a maker of educational history, is not in what he did for schools, nor in what he expressly said concerning them, but rather in the transfer, by other minds, of his thoughts concerning the promotion of knowledge in general to the narrower field of the school-room. Here the fertile ideas were, the need to push forward into a definite region of enquiry, and the purpose and general manner of the advance itself. These are summed up in the fragmentary *New Atlantis*, to which reference is made in the later chapter devoted to Bacon's most distinguished pedagogic disciple, Comenius.

With whatever limitations we may to-day invest Francis Bacon, he was, after all, the one man who set the thoughts of many, in this country and abroad, upon school reform. There is, of course, an obvious danger in too closely associating important historical changes with the labour and personality of the individual thinker. Nevertheless, the power exerted, for example, in the history of French education by such a man as Descartes cannot be questioned; Bacon's influence upon general, as distinct from national opinion in matters educational was even greater than that of his French contemporary. For that reason it seemed advisable to recall so well-worn a story as the subject-matter of this chapter, before considering the work of men who expressly turned their thoughts and activities to educational change.

CHAPTER II.

THE SCHOOL-ROOM IN THE EARLY SEVENTEENTH CENTURY.

"MANY of these men had greater wits far above mine own, and so are many in the universities of Europe at this day. But, alas! they learn nothing there but to believe: first, to believe that others know that which they know not: and after that themselves know that which they know not." So wrote Bacon in 1593 (*Praise of Knowledge*). Whatever was true of the general intellectual life outside the Church and the Universities, the old tradition was maintained in both, officially at least. The newer studies and the newer methods could not fail to interest many dwellers in those homes of an earlier culture, some of whom were led to engage actively in the new pursuit; but it was understood that these newer studies must remain unrecognised by authority. Venturing to regard this convention carelessly, Galileo suffered penalties: adhering to it, the Universities still compelled the student to argue his way to a degree through a series of disputations in the manner of his mediaeval predecessors.

The schools, as seed-plots of the Universities, were necessarily limited by their preoccupation with the future undergraduate. In intention, at least, the mediaeval curriculum in Arts was very comprehensive, embracing what may be called a literary group of studies (the Trivium of Grammar, Logic, Rhetoric), and a scientific (the Quadrivium of Arithmetic, Geometry, Music, Astronomy). The "revival of learning" had brought about a more liberal method of treating the first, but it had in effect discouraged zeal in pursuit of the second. A well-known passage in the first book of the *Advancement of Learning* tells how the sixteenth century devotion to Greek and Latin had made rhetoric the chief concern of the professional educator, who gave no attention to those studies of nature with which so much of contemporary thought was beginning to occupy itself. Bacon thus animadverts upon "the first disease of learning." "So that these four causes concurring, the admiration of ancient authors, the hate of the schoolmen, the exact study of languages, and the efficacy of preaching, did bring in an affectionate study of eloquence, and *copia* of speech, which then began to flourish. This grew speedily into an excess; for men began to hunt more after words than matter; and more after the choiceness of the phrase, and the round and clean composition of the sentence, and the sweet falling of the clauses, and the varying and illustration of their works with tropes and figures, than after the weight of matter, worth of subject, soundness of argument, life of invention, or depth of judgment. Then grew the flowing and watery vein of Osorius, the Portugal bishop, to be in price. Then did Sturmius spend such infinite and curious pains upon Cicero the orator, and Hermogenes the rhetorician, besides his own books of the Periods, and Imitation, and the like. Then did Carr of Cambridge, and Ascham, with their lectures and writings, almost deify Cicero and Demosthenes, and allure all young men, that were studious, unto that delicate and polished kind of learning. Then did Erasmus take occasion to make the scoffing echo, 'Decem annos consumpsi in legendo Cicerone': and the echo answered in Greek, Oνϵ, Asine. Then grew the learning of the schoolmen to be utterly despised as barbarous. In sum, the whole inclination and bent of those times was rather towards *copia*, than weight."

The separation in kind between the work of the school-room and the intellectual life of grown men and women of the hour outside the school walls is a separation which, in greater or less degree, has always been observable. It is very well illustrated, for the age under consideration, by two events in the history of education which occurred in the year 1612, that is, about midway between the appearance in print of the *Advancement of Learning* and of the *Novum Organum*.· The events are the publication in London of John Brinsley's *Ludus Literarius*, and at Frankfurt of Wolfgang Ratke's Memorial to the Imperial Diet assembled in that city. Brinsley is the successful practical schoolmaster, giving the benefit of his twenty years' professional experience to his brethren; Ratke is the adventurer, neither successful nor practical, who is pushing his fortunes by propounding schemes of a novelty well calculated to interest the great and powerful. Yet neither Brinsley nor Ratke has a suggestion which he owes to Francis Bacon or to the new men in Science and Philosophy, whose herald Bacon was.

Brinsley, father of a more celebrated son, the Puritan polemical writer, and himself suffering at the hands of eccle-siastical authority, was at one time Master of the school at Ashby-de-la-Zouch, and, later, a teacher in London. A writer of popular school-books, he was responsible for editions, with English "construes," of parts of Cicero, Cato, Virgil, and of Corderius's Dialogues; a catechism of Latin grammar by him, called the *Posing of the Parts*, was so much in request that it reached a 15th edition. He was, therefore, well known in his profession, and his books show that he regarded its practice with a critical eye, and, further, had certain definite reforms to propose.

The picture which the *Ludus Literarius* draws of the English secondary school of the time of James I is, therefore, an authentic one, which may be fully accepted as to its main features, though possibly a shadow here and there is over-deep; its account of the course of studies and of current methods is not to be questioned. The picture indicates unmistakeably that the New Philosophy, whenever applied to the school-room, would demand revolutionary changes.

The book bears the title "Ludus Literarius, or the Grammar Schoole; shewing how to proceede from the first entrance into learning to the highest perfection required in the Grammar Schooles." It is of the kind familiar to readers of English books on education; that is to say, its standpoint is frankly empirical, with little or no reference to general principles, and its aim is expressly practical. The writings and work of other schoolmasters are brought forward in support of the author's own experience, and all his recommendations are of plans which he has himself employed with success. As Brinsley says, on his title-page, his book was "begun to be sought out at the desire of some worthy favourers of learning, by searching the experiments of sundry most profitable Schoolemasters and other learned, and confirmed by tryail."

The author has adopted the dialogue as the form of his work; there are two speakers only, Philoponus, who stands for Brinsley himself, and his visitor Spoudeus, an anxious and much-tried schoolmaster, who desires to learn how his host succeeds where he himself has so entirely failed. The form chosen for the book not only enables Brinsley to state his own ideas, but also affords opportunities for animadversions upon the ordinary grammar school practice of the day.

The phrase in the title, "first entrance into learning," means learning to read, and for that purpose Brinsley would send the youngster to school at the age of five, thus anticipating the then customary practice by two or three years. He is careful to say that for these little ones the school must be made a "place of play," a statement which reflects the kindliness of the man who also saw a danger in "overtoyling and terrifying the Schollars" with rote-learning and who shocked his professional brother by proposing that every morning and afternoon school-session should be split into two parts, by a quarter of an hour's "recreation." The boys, then, of whom Brinsley is writing range from 5—7 years, till they were ready for the University somewhere between 15 and 17. Their chief study is Latin, and, with very much less completeness, Greek, Hebrew, "the ground of Religion," and Bible history. To this curriculum Brinsley adds a branch of study which came to be a characteristic note of the seventeenth century innovator in education, namely, the study of the mother-tongue. The establishment of the great modern literatures beyond all possibility of cavil was naturally followed by the appearance of the vernaculars in the class-room.

Brinsley, properly desirous that boys should "grow in our owne English tongue," shows how they may attain "to read English speedily," his method being the still only too familiar plan of beginning with the alphabet and then spelling out strings of syllables, b-a-t, c-a-t, f-a-t, etc.—a plan with good points when applied to phonetically spelt Latin, but radically unsound for the purpose of English[1]. As reading-book Brinsley recommends "their Abcie and Primer," "the Psalms in metre," the Testament, "The School of Vertue" (in verse), "The Schoole of Good Manner,"—very much the list of books which Locke, writing in 1693, would replace by "some easy pleasant book" such as Aesop (with pictures) or "Reynard the Fox[2]." At a later stage, Brinsley would have the boys "report a Fable in English," write letters to their friends in English as well as in Latin, and take notes of sermons, for subsequent report in the same languages. Following Roger Ascham, to whom he frequently refers as to a great authority, he makes much use of

---

[1] The transference of the "method" from the first language to the second, and its long retention in that connection, are excellent examples of the conservatism of the school-room.

[2] Locke, however, has practically no improvement to suggest as to the method.

double translation, and he says that one of several advantages secured by the practice is that these daily translations will keep up the boy's power of reading and writing his mother-tongue.

The Grammar Schools regarded this teaching of English as a burden, and Brinsley does not seem very hopeful about their adoption of his own practice, for he says of it, "Thus may any poore man or woman enter the little ones of a towne together; and make an honest poor living of it, or get somewhat towards helping the same. Also the Parents, who have any learning, may enter the little ones" etc. That the grammar schools thought English outside their province is well seen in a remark made by Spoudeus. "The trouble is this. That wheneas my children doe first enter into Latine, manie of them will forget to reade English, and some of them bee worse two or three yeares after they have been in construction, then when they began it"—a disagreeable discovery not confined to English school-rooms at that day, but reported from France also.

If the schools did little for the vernacular, they did even less for the teaching of arithmetic. Says the harassed Spoudeus, "For I am much troubled about this, that my readers and other above them are much to seeke in all matters of numbers, whether in figures or in letters. Insomuch, as when they heare the chapters named in the church, many of them cannot turn to them, much less to the verse." Philoponus assures his friend that his case is not peculiar. "This likewise is a very ordinary defect, and yet might easily be helped by common means in an hour or two. I call it ordinary, because you shall have scholars, almost ready to goe to the University, who yet can hardly tell you the numbers of pages, sections, chapters or other divisions in their books, to find what they should." The speaker then gives a few directions about the Roman and Arabic *notations*, and adds, "If you do require more for any; you must seeke Records Arithmetique, or other like Authors and set them to the *Cyphering Schoole"* (*i.e.* a thing apart from the grammar school).

The third " R " is in as poor a case as its fellows. " You shall find very fewe good writers in Grammar Schooles; unless eyther they have been taught by Scriveners, or be themselves marvellous apt hereunto, and very rare, or where the Master doth apply himself chiefly to teach to write."

A more thorough teaching of the mother-tongue was not the only school-reform which Brinsley desired to bring about. The principle which he calls his " first general observation " is of even more far-reaching importance. " For this is a matter which of all other concerneth the credit of schooles, and furthereth learning wonderfully ; *to teach scholars to understand whatsoever they learn, and to be able to give a reason of everything why it is so ;* and to doe this from the lowest to the highest." Both schoolmasters agree that this is not the common practice ; indeed, some traditional lumber would be turned out of the modern school-room if Brinsley's principle were universally practised to-day. There is another note of the educational reformer in the " second general observation " to the effect that scholars should " learne only such bookes and matters, as whereof they may have the best use, and that perpetually in all their learning, or in their whole life."

The practical reform on which Brinsley probably most prided himself was the grouping of children in fairly large classes for examination or instruction in common, the general practice being to have but few boys in a form, and these to come up to the master for recitation either singly, or in twos or threes. The innovation was an earlier one of the Jesuits, from whom also Brinsley may have borrowed the excessive use of emulation. He says that the whole school should be divided into " so few foarmes as may be," " though they be sixteene or twenty, yea forty in a foarme, it is not the worse." His reasons for preferring a fairly large group are, first it is the same labour to teach one as a thousand, " if all can heare alike " (a fallacy

which one does not expect from a practical schoolmaster);
secondly, the fewer the forms, the more thorough examination
is possible; and, finally, emulation and mutual help have freer
play. Jesuit-fashion, every boy is to have his "adversarius,"
and every form is to be divided "into two equall partes, to
strive alwaies whether side of the foarme should get the
victorie." This "strife for the Masteries," says Brinsley, will
"make the Schoole-house to bee Ludus Literarius, indeed a
Schoole of play and pleasure." A further "conveyance" from
the Jesuit school-room is the employment of monitors. "In
every fourme this may be a notable helpe, that the two or foure
seniors in each fourme, be as Ushers in that fourme, for overseeing, directing, examining, and fitting the rest every way
before they come to say; and so for the overseeing the
exercises." It is noteworthy that, with Brinsley, these monitors
are elected by the boys, to avoid suspicion of favouritism.
Similarly the boys choose the sides for the class-contests, as
they would at a game. Still, the schoolmaster does not
abdicate: "We use ever to appose the worst and most
negligent of each fourme above all the rest; though every
one something, yet them principally. This will make them
more careful, and cause all to come on together in some good
sort."

The great business of Brinsley's school is the teaching of
Latin, and he follows Ascham in advocating the employment
of double translation—"A child of 9 or 10 yeeres old, being
well entred, shall be able by the help of the translation, to read
of himselfe an easie Author, as Corderius, or Tullie's Sentences,
as fast out of Latine into the English, or the English into the
Latine." The translation and text should be separate, not
"interlineall," a mode which prompts too readily. A quite
inordinate amount of space, as it seems to the modern reader,
is devoted in the *Ludus Literarius* to describing what Brinsley
terms "the Golden Rule of Construing." This is no more
than the familiar device of requiring a boy, when construing,

to find the principal verb, then its nominative, next the adjuncts of the verb, and so on. The device cannot have been very familiar to Brinsley's readers, or he would not have found it worth while to publish editions of Latin authors "translated grammatically," that is, translated in the order and manner of a small boy's "construe." No doubt, the publication of these books is to be explained by the lack of scholarship in many of the teachers. All through the seventeenth and eighteenth centuries, up to Pestalozzi's time, this man and that is found proposing the use of school-books which should virtually make the teacher's ignorance a matter of indifference.

Greek construing is to begin, according to our author, with the New Testament, not only because of the intrinsic value of the book, but also because the familiarity of the subject-matter will make the learning of the foreign language easier. Generally, the pupil is first to learn the nouns and verbs in his grammar book, and next he is to begin acquaintance with the Greek author in a translation. Brinsley also thinks that the pupil should learn tables or lists of Greek roots. All of the practices here recommended were to reappear in the later history of classical instruction; so, too, were the reasons which he alleged for causing boys to make verses—with one exception. It is doubtful whether it occurred to anyone but Brinsley to set down, as a reason for requiring Latin and Greek verse, the use of such verses on occasions of "triumph and rejoicing, more ordinarily at the *funerals* of some worthy personages."

The scholastic tongue was Latin, and as instruction at the Universities and the official exercises there were in that language, the schools must do their best to prepare boys for the art of conversing in Latin. That boys did not take kindly to the plan comes out clearly in a passage which one may perhaps be pardoned for citing at length. Spoudeus, the visitor, who represents a sort of Greek chorus of "average schoolmasters," complains, "But this I have had too much experience of, that without great severity they will not be brought unto; but they will speake English, and one will winke at another, if they be out of the Master's hearing." Philoponus (*i.e.* Brinsley) replies: "It is exceeding hard to cause this to be practiced constantly amongst schollars. That is a usuall custome in Schooles to appoint Custodes or Asini (as they are tearmed in some places) to observe and catch them who speake English in each fourme, or whom they see idle, to give them the ferula, and to make them Custodes if they cannot answere a question which they aske. But I have observed so much inconvenience in it, as I cannot tell what to say in this case; for oft-times, he who is the Custos will hardly attend his own worke, for hearkening to heare others to speake English. Also there falleth out amongst them oft-times so much wrangling about the questions, or defending themselves, that they did not speake English, or were not idle, that all the whole fourme is troubled. So likewise when the Custodes are called for, before breaking up at dinner and at night, there will be so much contention amongst them, as is disquieting and trouble to the Master. Moreover, this I have observed, that ever, if there be one simple in some fourme, or harder of learning than the rest, they will make him a right Asinus, causing such to be the Custodes continually, or for the most part, if they cannot answer; and to this end they will be alwayes watching them; whereby many such are not only notably abused, but very much discouraged for being schollars, when they see themselves so baited at by all; some others are made over malipart thereby. Besides all these, I doe not see myself any great fitnesse, that one scholler should smite another with the ferula; because much malicing one another, with grudges and quarrels doe arise thereupon. So that the discommodities that follow the Custodes seem to me to be many moe then the benefits can be; chiefly in losse of time, and hindering more in other learning than can be gotten in that." Spoudeus confirms these inconveniences from his own experience. Philoponus is for doing away with the Custodes, and relying upon two seniors in each form and upon the master's eyes and ears. He would expect Latin only in the parsing and more formal exercises of the school-room, and would use books of dialogues, as Corderius, the Colloquium of Erasmus, Terence or Terentius Christianus.

The arrangements for religious instruction are thus described by Philoponus. "Every Saturdaie, before their breaking up the schoole (for a finishing their week's labour and a preparative to the Sabbaoth) let them spende halfe an howre, or more, learning and answering the Catechisme."..."For the Sabbaoths...let the Monitors see that all be most attentive to the Preacher." Everyone is to learn something at the sermon-time, the highest forms to be required to set down the whole sermon. "After all these you may (if you think good) cause them the next morning to translate it into a good Latine stile, instead of their exercise...or some little piece of it, according to their ability (I meane so many of them as write Latine)." On Monday, there is also an examination and "appoosing" on the sermon, exercises which will make them attentive and keep them "from playing, talking, sleeping, and all other disorders in the Church." Every day there is to be some short exercise, or lesson of religion, a Bible history, or reading from religious or moral books.

Brinsley has here been describing how he discharges the duty which was laid upon every licensed schoolmaster in England in the early seventeenth century. We have this officially set forth in the Canons of 1604, which were adopted by Convocation after the abortive Hampton Court Conference. Article 79, on "the Duty of Schoolmasters," is as follows: "All schoolmasters shall teach in English or Latin, as the children are able to bear, the larger or shorter Catechism heretofore by public authority set forth. And as often as any sermon shall be upon holy and festival days within the parish where they teach they shall bring their scholars to the church when such sermon shall be made, and there see them quietly and soberly behave themselves; and shall examine them at times convenient, after their return, what they have borne away of such sermons. Upon other days, and at other times, they shall train them up with such sentences out of Holy Scripture as shall be most expedient to induce them to all godliness; and they shall teach the grammar set forth by King Henry VIII, and continued in the times of King Edward VI and Queen Elizabeth of noble memory, and none other. And if any schoolmaster, being licensed, and having subscribed as aforesaid, shall offend in any of the premises, or either speak, write, or teach against anything whereunto he hath formerly subscribed (if upon admonition by the ordinary he do not amend and reform himself) let him be suspended from teaching school any longer."

The injunction here to make use of "none other" than the prescribed Latin grammar book, is to be noted. Brinsley has a chapter (xxxi.) on the "Inconvenience growing by diversitie of teaching, and of Grammar"—a complaint not confined to England at that time. Our author thinks that "the best courses" should be "found out by search, conference and trial," and the result made known, with directions for practice; meantime the best must be made of the " ordinary Grammar " of the Canon, that is, Lily's *Grammar.*

The *Ludus Literarius* has chapters on school-government, the use of rewards and punishments, and kindred matters, but as these are not of any special distinction they need not be repeated here. Brinsley arranges the school-day as follows. There are two sessions, the first from 6 till 11, or a little later, the second from 1 o'clock till half-past 5. The first morning hour is spent in preparation by the boys under the charge of the usher, the Master not appearing till 7. Following what Brinsley tells us is the Westminster custom, 15 minutes' interval is allowed for breakfast at 9 a.m.; and there is the same interval about 3 in the afternoon. Spoudeus looks askance at this half-hour, as likely to bring the reproach of idling upon a school. Brinsley gives a weekly half-holiday, "eyther the Thursday, after the usuall custom, or according to the best opportunity of the place."

The chapter which is practically the last in the book considers the kind of boy who should be sent to the University, and the age at which 'he should go. The "children who are to be kept to learning," and encouraged to go on in the same, are "those who after good time of triall shall be found fittest amongst a man's children, to be applied unto learning; as being the meetest to be offered to God in a more special manner, to the publick service of his church or their countries"—"those whom you find most ingenuous and especially whom you perceive to love learning best; which also do witness the same by their painfulnesse and delight in their books. The rest to be fitted so far as may be conveniently, for trades, or some other calling, or to be removed speedily[1]."

At matriculation the boy should be "a good Grammarian at least, able to understand, write and speak Latine in good sort": his age should not be under fifteen. This was the minimum age by statute, but Brinsley implies that the statute was evaded[2], and that some Heads wished to see 17 or 18 made the minimum. Before closing the *Ludus Literarius*, the title of one chapter (xxxiii.) must be quoted, if only to establish another bond of sympathy between the seventeenth century and ourselves; the title is: "Discouragements of Schoolmasters by unthankfulnesse of Parents." It is not necessary to rewrite *that* chapter.

In the grammar school as Brinsley knew it, the chief study was Latin; Greek, Hebrew, and Divinity occupied a secondary position. In the case of the younger boys, Latin meant the attempt to acquire that language ostensibly through spoken Latin, but as a matter of fact in very many schools

[1] Cp. xxxiv.

[2] According to the *Dict. Nat. Biog.* his own son, John, entered Emmanuel, Cambridge, under 14 (1614).

through a *grammar book* itself written in Latin. So it came about that the more formal and abstract part of the study fell to the lot of the younger scholar. The addition of the mother-tongue to the roll of school "subjects" is an innovation favoured by Brinsley, but the vernacular makes its appearance in the school-room under disadvantages, and amidst discouraging circumstances. The internal organisation of the school appears crude from our standpoint; its teachers were certainly often ill-equipped in respect of the knowledge they were expected to impart. In many European countries men were even then laying the foundations of Physical Science as it is studied to-day; no indication of the fact is to be got from Brinsley or from his colleagues of 1612.

In the year which saw the publication of the *Ludus Literarius*, Wolfgang Ratke made his earliest bid for public notice on the great scale. Time and place were admirably chosen. The German princes and prelates and the representatives of the Imperial Free Cities were assembled at Frankfurt on the Main, the business in hand being the election of the Emperor. Ratke, at that moment an unknown man of some forty years of age, ventured to present to this august assembly a "Memorial," wherein he professed himself ready to show how three things might be done "for the service and welfare of Christendom." First, he would show how both old and young might learn easily, and in a shorter time than usual, the Hebrew, Greek, Latin and other languages. Secondly, he had a proposal for the setting up of a school, wherein all arts and faculties might be learned in High German, as also in all other languages. His third idea was much more amazing, and, read in the light of subsequent history, has an irony which none of those at Frankfurt could have suspected. Within six years of the outbreak of the Thirty Years' War Ratke invites the Diet to consider plans, whereby there might be "conveniently introduced and peaceably established throughout the whole Empire a uniform

speech, a uniform government, and, finally, a uniform religion"!
That the Diet took all this very seriously is hard to believe;
but, in fact, some of its members certainly did so.

Around the person and work of the man who made these
fantastic proposals there grew up, some 60 years ago, a body
of assertions which finally took shape as a veritable Ratke
legend.   According to this story Ratke was a disciple of
Francis Bacon's, with whose writings he became acquainted
during a visit to England.   Following in his master's steps,
he advocated the study of natural science and of other
"modern subjects," including the mother-tongue.   Further,
he applied psychological principles to methods of teaching
(that is, he did so in a conscious way), improved the teaching of languages generally, was the fount of inspiration for
Comenius, and, in brief, was the originator of modern pedagogy.   Such is the story, the legend rather, which received
the *imprimatur* of Raumer, the historian of education, and
from his pages passed direct to other books.   It is reflected
in Mr Quick's paper on Ratke in the *Essays on Educational
Reformers.*

Like most legends, this one has a substratum of truth;
but it also includes misrepresentations and some sheer inventions.   The first modern study of Ratke was made by
Niemeyer, of Halle, an enthusiast who appears to have built
up his hero's fame by annexing the work of educators who
had been associated with "the Didacticus" (as he was called),
and labelling the proceeds with Ratke's name.   As this study
was based upon cotemporary documents in the archives of
the Grand Duchy of Anhalt, its truth was unquestioned for
a generation and more.   Then it was discovered that Niemeyer's examination of the documents had been very incomplete; closer investigation considerably reduced the claims
made on Ratke's behalf, and it became possible to regard
Ratke's work in a clearer light[1].

[1] "Wolfgang Ratichius," by G. Krause.

It will be noticed that Ratke's claim to high rank in peda-gogic history is made to spring from an assumed connection with Bacon. As a matter of fact, there is no evidence that he ever visited England, while there is strong presumptive documentary evidence that he did not do so. Similarly, there is nothing in the educational ideas which were undoubtedly Ratke's that requires us to assume any knowledge of Bacon's writings. Again, some at least of the innovations ascribed to Ratke were the invention of men who worked in collaboration with him. In short, much caution is necessary in accepting the details of the Ratke legend.

Wolfgang Ratke, or Ratichius, was born at Wilster in Hol-stein in 1571, and received his school education in Hamburg. His University studies, pursued at Rostock and elsewhere, included Lutheran theology as well as ancient languages; later he went to Holland, spending the eight years preceding the middle of 1610 in Amsterdam, where he occupied himself as a private teacher. He next visited Basel and Strassburg, and in 1611 took up his residence in Frankfurt. In May, 1612, he presented to the Imperial Diet in that city the " Memorial " already described. The three startling proposals of that document were accompanied by an " Explanation," and some ten months later by an " Elucidation for the pre-vention of disagreeable misunderstandings[1] " (March, 1613). In these Ratke insists upon the importance of the vernacular language as an instrument of education, and proposes to con-centrate language-study about that of the Bible, as a core, so to speak, assisted by concise and systematic text-books. " Now the right practice and course of Nature is that the dear youth should first learn to read, write, and speak, correctly and readily, their inherited mother-tongue (which in our case is German), and thereby they can the better understand and comprehend what they learn in other tongues. For this

---

[1] Rein's *Encyclop. Handbuch der Päd.*, *sub voce* " Ratke " (by Israel).

purpose the German Bible may be used with especial profit."
Similarly, Hebrew is to be studied from the Hebrew Bible,
Greek from the New Testament, and Latin, not from the
Vulgate, of course, but from Terence, the dialogue of whose
comedies lends itself to a colloquial treatment of the lan-
guage.

Ratke and his Memorial were much talked of in Frankfurt,
and the immediate result was a present of 500 gulden from
one prince (the Pfalzgraf, Wilhelm of Neuburg), and an
awakened interest in the mind of another, Ludwig of Hesse-
Darmstadt, who commissioned two Giessen professors, Helwig
and Jung, to enquire into Ratke's methods of teaching. Their
report was favourable, as was a second made in 1613, on the
reforms proposed in the " Memorial," by three Jena professors
for the information of the Duchess Dorothea Maria of Saxe-
Weimar[1].   The professors call attention to what they considered defects in the ordinary schools, defects which are
summed up in the phrases, want of uniformity in method
and in text-books (compare the quotation from the English
Canons of 1604 on p. 29 above), and the attempt to do too
much at once. As to methods, there are as many of these " as
there are cities and schools, and the multiplicity of grammars is
excessive, so that you shall find statements of grammatical rules
which are peculiar to schools and even to classes.   Boys are
called upon to study too many authors at once, whence it follows
that repetition, which is so necessary, becomes impossible."
Boys are expected to study Logic and Rhetoric, studies which
are beyond them[2], as well as many classical authors at the same
time. "Truly it is as if one were to cook flesh, fish, broth, and
peas together in one pot." Further, much time is wasted in
rote-learning, and in the making of notes from the teacher's
dictation.   Contrasted with all this, we have Ratke's proposed
reforms, which truly are not of a startling character.   He

[1] Krause, *ut sup.* p. 7 ff. gives the report in full (11 Mar. 1613).
[2] Cp. citation from Bacon's *Advancement*, p. 16 above.

would employ one standard grammar-book only, and keep
the boys steadily at one author till that author was mastered.
Since speech is an art, it can only be acquired by practice.
"The mode of teaching," says the report, "brought forward
by Herr Ratichius consists in continued and very frequent
repetition of one and the same thing; so that it is quite
impossible that boys shall not apprehend, in a short time and
easily, the one thing so often and so continuously repeated."
Instead of asking a boy to learn by heart words which he
often does not understand, Ratke repeats the subject-matter,
questioning the boys upon it, and going over it with them
so often that it sticks in their memory. "A boy learns more
easily and retains it, when the teacher goes over it with him
beforehand, than when he learns by heart without understanding. Possibly someone may say, that it is no great
matter which mode of teaching is adopted, if only the goal
is reached; many learned folk have been taught in the old
way. But we say that the mode of teaching matters greatly,
as a similitude will make clear. Suppose two persons who
wish to go from Leipzig to Vienna. One says he will go
through Bohemia and Moravia, the other through Thuringia,
France, and Bavaria, and thence down the Danube. Now ask
yourself whether anything depends on this difference of route,
seeing that in the end both get to Vienna," etc.

For these reasons, the professors express a mild approval
of Ratke's suggestions. The Duchess became Ratke's very
good friend, employed him to teach her Hebrew, introduced
him to her brother, the sovereign of Anhalt-Köthen, and, in
the days of his adversity, made him her pensioner.

The method of Ratke, as discussed in the foregoing report,
cannot be considered of much importance, but at the time
this report was being penned (March, 1613), Ratke had included in the "Elucidation" of his "Memorial" a proposition
which was capable of considerable application. It was that,
as Arts and Sciences are confined to no one language, a

complete school might very well be established in which all
teaching should be in High German[1].

In 1614 Ratke was invited by the town authorities of
Augsburg to set the administration of their school in order;
he was accompanied by Helwig, the Giessen professor, who
had been amongst the first to speak favourably of the "Memorial" of 1612. The two remained in the town for some
months, but their labours were not satisfactory. Mr Quick
alludes to the fact, and adds that the two men left Augsburg,
Helwig being "much discouraged but still faithful to his
friend[2]." Faithful he may have been, but Helwig had formed
a different opinion of Ratke after these months of attempted
collaboration. The professor was at home again at Giessen
in September, 1615, whence he wrote a letter to the Duchess
Dorothea Maria, in which Ratke is drawn in most unflattering
colours. "Slippery," selfish, getting credit for himself at
others' expense, "he tries industriously to fathom other men's
secrets, to use them for his own advantage," boorish and head-
strong, these and the like are the descriptions of Ratke which
Helwig sends to the Duchess. He says, too, that his late
colleague is "prodigal in promising the things which are not
in his power to perform[3]."

There was always more than a suspicion of the cheap-jack
and the quack about the Didacticus, and those who were
thrown into closer association with him did not fail to discover
it. The thing comes out in the absurd fuss and secrecy with
which he surrounded his *Didactica*, or "Christian project."
Between 1613 and 1618 he bound to secrecy respecting this
project quite a numerous company of officials and University
professors, and he succeeded in adding a reigning prince and
his consort to this company[4]. Here is part of a letter written

[1] Israel in Rein's *Handbuch*, art. "Ratke."
[2] *Essays on Educational Reformers*, p. 106.
[3] Krause, *ut supra*, gives the letter (on p. 159) from the Weimar *Acta*.
[4] Ludwig of Anhalt-Köthen.

by Ratke in January, 1617, to John Buxtorf, the celebrated Professor of Hebrew at Basel. "My *Didactica* consists, above all, in practice and in the use of the living voice, so that it cannot well be rightly shown or made clear in writing, still less in a letter. At this time I know not what better report or advice I can give, than that you should arrange to come here at the first opportunity, together with your son of whom you speak in your letter. Within 8 or 10 days I will then disclose to you my 'Methodus Linguarum' completely and in the most intimate way, and at the same time show in what manner in the future old and young, women and children, may in half-a-year teach, learn and converse in every tongue perfectly, not piecemeal....Before your son becomes practised and ready therein he will have no need to learn any one word by heart, a practice absolutely forbidden here. But he has only to devote to it an hour two or three [times] daily, according to opportunity, and in a fixed order, according to the natural method such as you will understand from me here later[1]." This letter was written from Frankfurt, where Ratke had again become resident, after the failure at Augsburg, and after seemingly fruitless visits to half-a-dozen widely separated German towns[2]. Buxtorf did not accept the invitation to Frankfurt, and Ratke went to Basel the following summer, with most untoward consequences. There seemed to him a reasonable hope that the city of Basel would undertake to carry out his "Christian project," when on a sudden his hope was shattered. His own picturesque explanation[3] was that the machinations of Satan and certain wicked people had hindered his plans. The more prosaic story is, that for certain smart but indiscreet words spoken in a tavern near Basel he became amenable to the law, and was at length committed to prison, where he remained from October to March, 1618.

---

[1] Krause.   [2] "Ratke" in Rein.   [3] Krause, p. 39.

On his release Ratke turned his back upon the Rhine, and conscious of opportunities for the display of his talents, made his way in April to Anhalt-Köthen, the seat of a sovereign prince who was well known as a man of culture, desirous of extending the benefits of education amongst his people. Prince Ludwig of Anhalt-Köthen, brother of the Duchess Dorothea Maria, Ratke's patroness and pupil, had been a member of the Florentine Accademia della Crusca during a long sojourn in the Italian city, and a little before Ratke's arrival he had founded (1617) with the help of other princes of his House a similar corporation in Anhalt. This *Fruchtbringende Gesellschaft*, of which he was the first president, aimed more especially at the cultivation of the mother-tongue, by maintaining the purity of German diction free from foreign contamination, and the improvement of German oratory : secondary aims were the building up of a system of education distinctively German, and the fostering of morality[1].

At Ratke's advent the prince was in communication with his brother sovereigns and with learned men for the purpose of improving the Anhalt schools. The Didacticus set forth his projects for reform, named a Basel professor (Lucius) as a possible collaborator, and asked for a numerous staff by whose aid alone his designs could be satisfactorily achieved. From April, 1618, to June of the following year preparations were made for establishing Ratke at Köthen, and scholars were recruited from the neighbourhood and from the Universities of Jena and Wittenberg who were to direct or themselves give instruction.

On Midsummer Day, 1619, all was ready. By the lectures of these scholars in the Castle of Köthen opportunities were afforded to students and teachers to learn Ratke's method, which was itself to be seen in operation in the schools for boys and girls held in the town. The boys' school contained six

---

[1] Paulsen, *Geschichte des gelehrten Unterrichts*, vol. i. p. 458.

classes, combining the primary and secondary stages. In the three lowest classes the course comprised the mother-tongue, reading, writing, summing, and singing; this also was the curriculum for girls, religion, of course, being taught in both schools. Latin was taught in the boys' school in the three highest classes, the highest class adding Greek—a school-course, in short, like that which was familiar to Brinsley.

After the work had been in progress for some weeks the prince left Köthen for the summer holiday, but kept up a correspondence with Ratke and the school-inspectors. So early as the month of August the latter reported that discipline had become relaxed, while the new system was not producing any notable improvement in other directions; to make things worse, Ratke was at open variance with his colleagues, his personal character and his manner of advocating theological and political ideas and changes partly accounting for the quarrels. Prince Ludwig summoned Ratke to Weimar in order to make explanation. Arrived there, a discussion began between the Prince and the Didacticus which ended in a declaration from the former that the operations under the new school-system must come to an end in consequence of its own defects and the scandals which had accompanied it. This was early in September. The relations between the two became even more difficult, and Ratke's display of personal disrespect to the prince was followed by his arrest on October 5, 1619[1]. He remained a prisoner till June 22, 1620, and was not released till he had signed a declaration that he had put the prince to great expense by promising and undertaking more than was in his power to perform[2].

In the two following years (1621–2) Ratke was at Magdeburg, by the invitation of the town-council; he does not

[1] Krause, pp. vii., viii.

[2] Krause, p. 165. Mr Quick's account is less than just to the prince and over-tender to the pedagogue.

appear to have achieved there anything considerable, but a statement of his to the council is worth remarking. He assured that body that the education of youth appertains solely to the political authorities, who, therefore, were acting within their rights in directing it[1]. Whatever the exciting cause of this pronouncement, it expressed a thought not very familiar during Ratke's lifetime; at an earlier date (1618) he had told Prince Ludwig that no one, boy or girl, young or old, should be excluded from the operations of his *Didactica*, "at least till he or she could read and write well and readily."

Ratke lived till 1635; we hear of him in two or three towns of Central Germany, a pensioner of Prince Ludwig's sister, the Duchess Dorothea Maria. Through that princess's good offices he had an interview in 1632 with Oxenstiern, the Swedish chancellor, who was desirous of learning what he could of educational projects and reforms. His judgment on Ratke was, that he had not unjustly disclosed the mistakes of the schools, but had no thorough reformation to propose.

Notwithstanding the advance in Natural Science and the advocacy of its study by Bacon, Brinsley's *Ludus Literarius* shows no trace of either in its discussion of school-reforms. There is the same omission from the recorded pronouncements of Ratke. The two men urge the great claim of the vernacular to a recognised and important place in the school-room; but their agreement shows that the claim was being generally put forward by the more enlightened educators of the day, a fact of which we are also reminded by the existence of Prince Ludwig's Association at Anhalt-Köthen. Von Raumer and those who follow him represent Ratke as a disciple of Francis Bacon; but in the matter of vernacular languages the opinions of Bacon and Ratke were clean contrary. The Englishman was always careful to give a Latin dress to such of his works as he deemed more important. When sending to

---

[1] Israel in Rein, *ut supra*.

Prince Charles the *De Augmentis* (the enlarged version of the *Advancement* in Latin) Bacon wrote, "It is a book that will live, and be a citizen of the world, as English books are not." This is a natural expression from a scholar who wished to secure a hearing from a scholarly public. But there was more in his distrust of the employment of the vernacular; he was doubtful of its future. "For these modern languages," he wrote to a friend, "will at one time or another play the bank-rowte with books, and since I have lost much time with this age, I would be glad if God would give me leave to recover it with posterity[1]." Ratke, on the contrary, shows full confidence in "these modern languages," and his claim to a place in educational history depends mainly upon the increased use of the vernacular which he desired to introduce into the school-room. Not only was German to be carefully studied as a branch of learning, but he would also employ it as the medium of instruction in the higher studies, in place of the usual Latin. This latter proposal, rather than an extended curriculum, would appear to be the true significance to be attached to Ratke's scheme of "a school for all arts and faculties[2]."

From Ratke's own accounts of his projects, and from responsible contemporary reports upon them, we are entitled to assert that these did not include the introduction into the school course of a knowledge of natural science, nor the employment of a method consciously psychological. Raumer and those who, like Mr Quick, have followed Raumer, made claims of this kind on behalf of Ratke which are contradicted by the evidence. The idea of the vernacular school, the belief that it was the duty of the magistracy to provide schools for the community, and that all should at least be taught to read and write are anticipations of Comenius;

---

[1] Church, *Bacon*, p. 210.
[2] "Memorial" to the Reichstag, Art. 2.

but so far from being an originator of modern pedagogy, Ratke's ideas in the field of method were, on the whole, not commendable. The problem of method with which he dealt exclusively was that of language teaching; and here he offers but two or three suggestions, of which the most valuable is the employment of the vernacular in the teaching of Latin. In effect, his language-method in other respects is : Fix a boy's attention on one thing and make him repeat it over and over again, a direction which makes the proscription of rote merely nominal. The use in all schools of a standard text-book, a great point in Ratke's scheme, had been anticipated long before in England by the prescribed employment of Lily's *Grammar*, the result not causing general satisfaction, as Brinsley's opinion goes to show.

NOTE TO CHAPTER II.

RATKE'S CLAIMS.

RATKE is so frequently said in English text-books to be the *fons et origo* of modern psychological pedagogy that one who ventures to question that assertion may crave indulgence while he states his reasons for dissent. The conception, due originally to Niemeyer and endorsed by Raumer in his *History* (1843), appears in two well-known books dealing with educational history, Prof. Laurie's *John Amos Comenius* (see pp. 16, 17) and the late Mr Quick's *Essays on Educational Reformers* (see especially pp. 109–115). Both writers repeat Raumer's statement of nine principles, which, Mr Quick adds, are gathered from a book published by Rhenius in 1626, the *Methodus Institutionis nova...Ratichii et Ratichianorum*. This book was, as a matter of fact, published at Leipzig in 1617, the year of Ratke's unlucky visit to Basel. As its title[1] states, Ratke is only in part responsible for its contents, his work being confined to the *In methodum linguarum generalis Introductio*. The nine principles quoted by Prof. Laurie, and of which Mr Quick made so much, are from a portion of the book (the third tractate) which the editor Rhenius states expressly was not written by Ratke, but by his fellow-workers in Augsburg. Still, with two very important exceptions, the principles of this third tractate are to be found in a document addressed to Prince Ludwig by Ratke within a few days after

---

[1] *Methodus Institutionis nova quadruplex M. Joh. Rhenii, Nicodemi Frischlini, Ratichii et Ratichianorum ter gemina Jesuitarum*, Lipsiae, 1617.

his arrival at Köthen. The first exception is the 9th and last principle of the tractate erroneously ascribed to Ratke, *Per inductionem et experimentum omnia.* This catch-word might have issued from the *Novum Organum* itself; but it is foreign to the thought of Ratke, who was no more a Baconian than was Brinsley. Secondly, Mr Quick, following Raumer not too exactly, makes the first principle of the tractate read as follows: "In everything we should follow the order of Nature. There is a certain natural sequence along which the human intelligence moves in acquiring knowledge. This sequence must be studied, and instruction must be based on the knowledge of it[1]." The "natural method," "the course of Nature" were phrases of not infrequent occurrence in Ratke's writings, but not with the well-defined meaning which Mr Quick has here assigned to them. Thus in the Explanation appended to the Memorial to the Diet, "course of Nature" means the employment of the mother-tongue in all studies, but especially the elementary. The subsequently written (1613) Elucidation of this Memorial asserts "that all should follow the *natural order*, which endeavours to proceed from the simple and the low to the great and high, and from the known to the unknown[2]." That the phrase "course of Nature," as understood by Ratke, means little more than these trite assertions, would appear also from such a passage as the following, written by Prince Christian, Ludwig's brother, in 1618, when the Anhalt princes were considering the advisability of employing the Didacticus. "As to the 'Modus' of Ratichius, it cannot be denied that he grounds it upon many fair foundations, as, that one must proceed from *generalia* to *specialia*, and from that which is easier to the more difficult, that one learns one thing after another and not much at once, that one ought to learn from

[1] K. von Raumer, *Gesch. der Päd.*, Theil ii. p. 29; and *Essays on Educational Reformers*, p. 109.

[2] Rein, *Handb.*, art. "Ratke."

standard books, and that through the mother-tongue other languages may be made clear[1]."

These are phrases expressing obvious truths, and many books upon teaching make a point to this day of solemnly asserting most of them. But they do not constitute that psychological basis for instruction which Ratke is said by some to have laid down. There is as little ground for ascribing a consciously psychological theory of teaching to Ratke, as there is for describing him as a disciple of Francis Bacon.

[1] Krause, p. 46.

CHAPTER III.

BACON AND COMENIUS

THERE are circumstances which render the Bohemian, John Amos Komensky, otherwise Comenius, especially interesting to the English student of educational history. Not only did he draw much inspiration and some concrete direction from the writings of Francis Bacon; he was resident in London during the nine months preceding the outbreak of the Civil War, an invited guest in his quality of educational reformer, and he remained the friend, the correspondent, and in a measure the master in educational theory, of some who were instrumental in bringing him to London, or who welcomed his presence there[1].

The achievement which entitles Comenius to a high place in the history of educational opinion is the composition of the *Great Didactic*. First written when its author was under forty, and published in its final shape a quarter of a century later, it

---

[1] This is not the place in which to narrate the chequered history of Comenius's life as schoolmaster, educational theorist and reformer, ecclesiastic and mystic; born in Moravia in 1592, he died at Amsterdam in 1670. Professor Laurie's *John Amos Comenius, Bishop of the Moravians*, has long been a standard authority in English. Under the title, *The Great Didactic* (1896), Mr Keatinge has translated the *Didactica Magna*, with biographical and historical introductions. A more exhaustive work than either is Kvačsala's *J. A. Comenius, sein Leben und seine Schriften* (Vienna, 1892).

contains all those principles which, owing to their general application, make Comenius's ideas on education worthy of attention to-day. Some of his contemporaries were conscious of the book's importance; its memory, however, did not long survive his and their decease. That its value was not widely recognised during the century and a half, or more, which followed Comenius's death is probably explained by insufficient knowledge of the book's contents. Written at first in the author's native Bohemian, it could not be generally accessible in that language; and though the practice of the time makes it probable that a limited number of manuscript or even printed translations was in circulation, there is no direct evidence on the point[1]. It could not appeal to many readers until it appeared in a Latin dress, in which form we now first know it in the Amsterdam folio of 1657. That book (Comenius's *Opera Didactica Omnia*) required a drastic editing such as its author did not give it. The various parts are very unequal in bulk and in merit, ranging from treatises such as the *Great Didactic* itself and the "*Methodus linguarum no-vissima*," through small books like the *School of Infancy* and the *Gate of Tongues Unlocked*, down to an announcement of the *Orbis Pictus*, a book which had not yet seen the light; this scholastic medley is loosely connected by passages, some long, some short, of an autobiographical kind, which are the authoritative source (frequently the only source) of our knowledge of the author's life up to 1657. The four "Parts" bound in one volume contain about 2,200 columns folio, in print often small; the *Great Didactic* is but a small fraction (58 pages) of a bulky work, amidst whose very miscellaneous contents it was only too likely to become *Vox clamantis in deserto*. Moreover, in his later years Comenius's reputation suffered from his innocent but not very wise association with

---

[1] Comenius (*Op. Did. Om.* vol. i. p. 4) says that he began a Latin version in 1638.

"prophets," some crazy, one, at least, fraudulent, and the fact would reflect upon his earlier work. The folio of 1657 became a rare book, and the *Great Didactic* shared with the rest of its contents that obscurity from which Raumer drew it by the account which he gave in his *Geschichte der Pädagogik* (1843–51).

Comenius relates the circumstances amidst which he wrote the *Great Didactic* between the years 1628 and 1632. For some twenty years he had, from time to time, thought over plans which might secure a wider extension of liberal studies, the provision of more schools, and the introduction of an easier method of learning. About 1628 these problems were more closely associated with the conditions of his daily life as a schoolmaster, and, in a course of reading expressly directed to their elucidation, he came upon the names of many who had begun to labour strenuously at reforming the method of study; amongst others he mentions Ratke, and "Campanella and Verulam, glorious restorers of Philosophy." His reading raised in him the hope that "so many different sparks would at last break out into flame. Hence when I seemed to note certain defects and gaps, I could not refrain from attempting somewhat which, supported upon a stable foundation and thoroughly thought out, would itself suffer nothing to shake it. Wherefore, after much cogitation, by bringing the whole matter to the immoveable laws and rules of Nature, there was born under my hand the *Great Didactic*, which sets forth a scheme for readily and soundly teaching everybody everything[1]."

The casual mention of "Verulam" in the foregoing passage, even when strengthened by the epithet "restorer of Philosophy," does not, of course, prove that Comenius had any great acquaintance with Bacon's writings. But, probability quite apart, there is superabundant internal evidence in Comenius's works

[1] *J. A. Comenii Opera Didactica Omnia* (Amsterdam, 1657). Part i. col. 442.

that he was fully in sympathy with that New Philosophy of Natural Science, which later generations came to associate with Bacon more especially. Nor is direct reference wanting. The following passage is at once an appreciation of Francis Bacon in his most characteristic philosophic aspect, and an assertion of aims on the part of the writer which transcended those of the author of the *Novum Organum*: the reference is to Comenius's own idea of an all-embracing system of knowledge which he named *Pansophia*. "We need standards to which we may bring Things and dogmas concerning them, so that necessary truths may be readily separated from contingent, useful from useless, true from false. Such a standard the illustrious Verulam seems to have discovered for scrutinising Nature, a certain ingenious induction, which is in truth an open road by which to penetrate into the hidden things of Nature. But this induction demands the incessant industry of many men and ages, and seems so laborious, and keeps certainty so long in suspense, that notable as the invention is, it is contemned by many as useless. And indeed it brings small help to me in building Pansophia, because (as I have said) it is addressed solely to the revelation of Nature's secrets, whilst I look to the whole Scheme of Things (*rerum universitas*)." (*Op. Did. Omn.* Part i. col. 432.)

In general treatment, as well as in things of detail, the *Great Didactic* is distinctly Baconian, that is, it bears marks of the influence of "the illustrious Verulam" rather than of the contemporary students who were actually constructing the foundations of scientific knowledge. The work, in short, shares the limitations and defects as well as some of the excellences of *The Advancement of Learning* and the *Novum Organum*. In conception and in execution, Comenius's book is deductive (its title-page declares that its "Fundamental principles are elicited from the very nature of Things"), and, persistent advocate of induction in the pursuit of knowledge as Bacon was, he himself preferred, as the *Novum Organum* shows, to develop his own

A.   4

theses in that deductive manner which was the more familiar logical instrument.

Both writers press analogy into their service, often very effectively in illustration of a point, sometimes trivially, or even so illogically as to allege it as proof. Examples are super-abundant in Comenius, since it is through analogy that he tries to establish the conformity to Nature of the principles, rules and suggestions which he brings forward. The following is typical of his manner: First, he states what he believes to be a "Principle of Nature," *e.g.* "Nature advances from the easy to the more difficult." This "principle" is illustrated from Nature; as, in the forming of an egg, the beginning is not with the hard shell, but with the yolk. Similarly, a bird first stands on its feet, next learns to move its wings, then to raise itself from the ground, and lastly attains to real flight. The "principle" thus stated and illustrated, he next shows its imitation in the arts and handicrafts: *e.g.* a carpenter learns first to cut down trees, next to saw the timber, then to join it, and lastly, to build houses. Comenius then sets forth the deviations of the school-room from this principle of Nature, as when the unknown is taught by means of the equally unknown, *e.g.* beginners in Latin learn the rules *in Latin*: youths of all nations (French, German, Polish, Hungarian, etc.) are informed in the same rules of grammar, though each of these vernaculars has its own relation to Latin, and, therefore, requires its own special treatment. Lastly, Comenius shows how these errors may be avoided, and the natural principle obeyed: *e.g.* the mother-tongue must be used as the basis of the language-teaching, the subject-matter of lessons must begin with the familiar, and pass thence to the remote, knowledge must be acquired first through the senses and later by way of generali-sation and judgment[1].

This is Comenius's normal course; first the statement and

---

[1] Abridged from the *Didactica Magna*, ch. xvii. fund. 4.

illustration of a supposed principle of Nature, next, a statement of the imitation of that principle in the arts, thirdly, deviations from the principle in the school, and lastly, rectification of these deviations. In this way Comenius brings before us the nine "Requisites of teaching and of learning," the ten "principles of facility," the ten "principles of thoroughness," and the eight "principles of compendious rapidity"; and in treating most of them he conscientiously follows his rubric of Principle, Imitation, Deviation, and Rectification.

To the modern reader it is no longer possible to consider seriously the manner in which the author seeks to give the sanction of "Nature" to his opinions on educational procedure. The arbitrary statement of an assumed principle of Nature, when backed by the practice of gardeners, painters, and builders (and what "principle," if only it be worded with sufficient want of precision, cannot be shown as related to such practice?), is taken as proving the necessity or reasonableness of all kinds of devices in school. Comenius scarcely makes amends for his flagrant misuse of analogy, and his readiness to commit fallacies of deduction, by his Baconian insistence on the need for Induction in scientific studies. Sometimes there is an obvious or, at least, an arguable *analogy* between Rectification and Principle; sometimes the analogy is forced to the point of absurdity. "The sun is not occupied with individual objects, tree or animal, but lights and heats the whole earth": "In imitation of this, there should be but one teacher at the head of a school, or, at least, of a class." "The sun, leading in spring, summer, autumn, and winter, makes all things germinate, flower, and produce fruit at the same time throughout all regions: Therefore one and the same task should be imposed upon the whole class[1]."

But whether the analogy be a real or a fictitious one, the educational method, process or principle advocated is logically

[1] *Didactica Magna,* ch. xix.

independent of the proposition on which the writer professes
to ground it. The despised schoolmen knew very much better
than to confound analogy with proof, and they would have
made short work with Comenius's "arguments." Still, it is
significant that the seventeenth-century writer, having cast off
the ties of Authority, turns, however blindly, to natural process
and natural law for light in the attempt to construct a theory of
education. And even Bacon is not richer in the wealth of
concrete illustration, usually of a familiar, every-day kind, with
which Comenius makes his meaning clear.

The author of the *Great Didactic* is a Baconian, too, in the
essential points of refusing to defer to Authority, and insisting
on direct, first-hand observation of natural phenomena—in
Bacon's phrase, *Ipsis consuescere rebus*. "As far as possible,"
writes Comenius, "men are to be taught to become wise, not
by books, but by the Heavens, the Earth, oaks and beeches;
that is, they must learn to know and examine the things themselves, and not the observations and testimony of others about
the things[1]." Again, "The truth and certainty of science
depend not otherwise than on the testimony of the Senses;
for Things impress themselves at once and immediately upon
the Senses, but afterwards upon the Understanding by inter-
mission of them....Wherefore, Science is the more certain the
more it rests upon Sense[2]." Contrast these dicta with the story
which is told of the monk, Scheiner, one of the discoverers of
Sun-spots. Having reported his discovery to his Superior, he
met with the following assurance, "I have searched through
Aristotle, and can find nothing of the kind mentioned: be
certain, therefore, that it is a deception of your senses, or of
your glasses[3]."

But in nothing is Comenius more directly inspired by
Francis Bacon than in the conviction, held by both, each in

[1] *Did. Magn.* ch. xviii. 28.
[2] *Did. Magn.* ch. xx. 8.
[3] Baden-Powell, *History of Nat. Phil.* p. 171.

his own province, that he had discovered a method of universal application, *the* method, in short, whether of knowledge, or of imparting it, and of a kind that any man of ordinary intelligence could employ with success. Says the *Novum Organum*: "Our method of discovering the sciences is such as to leave little to the acuteness and strength of wit, and indeed rather to level wit and intellect. For as in the drawing of a straight line, or accurate circle by hand, much depends on its steadiness and practice, but if a ruler or compass be employed there is little occasion for either: so it is with our method." (Bk. ı. Aph. lxi.) Now, the *Great Didactic* is the *Novum Organum* of pedagogy. Just as Bacon had discovered his new instrument for advancing the knowledge of science, so Comenius has discovered his new instrument for educating children. The title of his book asserts this conviction. It is, "the Great Didactic [Art], setting forth a universal system for teaching everybody everything." [Didactica Magna: Universale Omnes Omnia Docendi Artificium Exhibens.] Added to the belief that he had discovered *the* method, is the further belief (implied, perhaps, in the other) that, given a good method, all things are possible. Says Comenius: "It is certain that any man can attain to any height whatsoever by means of steps duly arranged, adequate, solid and safe[1]." Again, commenting on the practice of apprenticeship, he says that "a proper scholastic discipline would get through the whole Encyclopaedia of Learning within a certain number of years and turn out from the schools ('man-manufactories,' *humanitatis officina*) men truly erudite, moral, pious[2]." These two beliefs, or rather the one belief that a method was discoverable whose powers were well-nigh unlimited, proved to be a will o' the wisp for thinkers on education from Comenius's time onwards. It explains the wide range of things knowable which Milton and Locke, for example, would bring before the boy and

---

[1] *Did. Magn.* xii. 15. [2] *Ibid.* xxvii. 1, 2.

youth: it excuses Basedow and Pestalozzi for their attempts to produce text-books so far in accordance with "the method" that even a comparatively ignorant person might be entrusted to, shall we say *teach*? with their assistance.

It was clear to the minds of both the English philosopher and the Moravian schoolmaster that, in the field of Knowledge, the prime requisite of their day was research, carried out on a scale so liberal and extensive that only the State could provide the means, and so organised as to employ the most able scholars. In Bacon's case, this idea has its most complete expression in his picture of "Solomon's House"; Comenius's project called "Pansophia" embodies a very similar thought. Comenius, it is true, never so thoroughly divested himself of purely metaphysical principles as did his master, and the day came later in his life when he ventured to expostulate with the Royal Society for its members' too exclusive interest in mere phenomena[1]. But the general likeness of the fundamental conceptions of *Pansophia* and *Solomon's House* is too evident to be missed: and, moreover, the notion of State-organised research on the great scale exerted much influence amongst English educational reformers of the generation succeeding Bacon's.

From the days of his earliest writings, Bacon often endeavoured to impress others with his own deep conviction that it was the duty, the privilege and the manifest interest of the State to provide liberally for the prosecution of scientific studies. He had pleaded earnestly in that sense in the *Advancement of Learning*: nowhere does the idea find fuller expression than in the *New Atlantis*, the first version of which (in Latin) appeared in print in 1627, the year following the author's death. Written within the last two or three years of Bacon's life, and subsequently to his disgrace, the *New Atlantis* depicts a "good time coming," after the manner of *Utopia* and the many similar fables that have presented men's

[1] See Keatinge, p. 96.

dreams, hopes, and aspirations, from Plato's day to our own. Bacon's first editor (Rawley, 1627) put it forward as a "fragment," and as a work of art it is obviously incomplete: but it would seem to have had but one purpose, the description of a new seat of learning, and that purpose is achieved in the account of "Solomon's House." Bacon has been at the utmost pains to impress his readers with the national importance of this institution, not only in setting forth particulars of its work, but in ascribing a dignity almost more than human to the men who directed it. The house is, we are told, the "very eye of this kingdom," Bensalem, "the noblest foundation...that ever was upon the earth, and the lantern of this kingdom." Its purpose is "the finding out of the true nature of all things (whereby God might have the more glory in the workmanship of them, and men the more fruit in the use of them)." "The end of our foundation," says one of the Fathers of Solomon's House, "is the knowledge of causes, and secret motions of things: and the enlarging the bounds of human empire, to the effecting of all things possible." To discharge this great office, the House employs a whole hierarchy of workers in Natural Science, who are constantly engaged in research, according to the method which Bacon had described in the *Novum Organum*. The chief of these men of science are, by virtue of their office, of the first rank in the kingdom; and when one of them visits a city there, he is received with more than kingly honour. His office is sacerdotal, episcopal: his chariot is preceded by crozier and pastoral staff. "He held up his bare hand as he went, as blessing the people, but in silence." Of the particular Father of Solomon's House who is presented to us in the fable, we are told that he was a man of middle stature and age, comely of person, and had an aspect *as if he pitied men.*"

All branches of natural science, and all kinds of useful arts occupy the minds of the workers in Solomon's House. Provision is made for observation and experiment in the study

of soils, of horticulture and arboriculture, of meteorology, of
air, and of temperature, of water-power. The cure of diseases
and the preparation of medicines are studied, and vivisection
is practised : careful attention is bestowed upon food-stuffs,
sweet-meats, and perfumes. "We have also divers mechanical
arts which you have not, and stuffs made by them, as papers,
linen, silks, tissues, dainty works of feathers of wonderful
lustre, excellent dyes, and many others." Elaborate provision
is made for the experimental study of Sound, of Light, of
Optics. "We have also engine-houses, where are prepared
engines and instruments for all sorts of motions :...We imitate
also, flights of birds : we have some degrees of flying in the
air : we have ships and boats for going under water, and
brooking of seas," etc.

One of several parallels from Comenius is furnished in
a chapter (the thirty-first) of the *Great Didactic*, which closes
in the following way. "There is," says Comenius, "no need
to mention how necessary is a School of schools, or Didactic
College, wheresoever it ought to be founded : or, if there be
no hope of such a foundation, corporations being left wherever
they are, the design itself should be cherished with a holy
faith among the learned, sworn as they are to the promotion
of God's glory in this very matter. Let their societies tend to
clarifying and dispersing amongst the race of men the light
of Wisdom, that the principles of Science be more and more
elicited, and man's estate be improved by new and most
advantageous discoveries. For unless we desire to stick ever
in the same spot, or even to go back, we must take thought
for the good progress of what has been begun. To which
business neither a single man nor a single age is sufficient,
but many acting in concert and in succession must continue
what has been begun. This universal college would bear the
same relation to other schools that the belly bears to the other
corporeal members, that of a living laboratory supplying sap,
life and strength to all."

In this paragraph there is the hint of an idea which, developed later under the name of *Pansophia*, was in brief the translation into matter of fact of that Solomon's House of which Bacon had dreamed. Comenius spent years of toil in working out the conception, but in vain, so far as immediate results are concerned. Most probably his fame is the gainer by the failure; he was not the man, either by attainments or training, to rear from its foundations a home for scientific research, as, indeed, his pronouncements on Natural Science show. Like his master Bacon, he saw the necessity for a more direct interrogation of Nature, but his notions concerning scientific method were the vaguest; both men had the wide outlook over the Promised Land of Knowledge which enabled them to discern in which direction success was probable: they had not at all accurately charted the route, but they knew its bearings. So long as they remained in the region of generalities, their utterances made for an essential reform in studies and in method; so soon as they left that region they ran the risk of becoming nugatory, or even harmful.

However, *Pansophia* was the darling of its author's later years, his pedagogic work seeming trivial to him in comparison. His visit to this country (1641–2) was most probably owing to the interest aroused by his pansophic schemes in certain public-spirited Englishmen, rather than to their regard for his scholastic reforms. From the date of that visit till the close of the century repeated attempts were made to erect a school, or college, which should be either a Solomon's House, or an institution preparatory thereto. The men who made these attempts had a clearer vision of what was requisite than had Comenius, and if political conditions had been different they might have succeeded, to the advantage of subsequent English educational practice. To-day, we are tentatively groping our way to the establishment of that modern form of the pansophic college which is partially realised in the great Technological Institutions and Technical Universities of Germany and Switzerland.

CHAPTER IV.

THE GREAT DIDACTIC.

THE opening chapters of the *Great Didactic* disclose the author's conception of human nature, whence he deduces the essential character of education, its universal necessity, and the consequent obligation of the community with reference to it. Man, last work of Creation, is the acme of all, the creature absolute, whose true end is to participate with God in the life of eternal blessedness. The present life of earth is but a preparation for the beatific life hereafter, and of this preparation there are three grades, commonly named Learning, Virtue, Religion. Nature gives the seeds of Knowledge, of Morals, and of Religion,—but themselves are not so given; they must be acquired by prayer, by learning, and by action. Therefore man is not badly defined as the *disciplinable animal*; deprived of discipline, he fails to become man. Indeed, Comenius is so convinced of the need of this discipline, that he asserts that a school was opened in Paradise for man before the Fall. He argues thus: Although the earliest human beings had from the beginning the powers of locomotion, speech and reasoning, yet they wanted the concrete knowledge of things which comes from experience. (They were not, in short, inductive Baconians.) This, he says, is manifest from Eve's conversation with the Serpent: for if she had had a fuller experience, she would have known that this creature has not the faculty of speech, and she would have been certain that there was some deceit (*Op. Did. Om.* 1657, col. 35 ; ch. vi.).

To lead the social life, to get knowledge and to refer himself and all else to God are man's natural tendencies : education is the process by which these are made actual and effective. Every human being, simply by virtue of his humanity, claims the benefits conferred by education, irrespective of rank or sex. Comenius's protests against the neglect to instruct girls, to educate the poor and those of but modest intellectual power are the more prominent, when compared with the common opinion of his day, which he dared to brave in words like these. "With God is no respect of persons, as He Himself so often protests. If, therefore, we admit some to intellectual culture, excluding others, we wrong not only those who have the same nature as ourselves, but we also wrong God, whose will it is that He be confessed, loved and praised by all upon whom He has impressed His image....It is not given us to know to what uses Divine foresight has destined this man, or that ; but it is known that God has sometimes framed excellent instruments of His glory out of the poorest, the most abject, the most obscure. Let us, therefore, imitate the sun in heaven, which warms and gives light to the whole earth, so that whatever is able to live, to flourish, to flower, and bear fruit, may do these things. That some seem naturally dull and stupid is no objection, but rather a reason for commending and urging this universal culture of minds. The slower and the less endowed by nature one is, the more he needs to be helped, that he may be delivered, as far as may be, from his brutish dulness and stupidity. Nor can anyone be found whose intellect is so unfortunate that it cannot be somewhat amended by culture....Some wits are precocious, but soon become feeble and blunt, others, dull at first, grow sharp and penetrating....Why, therefore, should we wish that only precocious and quick wits should be tolerated in the field of letters? Let nobody be shut out, save him to whom God has denied senses or a mind."

In a time when all but the barest rudiments of instruction were denied, irrespective of genius, of wealth, or of lack of either, to half the human race, the Moravian reformer said, "No satisfactory reason can be given why the weaker sex ought to be entirely excluded from the study of Wisdom, whether treated in Latin or in the vernacular, for they are equally in the image of God, are equally participants in His grace, and in His future kingdom. They are endowed with minds quick and capable of wisdom, often beyond our own sex....Why, therefore, should we admit them to the alphabet indeed, but afterwards drive them away from books? Do we fear their rashness? The more we occupy their thoughts, the less will there be place for the rashness which springs from an empty mind....If anyone says, What will happen, if mechanics, peasants, day labourers and even wenches become literate? the answer is, that, this universal education of the young being duly constituted, no one will be without the means of thinking aright, of choosing, following, nay of doing what is good. Everyone will know how to prepare himself for all the actions and desires of life, within what bounds he should advance, and how his present situation should be secured[1]." "Those in subordinate positions are to be enlightened, that they may know how to obey their rulers wisely and prudently: not by compulsion, nor obsequiously, like asses, but freely, moved by the love of order" (ch. vi. 9). The sentence that follows is italicised, and marked in the margin, "N.B.": no doubt the writer's indignation had a touch of personal bitterness as he recalled recent experiences. "For a rational creature is not to be led by shouts, by fear of prison,. by

[1] *Did. Magn.* ch. ix., " All youth of both sexes should be put to school" is the title of the chapter.

cudgels, but by reason. Where it is otherwise God receives the insult inflicted on those whom He has equally made in His own image, and human affairs are filled with violence and unrest."

The State, therefore, has an obligation in the matter of education towards every one of its members. "It remains, then, that all who are born men stand in need of instruction: they need it that they may be men, not wild beasts, brutal monsters, nor lifeless stocks." Comenius shows, at length (chiefly in the 27th and following chapters), how the State may discharge this obligation by instituting a system of schools, attendance at which shall be universal and compulsory in the primary stage, whilst the privilege of continuing education a stage higher is reserved for those who, being intellectually fitted to receive it, are most likely to turn higher education to profitable account.

Comenius postulates that *the* business of youth is education, expressly grounding himself upon the prolonged infancy and slow growth to maturity which characterise man above all created beings, small and great. Where ability, knowledge, and circumstances allow, he would continue the period of formal education up to the age of twenty-four; in no case should it terminate before twelve. Sharing to the fullest that seventeenth-century belief, born of faith in Method, that a pupil under favourable conditions might master all things knowable, he proposes a curriculum arranged concentrically, so to say. That is, the same branches of knowledge are to be studied in each of the four periods into which the twenty-four educable years are divided, the differences being those which the varying stages of mental development in the pupil make inevitable.

From birth to the age of six, the child receives his education at home in the domestic kindergarten which Comenius has sketched in the *School of Infancy*. Every family should be such a school, and the educator would serve it best by furnishing mothers with a simple hand-book and a book of pictures pourtraying well-nigh everything picturable. Comenius, like the German-speaking communities of to-day, was of opinion that the right age for beginning formal schooling is six. From six to twelve, children are to attend the Public Vernacular Schools, of which there should be at least one in every well-ordered habitation of men, whether hamlet, village, town or city, the towns and cities, of course, requiring each many primary schools, according to population. In every city there should be a gymnasium, or Latin School, whose pupils having passed through the Vernacular School, spend the years from twelve to eighteen in secondary school studies. The years from eighteen to twenty-four belong to foreign travel and the Academy, there being one such institution in every kingdom.

The Mother School and the Vernacular School contain the whole school population up to the age of twelve, without respect to rank, wealth, or sex. The Vernacular School is the Common School; all there pass through the common minimum curriculum which it is thought Education demands, and out of which all advanced studies spring. Class distinctions must not be encouraged, and at the early age of six it is impossible to say whether a particular boy is better fitted for manual labour or for a learned profession.

The Latin School gives a more thorough education to those who aspire higher than the workshop, while the Academy trains the future teachers and leaders in Church, in School, and in State.

The children who show aptitude for learning, though their parents be poor, are not to be refused admission to the Latin School on that ground. Comenius does not say so, but he seems to be contemplating some scheme of exhibitions, or scholarships, by which poor but capable children may continue their education. At all events, much of his plan is impracticable and many of his expressions pointless, unless we assume a scholarship scheme of some kind. School-education is closed at eighteen by a public examination whose purpose is to discover who should go to the University, who to occupations which do not demand the highest education.

The constitution and courses of study of the Vernacular and Latin Schools are fully described: the more noteworthy points only can be briefly considered here. The aim of the Vernacular School is said to be that general instruction in human concerns which it befits all men to receive[1]. It does not follow the practice of most schools, which is to give the place of honour to Latin. On the contrary, no Latin is taught, because "to attempt to teach a foreign language, before the mother-tongue has been learned, is all one as to try to teach your son to ride before he can walk." The school seeks to make the pupil learned in Things, as distinct from Words, to give him Real Learning, the knowledge of *Res*, "Reals," Realien[2]; such knowledge is best conveyed through the vernacular. This postponement of Latin till the 12th year will be compensated in the more rapid acquisition of the language by the better-instructed and mentally stronger pupil.

The Vernacular School course includes, in addition to instruction in Religion, Morals, and the three R's, certain striking novelties. Thus, the boys and girls must learn "to measure skilfully in the accustomed manner length, breadth, and distances, they must learn so much of economics, of politics, and of mechanical principles as will enable them to understand ordinary daily life at home and in their State, nor may they be ignorant of the course of the world's history as set forth in the most general way; to this must be added the chief things in Cosmography, as the rotundity of the heavens, the globe of the Earth hanging in the midst, the movement of the Ocean, the various straits of Seas and Rivers, the chief

---

[1] " Generalem nos intendimus institutionem, omnium qui homines nati sunt, ad omnia humana " (*Did. Magn.* ch. xxix. 2).

[2] "Tandem, quia nos Eruditionem querimus realem" (*ibid.* 5).

divisions of the World, the chief Kingdoms of Europe: but, above all, the Cities, Mountains, and Rivers of their Fatherland and whatsoever is memorable therein[1]." The pupils of this very modern elementary school are to be taught in six classes, that is, they pass through a class each year: and as far as possible, each class should be so separated from the rest that mutual interference is prevented[2]. Finally, if any boys are to learn a modern foreign language let it be done at about the 10th, 11th, or 12th year, that is, between the Vernacular School and the Latin School. The most convenient plan is to send the pupils where they will hear the foreign language, and not the vernacular, daily; there let them read, write, learn by heart and otherwise exercise themselves in their familiar Vernacular School books, but these expressed in the new tongue. The familiarity of the subject-matter will greatly facilitate the learning of the foreign language.

The Latin School is the weak point of Comenius's School-system, since it aims at the impossible combination, in the mind of every pupil, of erudition of the older type with the knowledge of physical science that was to mark the new. Such a combination could not be effected in six years of study, from twelve to eighteen, unless, indeed, a mere smattering of everything was to be considered sufficient. Sciolism was the bog into which their superstitious trust in Method drew many of the scholastic innovators. Thus, Comenius proposes to teach in the Latin School the Mother-tongue, Latin, Greek and Hebrew (the three foreign languages virtually constituting the ordinary secondary curriculum of the time), and further "to exhaust the whole encyclopaedia of the Arts[3]." The study of the seven liberal arts which the Masters of Arts (Philosophiae Magistri) are popularly supposed to

[1] *Did. Mag.* ch. xxix. 6.

[2] "Sex in Classes—quantum potest loco etiam separatas, ne se mutuo impediant—dispescitor." *Did. Mag.* ch. xxix. 8.

[3] Opening words of ch. xxx. *Did. Mag.*

complete, is not· at all sufficient, says Comenius, for these lads of eighteen. They must also master the principles of Physics so as to apply them practically to the various uses of life, as in Medicine, Agriculture, and the mechanical Arts. They must have a competent knowledge of Geography and World-History; and Ethics and Theology must be studied to good purpose.

This excessively overburdened course is distributed through the work of six classes, whose names, beginning at the lowest (the boys of twelve to thirteen) are : Grammar, Natural Philosophy, Mathematics, Ethics, Logic, Rhetoric. Comenius calls attention to the precedence of Natural Philosophy over Ethics and Logic in this arrangement, and defends it as the only satisfactory plan. "I have already convincingly demonstrated," he says, "that before we treat of the relations of Things in general, we ought to consider the concrete Thing itself (*Res ante Modum rerum tradi debere*), that is, Matter before Form. I have also shown that the one method fitted to ensure sound and speedy progress is that we be instructed in the knowledge of Things before we are called upon either to judge them acutely, or to speak eloquently concerning them. Otherwise, you may be ready with all the shifts of Logic and Rhetoric, yet if you are destitute with respect to the things which you are examining, or about which you intend to persuade, what in truth will you examine, or whom will you persuade?... Reasoning and speech turn so much about things, and depend so much upon them, that, without Things, these two either vanish away, or become sound without meaning, a stupid or ridiculous effort. Since, therefore, reasoning and speech are founded upon Things, sheer necessity demands that the foundation be laid in advance." (*Did. Magn.* ch. xxx. 5.)

Comenius disclaims any desire to propose University reforms or innovations ; still, he has some interesting suggestions in this field also. The Latin School course is to be closed by a public examination, held by the Scholarchs, whose judgment shall decide which pupils are fit for the University, the rest

A. 5

betaking themselves to the plough, the workshop, or to traffic. The select intellects, the very flower of humanity, proceed to the Academy, there to study Theology, or Politics, or Medicine, or whatever branch of Knowledge each desires to become expert in, it being reserved to a few (the very quintessence, let us say) to adopt Bacon's boast, and take all Knowledge for their province. "Care must be taken that the Academies nourish only the diligent, industrious men of good life: let them not tolerate sham students who squander their patrimony and time in ease and debauchery, an evil example to the others." Once a year the Academy should be visited by Royal Commissioners, whose duty it would be to test the work of students and teachers[1]. Amongst the suggestions which Comenius makes for the University life is the Baconian idea of a Great College devoted to research, the idea which was the parent of *Pansophia*.

The curriculum which Comenius proposed to introduce into his schools suffers from the obvious defect of including too much; this should not obscure the excellent principle on which it is based. Again and again its author enunciates Bacon's assertion that one great end of knowledge is the practical every-day service of mankind. It was an old reproach against the class-room that it dealt with a world which was unlike the world outside its walls, and that pupils got very much less out of their sojourn in the school than they would if only the two worlds were in living, organic connection. Says Comenius, "Whatever is taught should be taught as a thing which is actual (*res praesens*) and of a certain use. Let the pupil see that what he learns is not something from the land of Nowhere, or matters relating to the Platonic Ideas, but things which verily surround us, a true knowledge of which will confer real advantage in our

[1] This same chapter (xxxi.) also suggests something like the University *Seminar*: the professor's lecture of the morning becomes the text of the afternoon discussion by the students, the professor acting as moderator or chairman.

life. So will his mind be keener in attack, and more accurate in discernment" (ch. xx. 16). This is the cry of Pestalozzi, "It is *Life* that educates." It was the principle which was in the end to assure a place in the ordinary school-course for modern studies.

Whatever his personal opinions the seventeenth-century schoolmaster was beyond all else a teacher of language, and particularly of Latin. So true was this, that even Locke, though a writer on education who was not a schoolmaster, and a writer who was convinced of the importance of "real" studies, yet makes his most practical suggestions on method when he deals with the problems of language-teaching. Comenius did not escape from the burden laid upon him by his age and profession ; much of his time and thought he regretfully gave to improving the teaching of the Latin language. But it is one of his limitations that he failed to grasp the possibilities of literature as an instrument of education. The twenty-fifth chapter of the *Great Didactic* bears this title: "If we wish schools to be wholly reformed in accordance with the true standards of true Christianity, either the books of Pagans must be removed from them, or, they must be treated more cautiously than hitherto." With one of his reasons most people would entirely sympathise, namely the unfitness, to say the least, of presenting to young people some aspects of a civilisation, which was not always and in all things controlled by modesty and shame, as both the seventeenth and twentieth centuries agree in understanding these. But Comenius goes much deeper than this in his aversion from the old literatures. He thinks that "our dignity as Christians...does not permit us so to cast away ourselves and our children as to consort with profane pagans, and to hold dalliance with them" (ch. xxv. 10). It is not that he objects to writers who may be adjudged impure, either by ancient or by modern standards. All, or well-nigh all, fall under the same condemnation. Thus, he speaks of "the ravings (*deliramenta*) of the heathen philosophers

and poets," citing St Paul in justification (xxv. 14). To
the objection that all are not impure, he replies, "Yet are
they blind pagans, and turn the minds of their readers from
the true God to gods and goddesses." The temper here
displayed was shared in some degree by well-nigh all the men
who were prominently associated during the seventeenth
century with proposals for educational change : their hard
Puritanism suspected the grace of letters and the beauty of art
as being trivialities, at the best, and darkest evils at the worst.
"O vain man !" cries Comenius, "whoso seeks a clear light
in the darkness of the human reason." The Bible excepted
(and, of course, it is a great exception) he would prefer to
banish literature from the school ; but, if any pagan is to be
admitted, let it be Seneca, Epictetus, Plato, or some similar
teacher of virtue and honesty, in whom less error and super-
stition are to be noted.

An admission must be made which is still more damaging
to Comenius's fame as an educator; he sometimes thinks and
speaks of teaching as a very mechanical process. Thus in the
nineteenth chapter of the *Great Didactic*, he writes : "I affirm
that it is not only possible for one master to preside over
several hundreds of scholars, but I assert that it ought to be
so, because the arrangement is most convenient for him who
teaches and for those who learn." He goes on to clinch this
in a passage calculated to impose a modest diffidence upon the
teacher. "In a word, as by one kneading of material and one
heating of the oven a baker makes many loaves and a brick-
maker burns many bricks ; a printer with one setting-up of type
prints hundreds or thousands of copies of a book, so certainly
a schoolmaster can at one and the same time serve an immense
multitude of scholars by the same studious exercises, without
inconvenience to himself." He becomes complimentary, even
insinuating. "Do we not see that a single trunk suffices for
a tree, however many its branches, and however great the
needful supply of sap? So, too, we see that the sun suffices

for the whole teeming earth." The sun-simile is engaging, but later passages show that the troughs of the baker or brick-maker are the more exact figure of the humble function of teaching as Comenius sometimes conceived it. He says that by employing the perfect method, "even those will be fortunate in teaching who naturally are not so, since the things to be taught and the manner of teaching them will not be brought forth from the mind of the individual teacher, but the learning being ready prepared and suitable means being supplied, he will forthwith instil it, or pour it into youth" (ch. xxxii. 4). This desirable state of things will be more readily attained, when *Informatories* are written for the use of teachers, "which will impress upon them what to do, and where and how to do it, so that they mistake not" (*ibid.* 14). Comenius was a great systematiser, instinctively reducing his projects to time-tables and other tabulations of a like kind : here, at least, he seems to fall into the pit which gapes for the man who over-systematises, he comes to value machinery above its real worth.

But what, it may be asked, is Comenius's conception of that childish mind which is the object of school-administration, of curricula and all the other machinery of education? The answer must be qualified by the fact that our thinker was a man of his own age, not of ours. He viewed the question from a standpoint which was very much that of John Locke's *Essay on the Human Understanding*, though that great book only appeared when Comenius had been dead for twenty years. That is, Comenius's philosophy is a sensationalist philosophy: the mind of the little child is figured by Aristotle's blank tablet, his brain by wax. All the writing subsequently found on that tablet, all the mouldings of that wax are to be explained as the outcome of sights, sounds, and all other varieties of sense-experience conveyed to the mind through the organs of sense, and connected with each other by powers which Comenius calls "internal senses" (ch. xxvii.). *Nihil in Intellectu quod non prius fuerit in Sensu.* To-day we cannot regard the dictum as adequate: but much was to be done in philosophy after Comenius's day before there could be much cogency in our criticism.

To this sensationalist, or experiential theory (it is, perhaps, unfair to use the former epithet alone), Comenius added a belief in the then still established physiology and psychology which, after their long dominance, began to fall into disuse during his lifetime. The bodily "humours" and the "vital spirit," which were made to account for many mysteries in the pre-scientific age, meet us in the *Great Didactic.* Thus, cleverness is said to be the manifestation of a fine, rapid movement of the vital spirit in the brain; excess of that spirit means insolence, intractability; while stupidity is accounted for by a clammy viscous state of the humours in the brain (ch. xii.). The psychology of the book is that account of mental phenomena usually called the Faculty psychology, which though dead long since in the minds and writings of professed students of the science, still stalks abroad in the pages of many writers on the art of teaching. Comenius (ch. xxvii.) sets forth a whole hierarchy of faculties, Senses external, Senses internal (Imagination, Memory, Recollection), Comprehension, Judgment, the Will. He bids us suppose that these in turn are evolved by the growing, or developing mind, that they retain a large measure of mutual independence, and that each is therefore susceptible to a particular cultivation. "It is lost labour to try to form the Will before the Understanding, or the Understanding before the Imagination, or the Imagination before the Senses." Accordingly the School of Infancy trains the external senses, the Vernacular School trains the internal senses, Comprehension and Judgment occupy the Latin School, while the Academy concerns itself especially with the Will[1]. A closer analysis has taught us how

---

[1] *Great Didactic*, ch. xxvii.

artificial such psychologising is : but we cannot fairly require any other from one who had to take his mental science as he found it. If he needed an excuse, the persistence of the theory excuses him.

And yet one of Comenius's legitimate claims to be regarded as a founder of modern pedagogy is grounded upon the association of psychology with teaching. Where his predecessors and contemporaries were content to proceed according to use and wont, to apply rule-of-thumb, and to suffer their psychology to be of the unconscious type shared by all human intercourse, this man consciously brought into the school-room such mental science as was available, used it as a criterion of his practice, contrived new modes of work in the light which it gave, and, by so doing, established the idea of pedagogic method. Until that idea arose, teaching could not be regarded as anything other than a purely empirical art.

The faculty psychology was very artificial : yet it was also an attempt to set forth the truth, that mind develops in an order which, within limits, is a normal order. It is Comenius's merit to have seen that an instruction which aspires to deal successfully with a developing intelligence must conform itself to that normal order. That he was over-dogmatic, and insufficiently informed as to the character of that order, is excusable, his circumstances being remembered : that he rightly grasped the general point of view, and made it a standpoint for his educational theory, is what chiefly matters. He desired to discover a general theory of instruction which should justify, or rather initiate practice, so that the uncertainty which baffled so much of the labours of the school might be replaced by a progress towards better things.

To find that theory he turned to what is loosely called Nature, and in spite of the unjustifiable use of analogy which his procedure implied, he brought back principles, rules, and warnings which have a rightful place in a sound theory of instruction. The dismal picture which he draws of the contemporary school-room may be suspected of exaggeration, as coming from one who had reforms to advocate : but there is enough independent testimony to show that his picture displays only too much that was unhappily true. The guiding principle of the school-room was obedience to authority, rather than scrupulous attention to things as they are. "Scarcely any one teaches physics by ocular demonstration and experiments : all recite the Aristotelian and other texts" (*Did. Magn.* xviii. 25). Teaching by precept took the place of an appeal to the understanding : boys learned rules, exceptions to the rules, and exceptions to the exceptions, until nothing but confusion reigned in many minds. Where fidelity to the written word and the "ipse dixit" stood so high in esteem, the abuse of learning by heart quickly followed. Boys were overburdened by these rote-tasks ; as Montaigne had said, they were asses, loaded with other people's learning, forced to keep the road by dint of blows. Thus a discipline frequently harsh, seldom gentle, united with a preposterous method to make the school a place of terror to children. As though these were insufficient, the school insisted that the naturally active boy, curious concerning the things and the operations about him, should devote the greatest share of his time to learning a foreign language. Yet this chosen task of the school was discharged badly. The earliest study of Latin was the study of *grammar*, written in Latin, and arranged or disarranged in that welter which Comenius calls *Praecepta certe et Regulae et Regularum exceptiones, Exceptionumque limitationes* (ch. xxi.). The outcome of the boy's sojourn in this wilderness was not invariably a working knowledge of the Latin language.

The Method which Comenius drew from a consideration of the minds of children as he had watched their manifestations in the school-room and out of it, the Method which he professed to see obeyed in "Nature," was to bring order into chaos ; henceforth children were to learn "quickly, pleasantly, thoroughly" (*Gt. Did.* Title). The first object of his attack ın the older practice is the excessive employment of teaching by rule: he repeats, unwittingly of course, the injunction of John Brinsley. Children should *understand* that which they are required to learn. To ensure this is partly a matter of curriculum, partly a matter of method. As to curriculum, the first things that the child is called upon to study should be those which are nearest to his intelligence. Convinced of the soundness of the sensationalist psychology, Comenius declares that these are the things of sense. The first studies are to be studies of things: and all studies are to begin with a concrete stage. Where the actual objects cannot be placed before the pupil, then copies, models, pictures, diagrams, or other sensible representation must be submitted to him for observation. Not Pestalozzi himself is more convinced that the foundation of instruction lies in sense-perception.

Curriculum and method must combine to awaken interest ın the scholar's mind: parents, masters, even the State itself should kindle the desire to learn. The school-premises themselves should be pleasant places: bright, clean, ornamented with pictures within, and without supplied with a playground, and also a garden where scholars may "feast their eyes by the inspection of trees, flowers, and plants" (ch. xvii. 17). Individual capacities, incapacities, dispositions, and repulsions ought to be noted by the educator, and his practice regulated accordingly. No child should be tasked otherwise than suitably to his age and mental strength.

Comenius's quarrel with the teachers of Latin was that they violated the general canon of Method, which bids the teacher deal with Matter (in this particular case, the written or spoken language) before Form (here, the grammatical *schema*). He declares that this canon is inverted in other studies also: for example, children learn the classification of objects before they are familiar with the objects themselves. The usual practice is to follow the logical order in dealing with branches of knowledge; Comenius would follow the psychological order: that is, at the outset he would keep chiefly in view the particular *minds* under instruction rather than the logical connections of the subject-matter, connections which are more evident as instruction proceeds.

Another principle which Comenius states is, that the teacher should begin with the general and pass thence to the special, a statement which may be paraphrased as, Pass from the indefinite to the definite. The phrase describes the process of analysis, which, with synthesis, Comenius declares to be indispensable. Contrary to present opinion, he says that of the two, synthesis should come first; but the illustrations which he gives serve to show that analysis is "naturally" the prior[1]. There is, in fact, some inconsistency in his dealing with synthesis, just as he contravenes the canon "Matter before Form," in the Latin School, by making boys of twelve to fourteen study "Universal Science," or First Philosophy—the science which "lays bare the basal principles of Nature, for example, the essential presuppositions of the universe, attributes and differences," etc.[2]

All, however, would agree that he is right when he insists that gradation and concentration must rule studies:—" Let all studies be so arranged that the later be based upon the earlier, which, indeed, are more firmly established by the later studies[3]." Things naturally associated should be associated in teaching[4], words with things, mutually related sciences in correlation. So, too, his criterion for rote-work is excellent: "They should not be required to commit anything to memory but what is properly understood." "Fatigue the memory as little as may be, that is, with fundamentals only, letting the rest flow freely[5]."

---

[1] *Did. Magn.* ch. xxi. 14, 15.
[2] *Ibid.* ch. xxx. 9.—" Scientia generalissima, sapientia prima."
[3] *Ibid.* ch. xviii. 32.
[4] *Ibid.* ch. xix. 5.
[5] *Ibid.* ch. xvii. 38, 35.

The *Great Didactic* is the work of one who united the purely theoretic study of education with an extensive knowledge of pedagogic questions as they present themselves in the school-room. He had found solutions for some of these, either in his own experience or in the successes of others, and his book contains advice on the more practical side of school-management as helpful as are its pronouncements on method. As in Brinsley's book, so in Comenius's, there is testimony to the success of the Jesuit manner of keeping school : both writers urge the advantage of teaching classes rather than little groups or individual pupils, and both advise the employment of monitors. Comenius holds that mutual stimulus, rivalry, example, assistance, all make the class itself a sort of instrument of instruction : while the monitors (*decurions*, as in the Jesuit school) by repetition of their tasks with fellow-pupils get a deeper insight into their studies and a firmer grasp of them. The practical school-craft of the *Great Didactic* is also revealed in the almost over-elaboration of time-tables and syllabuses of work ; the latter are laid down beforehand with a completeness that not even the present-day English elementary school can surpass.

These things show Comenius as the organiser of the work of others but his directions for the management of a class prove that he could carry out as well as plan. His nineteenth chapter ("The Principles of Compendious Rapidity in Teaching") may be safely commended to novices at this hour. For example : Begin a new subject by tacking it on to an old one, ask questions with that purpose, and ask questions which will convince the class of ignorance, while stirring them to turn their ignorance into knowledge. Stand where you can see all, and allow no eye to wander from yourself. Make pauses for recapitulation, and interrupt your own discourse by questions. At the conclusion, permit pupils to put questions— and so on[1].

---

[1] *Did. Magn.* ch. xix. 20.

The *Great Didactic* has one chapter (ch. xxvi. *De Disciplina Scholastica*) which contains a protest against the indiscriminate use of punishment, so common in its day. Severity, Comenius rightly says, must be reserved for moral offences: it is out of place when enforced against intellectual shortcomings. "An offence against Priscian is a stain to be wiped out by the sponge of rebuke." There is a caustic parable for those who think otherwise: "When a musician's instrument emits a discordant note, he does not strike it with his fist, or with a club, nor does he bang it against the wall: but continues to apply his skill to it, till he brings it into tune" (ch. xxvi. 4).

Nevertheless, discipline must ever be watchful, and when punishment is due it should be meted out there and then (ch. xxiii. "The Method of Morals," *ad fin.*)—a precept of greater humanity and wisdom than that which bids the parent or teacher punish "in cold blood." Comenius agrees with Locke in holding that there are moral offences for which the rod is a fitting penalty. The abnormal and the servile must be treated in the spirit of the old dictum—Nothing but a beating improves a Phrygian.

The chapter on the Method of Morals reads like a rough draft of Locke's *Thoughts on Education.* Here we read that the aim of moral training is to subdue impulse by reason, that virtues are acquired through habits, that example, whether from parents, servants, tutors, or school-fellows, is a potent force ("for boys are like apes"), and that precepts and rules of conduct are necessary in training of this kind.

In the last chapter of the *Great Didactic* its author enumerates the things requisite to the institution of that system of schools which he has been describing. He calls for a company of well-instructed and enlightened scholars who, working in a great library, shall prepare those school-books without which the work of the Vernacular and Latin Schools could not be. The books compiled, the provision of teachers demands attention: and, assuming that teachers and books are available, there is still the difficulty of compelling children to attend school. Comenius is therefore driven to make appeal to Kings, Princes, and Rulers of all sorts, in the name of God, that they may open the gate to universal education. Well said Martin Luther: "Where one gold coin is spent on the building of cities, fortresses, monuments, and arsenals, one hundred ought to be spent in rightly educating a single youth who, when he becomes a man, may be a leader of others in honourable enterprises. For a good and wise man is the most precious possession of the whole commonwealth, in whom there lies more than in shining palaces, heaps of gold and silver, in brazen gates and bolts of iron" (ch. xxxiii. 19).

The next chapter gives an account of the institution during Comenius's lifetime of a State school-system resembling that which he outlined in the *Great Didactic*. His own performances were slight: even when actively engaged in school-reforms he did not get the opportunity to initiate a great administrative scheme. In Hungary, his labours were confined to a single school: in Sweden, though his scope was wider, he was required to devote himself to the Gymnasia which Gustavus Adolphus had founded a generation earlier. The first special code for these schools, containing an 8 years' course, was the work of Comenius in 1649: but it is said that the code was never completely enforced[1].

While this is true, Comenius has been abundantly justified by the subsequent course of educational history. Universal compulsory instruction, of some sort, is a postulate of modern school-administration: even in things of detail, modern practice has endorsed ideas to be found in the *Great Didactic*. For example, the Abiturienten-examen, which did so much for German secondary and university education since its intro-

---

[1] *Special Reports on Educational Subjects*, vol. viii. p. 112.

duction late in the eighteenth century, is anticipated in the leaving examination placed by Comenius between the Latin School and the Academy The arrangement of a school-building in separate class-rooms, which has become so common since Prussia applied it to her elementary schools, is implied in principle, if not in fact, in Comenius's account of the Vernacular School. The liberal curriculum proposed for that school ante-dated by more than two centuries the wider course which modern needs have increasingly made incumbent upon schools devoted to the mass of the population in all civilised countries. Of those countries only a few have ventured to make the elementary school the Common School for all ranks : amongst the few is America, where the Common School was founded in Comenius's own day, and by men who most probably had felt his influence. The postponement of Latin till the age of twelve, and the study of a modern tongue before Latin, both essential parts of Comenius's secondary school course, constitute an attempt at reform which is associated with the schools of Frankfurt-am-Main at the close of the nineteenth century. Indeed, if we make allowance for the growth of knowledge and the wisdom which administrators have learned from experience, we may see school-systems at work to-day, *e.g.* in Switzerland, which recall the pages of Comenius.

In sum, the essential thing in the *Great Didactic* is its absolutely modern outlook. Its deductive method, its falla-cious employment of analogy, even many of its appeals to authority are excrescences. These and a well-nigh superstitious confidence in the power of method, Comenius shares with Bacon : but the two men also foresaw the general direction which progress in knowledge was destined to take, and each did his best to quicken the march.

It is a matter of some little historical interest to trace the influence of the Englishman upon the history of education, exercised as that influence was through the work and person of the Bohemian. But, after all, the real interest of the *Great*

Didactic is much more general than this, and belongs more particularly to Comenius himself as a man of original genius. Let the main doctrines of this seventeenth-century book be recalled for a moment, and we have to admit that, after two centuries and a half, we have only in part reached its standpoint. In spite of some errors Comenius was a true prophet, and the world from his day to ours has been trying to convert his visions into realities. No man ever held a more thoroughgoing belief in the universal need of education, whose benefits were to be monopolised by no caste, wealth, sex, or condition.

The newer life which entered into Europe with the changes of the sixteenth century, and the wider sweep of the educational net which Comenius desired to make, were incompatible with the purely scholarly, or erudite school-course of the earlier time. The curriculum devised by Comenius is not literary only, nor scientific only, but is typical of human experience as a whole : place is given to "modern studies," the vernacular is held in high honour, and if the humanist receives somewhat hard measure, he is not ruled out of the account. Most important of all, the Father of modern pedagogy tries to survey class-room problems from the standpoint, not of the pedagogue, but of the child. Instruction is only learning looked at from without : the two are united in following the normal processes of the learner's intelligence. On the side of method, the *Great Didactic* is especially rich : when its author drops his little pedantries, and speaks freely of the work which he knew so well, he is prodigal of invaluable principles, rules, warnings, hints, which have lost none of their pregnancy by lapse of time.

It is on grounds such as these that are reared the claims of Comenius to be regarded as the founder of modern educational theory. On this point and on that he had been anticipated ; he stands alone in bringing all together into one connected, self-contained, and consistent system.

CHAPTER V.

THE NEW PEDAGOGY IN LONDON AND IN GERMANY.

THE fame of Comenius burned low during the eighteenth century, and incongruous as it now may seem, and distressful as it certainly would have been to the man himself, the flame was kept alight almost entirely by a school-book or two which proved helpful in teaching children Latin. The *Janua Linguarum Reserata* and the *Orbis Sensualium Pictus*, though nearly 30 years apart, illustrate a fundamental principle of their author's pedagogy. Both attained a most extraordinary popularity, followed by a long lease of life not singular, however, amongst seventeenth-century school-books. Owing to its distinctive feature (the presence of pictures) the *Orbis* outlasted the *Janua*; Goethe knew it as a child, and German versions of the book were issued in the first quarter of the nineteenth century.

The principle underlying these two small books was, that the everyday objects, sights, and occupations of the child had an educative influence which it was the teacher's duty to employ in his own particular task. Granted the boy must learn to read and speak Latin, the readiest way to secure this power, and at the same time to furnish him with the educationally essential knowledge of his surroundings, would be, so Comenius held, to compile a great number of sentences in Latin and the vernacular, dealing with everyday life chiefly, but not exclusively. The needful grammar exercises could be got from these sentences, while their diction and subject-matter would afford information of the desired kind, and give the pupil facility in speaking Latin of a conversational sort. Such, in effect, is the *Janua*: reduce the number of sentences, simplify them, add pictures (over 300 in all), and you have the *Orbis Pictus*, which was designed as an introduction to the earlier book. Amongst its multifarious contents are sections on the celestial bodies, metals, minerals, animals, man, country life, trades, handicrafts, modes of government, worship, forms of social life and relationship, in short, an encyclopaedia, Latin and vernacular, in little.

This utilisation of the child's surroundings for scholastic purposes, and the cultivation of a habit of observing things, are Baconian traits already noted in the *Great Didactic*. There is a chapter (the 28th) of that treatise which sets forth the kind of teaching which a child might receive before the age of six: the writer thought its importance justified him in enlarging its contents and printing it as a separate treatise (the *School of Infancy*) in the 1657 folio.

It is a mere by-path in Comenius's pedagogy, but its spirit is a remarkable anticipation of those reforms in the teaching of little children which are usually associated with the Kindergarten. The child is to be taught "to move things hither and thither, to arrange them so and so, to set up and pull down, to make knots or undo them, etc., as at this age it is a pleasure for boys to do. As these actions are nothing but the attempts of an inventive nature, addressed to the productive arts, they should not be prevented, but encouraged and wisely directed[1]." Would Froebel have said otherwise?

Comenius's name became familiar to English schoolmasters long before his visit to London in 1641–2, and the improvements which he introduced into school-books were much

---

[1] *Did. Magn.* ch. xxviii. 12.

appreciated by them, the *Janua* being the work on which his fame more particularly depended. The bibliography of the earliest English editions of that extremely popular book shows that its success was as rapid and complete in this country as abroad. The preface to the original issue by Comenius is dated March 4, 1631[1]. The earliest English version in the British Museum is Anchoran's *Porta Linguarum Trilinguis* [*i.e.* Latin, English, French] *reserata, the Gate of Tongues Unlocked*, which was published in London in 1633: but this is a *second* edition, Anchoran's first edition being dated 1631[2]. Editions subsequent to the second were issued in 1637, 1639, 1643. These later copies contain an alphabetical vocabulary arranged by William Saltonstall, who says that Anchoran was attracted to the original work by its popularity in Norway, Sweden, and Denmark. If this be so we have within some twenty months, or less, the following series of events: the appearance of Comenius's *Janua*, its popularity in the Scandinavian countries as elsewhere on the Continent, the preparation and publication of an English version, and the call for a second edition of the latter.

At first Comenius's name was not too obtrusively associated with these English copies of his book: indeed the Dresden copy is said to be without his name, and the long preface in the edition of 1633 stands over the signature of John Anchoran, the real author's name following in smaller type. The editions of 1637, and later, print two scraps from a letter of Comenius to Anchoran, which indicate that the two men were in courteous, but rather formal communication in the autumn of 1632.

But the man to whom Comenius owed his closest association with English education was undoubtedly Samuel Hartlib, that unwearied friend of education whom Milton described

---

[1] *Op. Om. Did.* p. 254.

[2] Kvacsala, p. 239, and note thereon in Part iii.; a copy of the 1631 Anchoran is here said to be in the Royal Public Library at Dresden.

as "a person sent hither by some good providence from a far country to be the occasion and the incitement of great good to this Island[1]." Born at Elbing in Prussia about the year 1600, the son of a Polish father and an English mother, Hartlib from 1628 had been resident in London, where he became a noteworthy figure in the days of the Civil War and Commonwealth. It has been suggested[2] that he and Comenius got to know each other between 1625, when Comenius perceived that the Moravian community must suffer permanent exile, and 1628, when Hartlib quitted Prussia for London. However that may be, the names of the two men are publicly associated as early as March, 1636, in a letter reproduced in the Amsterdam folio[3]. The letter sketches a school course in Latin based upon the rudimentary studies already arranged by Comenius, to whom the epistle is addressed as to the "first Author of the Janua Linguarum," joining with his name those of "his very well-known helpers in publishing the same"— and first of the five names comes "Mr Samuel Hartlib in royal London."

Comenius was known in his own community as having greater claims to fame than a successful school-book could justify. Spiritual head of that community, rector of its gymnasium at Lissa, writer of the *Great Didactic* (which he now began to turn into Latin), he was also understood to be meditating a work on the advancement of knowledge in general, and of "science" in particular. Certain zealous Moravians, who had gone to England, spoke freely there of their Bishop's studies and projects, in which they found some Englishmen were greatly interested. Three or four disconnected passages of the Amsterdam folio tell in what manner this interest was shown[4]. Some "English friends"

---

[1] "Of Education," *ad init.*   [2] Kvacsala, p. 239.
[3] *Op. Did. Om.* (1657), I. 318.
[4] *Op. Did. Om.* I. pp. 4, 403, 454, 459.

made enquiries of the Bishop himself, amongst them being "a distinguished man, S. H.," "an intimate friend," "a man dutifully zealous for the public good." The man so described requested Comenius to communicate some idea of the coming book. "I sent to him," says Comenius, "what I aimed at in the form of a preface to be prefixed at some time or other to a book. Quite beyond my expectation (indeed I was not consulted at all) this was printed at Oxford under the title *Conatuum Comenianorum Praeludia*. The intention was of the best, to facilitate the knowledge of the project amongst many of the learned, and to seek their judgment thereon : but the result did not in all respects answer to the expectations of my excellent friend[1]."

The unauthorised publication referred to in this passage was a small quarto (some 60 pages) printed at the University press in 1637; its title may be Englished, "*Prelude to the Comenian Attempts from the Library of S. H....* The Gate of Wisdom unlocked, or a seminary of Christian Pansophia, by J. A. Comenius." The last three leaves contained the titles of the chapters which made up the *Great Didactic*[2]. Early in 1639 Hartlib reissued the book, still in Latin, but printed in London, in duodecimo, and under a new title, "The Fore-runner (*Prodromus*) of Pansophia, by the famous reverend gentleman, John Amos Comenius." The earlier book had elicited criticism both favourable and the reverse, and the Bishop had taken his defence into his own hands by issuing in 1638 a pamphlet called *Conatuum Pansophicorum Diluci-datio*, which Hartlib bound up with the *Prodromus*. On the whole Comenius had no reason to regret what must have at first seemed a premature divulging of his "pansophic" scheme. The emphatic character of the criticism, friendly and hostile, which the little quarto evoked, showed that learned Europe

---

[1] *Op. Did. Om.* I. 459, *Praefatio: Pansoph. Dilucidatio.*
[2] Dircks, *Memoir of Samuel Hartlib*, p. 51.

was ready for the most part to take Pansophia seriously. One
enthusiast declared that no greater benefit had been bestowed
upon mankind since the revelation of the Divine Word;
those of the practical sort said that Comenius must be
furnished with collaborators, and a Pansophic College founded,
because one man's shoulders were not sufficient for so great
a burden. As usual, the prophet found least honour in his
own country, where there were those who greatly suspected
the whole pansophic business, "as a dangerous mingling of
Theology with Philosophy, of Christianity with Paganism, and
therefore of Darkness with Light" (*sic*). These brought over
to their opinion certain of the Polish notables, and Comenius
deemed it advisable to pen the *Dilucidatio* already mentioned.
The troubled philosopher must have been comforted when he
read the words of Tassius, Professor of Mathematics at Hamburg, addressed, in the first instance, to Hartlib: "The zeal
for Pansophia and for a better didactic burns in every corner
of Europe: if Comenius had furnished nothing more than the
great crop of incentives which he had scattered in the minds
of all men, he might be considered to have done enough[1]."

The next point in the story of the association of Comenius
with England belongs to the years 1641–42, that is, the early
days of the Long Parliament and the eve of the Civil War.
The story presents features of great interest, and furnishes the
historian of English education with at least one unsolved
problem. It will be best to give the story first as Comenius
himself tells it. "Man proposes, God disposes: so it happened
in my case, when I seriously intended to abandon the thorny
studies of Didactic, and pass beyond to the delightful pursuit
of Real studies: nevertheless I slipped back amongst the
thorns. I will touch upon the manner in which this came
about: that, if anything prove to have been done otherwise

[1] *Op. Did. Om.* pp. 454, 455. *Ad Lectores,* introduction to *Con. Pans.
Dilucidatio.*

than for the best, *they* may take a share in the blame who
drove me to those rocky heights. The "Forerunner of Pansophia" (*Prodromus Pansophiae*) having been published, and
dispersed throughout the different kingdoms of Europe, many
of the learned approved the sketch of my projected work,
though indeed they doubted the power of one man to finish
that work, and therefore advised the institution of a Society
of learned men for the purpose. The man who had introduced
the *Forerunner* to the light, that strenuous man of affairs who
is nicknamed the Pursuer of Work, Mr S. H., was very
active in this matter to engage therein as many interested
persons of intelligence as possible. So, at last, he secured one
or two, and with much entreaty summoned me also to his side
in the year 1641. When my people had consented to my
departure, I set out and reached London on the very day
of the autumnal equinox: and there at length I learned that
I had been summoned by order of Parliament. But the King
being away in Scotland, and Parliament prorogued for three
months, I was kept there during the winter, my friends
surveying (*lustrantibus*) the Pansophic equipment, slender as
it was. This gave occasion to my preparing a tractate, under
the title *Via Lucis* ... for the better understanding of that text,
'At eventide there shall be light.' Meantime the Parliament
had met, and my presence in London being made known,
I was ordered to wait until they had leisure from other business
to commission learned and wise men from their own body to
hear me, and to become acquainted with the fundamental
parts of my project. They also communicated at the outset
their thoughts of assigning to us some college with an income,
by means whereof a number of learned and industrious men,
invited from all nations, might be honourably maintained,
either for a certain number of years, or permanently. There
were even specifically named the Savoy, in London ; Winchester,
outside London ; and, again, nearer the City, Chelsea, an
account of whose income was communicated to us, and nothing

seemed more certain than that the project of the great Verulam was about to be realised, of opening in some country a Universal College, solely for the advancement of learning. But there intervened the rumour of a rising in Ireland and of the massacre in one night of more than 200,000 English [November, 1641], the sudden departure [Jan. 10, 1642] of the King from London, and the unmistakeable tokens of the bloody war about to break out; these things disturbed my project, and compelled me to hasten my return to my own people. A letter had also been sent to me from Sweden by way of Poland and thence to England, in which that great hearted and earnest gentleman, Ludovic de Geer, offered promptly to further my designs, and to associate one or two learned men with me, if I should so desire. I left [England] after having consulted my friends, who protested that I ought to devote myself to nothing else but Pansophia. In August, 1642, I was conveyed into Sweden, and found the modern Maecenas at his home in Nordkoping." Comenius then goes on to tell how Chancellor Oxenstiern and the Chancellor (Skyte) of the Upsala University agreed in advising him to postpone Pansophia in favour of a much-needed reform in the teaching of Latin: and as his patron, de Geer, was of the same mind as the two Chancellors, Comenius felt, reluctantly enough, that he must again betake himself to the thorns and craggy rocks of Didactic. He continues his narrative: "But my complaisance towards the Swedes displeased my English friends exceedingly, and in a prolix but pregnant letter they attempted to draw me back. They wrote: 'What has been done as a model in Didactics is sufficient, the way of rectifying all its errors is now plain enough: but it is not so with respect to scientific studies (*nondum in realibus*). Others may be left to deal with the former, and teachers are already arising here and there who will provoke each other to industry by their competition. But not even the very rudiments of Pansophia are as yet made known. Infinitely more advantage will accrue to the public from explanations of the ways of true wisdom than from Latin grammatical studies (*a literalis Latinis*)': and more to the like effect[1]."

Expostulation and entreaty alike failed: Comenius was fast bound in the chain of circumstance, and England saw him no more, though he kept up a correspondence with individual Englishmen for many years after 1642.

A stray allusion in a letter of Hartlib's goes to show that Comenius's sojourn in London excited sufficient interest at the time to be remembered in those later years when the educational reformer had become a controversial divine and the friend of enthusiastic prophets. The letter is addressed, under date 25 March, 1658, to Pell, Cromwell's political agent at Zürich: "Just now I heard that one of our preachers here [London] had been still railing against Comen. What! such a man to come and prescribe us a new method here! And oh! what a crime it is, in his eye, that he published *Lux in Tenebris*[2]" [1657]. Though the foreign visitor stood thus prominently in the public eye, his visit suggests questions which we are now unable to answer. Particularly, what Hartlib's precise relationship to Comenius was when he invited the latter to England in the summer of 1641 is a question which has baffled research. From Comenius's own account (whose absolute honesty we have no reason to doubt) it is clear that Hartlib was more agent than principal in extending the pressing invitation. "I learned," says Comenius, "on my arrival that I had been summoned by order of Parliament." No trace of a formal order in this sense having been found in the Journals of Parliament, or in other official records, the inference seems to be that Comenius had not perfectly understood his position. Hartlib was a man with many connections

---

[1] The foregoing narrative is from the *De Novis Studia Didactica continuandis occasionibus*, the highly interesting introduction to Part ii. of *Op. Did. Om.*

[2] Hartlib's letters to Pell in Vaughan's " Protectorate of Cromwell."

in the great world, a man enthusiastic for the advance of public education, and, withal, an invincible optimist. There were men in the House of Commons at that moment who shared Hartlib's desire for educational improvement, as the records still show. Had Hartlib interested these so far in Comenius's projects that they had used expressions which might be interpreted informally as the invitation of Parliament, or, at least, of the majority in the House of Commons? To put it otherwise: while the desire for the spread of education and the employment of newer methods was undoubtedly in the minds of certain Members of Parliament, was the desire to employ Comenius confined mainly to Hartlib? An authoritative answer seems impossible, but an expression in Comenius's narrative may point to a reply in the affirmative. The Bishop says that "they" told him of a plan whereby "a number of learned and industrious men, invited from all nations, might be honourably maintained"—just the kind of cosmopolitan society of scholars which would occur to a man of Hartlib's antecedents and sympathies. Comenius names amongst possible and suitable homes for these native and foreign men of learning that unlucky Chelsea College which Hartlib afterwards [1652] recommended to Parliament as a foundation that could "maintain an Evangelical Intelligence and Brotherly Correspondence with foreign Divines[1]." Again, Comenius says that Hartlib's invitation was sent after the latter had found "one or two" learned men ready to co-operate in founding the Pansophic College; this may be a reference to the educational pioneer, John Dury, then in England during one of the infrequent intromissions of his arduous and unsuccessful task of reconciling Lutherans and Calvinists. Hartlib, in this very year 1641, had told Dury's story in one of the pamphlets with which he was constantly edifying London[2].

[1] *The Reformed Spiritual Husbandman*, p. 37.
[2] *A Briefe Relation*, 4to, 1641.

But, whatever the answer to these questions, it is certain that the early days of the Long Parliament deserve the careful attention of the historian of English education. Beneath all the stress and turmoil which marked its progress, there are unmistakeable signs of an interest in public education, and of attempts to extend and improve it both in England and elsewhere As usual these attempts were not kept clear from the burning controversies in Church and State which divided Englishmen, and at the Restoration they shared the fate of projects associated with the Commonwealth *régime*. Had it been otherwise England would have had a system of popular education, and a wider curriculum in her schools some two centuries earlier than these things were vouchsafed to her.

In the summer of 1641 Parliament was rapidly undoing the system of personal government which Charles had constructed since the Houses had ceased to meet in 1629. Strafford had been brought to the block in May, the impeachment of Archbishop Laud had begun, and the Commons were debating the manner in which the system of Church government should be revolutionised by the abolition of Episcopacy. On June 15, 1641, the House of Commons went into Committee on this last business, the sequel being thus narrated in the Journals of the House for that day. " Upon Mr Hide's Report from the Grand Committee it was by this House *Resolved* upon the Question, That all Deans, Deans and Chapters, Archdeacons, Prebendaries, Chanters, Canons and Petty Canons, and their Officers, shall be utterly abolished, and taken away out of the Church. *Resolved* upon the Question, That all the Lands, taken by this Bill from Deans and Chapters, shall be employed to the Advancement of Learning and Piety : Provision being had and made that his Majesty shall be no loser in his Rents, First-fruits and other Duties : and that a competent Maintenance shall be made to the several Persons concerned, if such Persons appear not peccant and delinquents to this House."

The Commons decided to the same effect on June 18, and again on July 9[1]. Comenius, it will be remembered, says that he reached London on the day of the equinox, September 22. Communication between London and Lissa in Poland, where the reformer then was, could not be established direct in 1641: the quickest route would be by sea from Hamburg, involving a very long land-journey (say 300 miles), or with a shorter land-journey and longer sea-route, from a Baltic port. If we allow three or four weeks for Hartlib's letter to reach Lissa and an equal time for Comenius to get to London, and add the time occupied in coming to a decision and getting the consent of the Moravian community, it appears that Hartlib's invitation was despatched very soon after the Commons declared the confiscation of Church property in the interests of "learning and piety." Possibly that invitation was the consequence of an understanding with influential Commoners who had a special interest in education.

Parliament adjourned for the recess on September 8, appointing a Committee of both Houses to carry on necessary business till the reassembling on October 20. The report of this Committee, brought up by Pym, makes no mention of education, or of any like matter.

Five days after the opening of the new session Hartlib published a thin quarto tract, " A Description of the famous Kingdom of *Macaria*, showing its excellent Government, wherein the Inhabitants live in great Prosperity, Health and Happiness: the King obeyed, the Nobles honoured, and all good men respected; Vice punished and Virtue rewarded. An example to other Nations," etc. As this title indicates, the little book expresses Hartlib's notion of Utopia, or a New Atlantis: it is chiefly remarkable for its insistence on the experimental study of science, and the application thereof to

---

[1] See also " The Diurnall Occurrences or Dayly Proceedings of Both Houses, in this *Great* and Happy Parliament," Nov. 3, 1640—Nov. 3, 1641 (Burney Newspaper), also Journals of House of Commons, under date.

the advantage of the community through State departments, or boards, of Agriculture, Health, Industry and so on. "All such as shall be able to demonstrate any experiment for the health or wealth of men, are honourably rewarded at the publike charge, by which their skill in Husbandry, Physick and Surgerie is most excellent" (p. 5). Its author is not amusing himself with fancies; he is trying to arouse a general interest in that *Solomon's House* of which Bacon had dreamed, but whose actualisation was thought to be possible in the Pansophic College conceived by Comenius. The better to secure influential readers, Hartlib dedicates his tract "To the high and honourable Court of Parliament."

The moment was inauspicious. The breach between the King and the Parliamentary majority was rapidly widening, while a King's party was growing stronger within the Parliament itself. In November the House of Commons passed by a small majority that "Solemn Remonstrance" which was, in effect, an appeal to the nation at large against the government of the country as carried out by Charles and his advisers. A little later, and the streets of Westminster were thronged daily by excited crowds bent on demonstrating their agreement with Parliament, their hatred of Bishops and their distrust of the Court. Then in the early days of January, 1642, Charles was defeated in his attempt to arrest the five members of the Commons in their House, under circumstances contrary to Parliamentary privilege; on the tenth of the month he quitted Whitehall and withdrew to the North, London being abandoned by the Queen and Court also.

During all these anxious months of autumn and early winter Comenius had been patiently waiting in the troubled city for the appointment of that Committee of "learned and wise" members of Parliament which was never made. Hartlib's *Macaria* had failed in its chief purpose; still undaunted, he tried once more to call public attention to Comenius's projects by publishing on the 12th of January, two days after Charles left London, a translation of those two Latin productions of the Moravian, by which he had introduced Comenius to Englishmen in 1637 and again in 1639. The intention was obviously to make known the pansophic schemes in quarters inaccessible to the original, and for the same purpose Hartlib gave a new and more "popular" title to the work. Part of that title is "A reformation of Schooles, designed in two excellent Treatises: The first whereof summarily sheweth the great necessity of a general Reformation of common learning. What grounds of hope there are for such a Reformation. How it may be brought to Pass. The second answers certaine objections ordinarily made against such undertakings," etc.

Comenius's patience and Hartlib's quartos were alike powerless before the tide of civil war which was steadily rising, and in the end the Bishop betook himself to his thorny Didactic in Sweden, and in England Pansophia became but a fleeting memory.

But at the very time when Comenius's theories failed to gain the public ear of London, scholastic reforms of an epochmaking kind were putting those theories, or some of them, to the test in Central Germany. The tradition of princely interest in popular enlightenment there associated with the name of Ludwig of Anhalt-Köthen was continued by Duke Ernest of Saxe-Gotha and Altenburg, who ruled in Gotha from 1640 to 1674. Ernest is distinguished from others of his House by the surname "the Pious," an epithet which recalls but one aspect of a very fine character. In his younger days he proved himself a brave and skilful soldier, and a capable man of affairs: as sovereign prince he was deeply concerned for the well-being of his people, and devised means by which it could be attained in various ways. By family compacts and subsequently by inheritance from his elder brothers, Duke Ernest became sovereign of an extensive Saxon territory, which he ruled after the paternal manner customary amongst German monarchs of his day.

His reign began some eight years before the conclusion of the Thirty Years' War, and it was a troubled heritage to which he succeeded, but under his inspiration and leadership reforms were commenced and steadily pursued in the administration of justice, the incidence of taxation, the conduct of trade and of agriculture. The Duke's surname of the "Pious" owes its origin no less to his vigorous attempts to better the moral and religious condition of his subjects than to his own personal attributes. Coming to a dukedom whose churches, parsonages, and school-houses were in great part burned to the ground during the war, he left to it the beginning of an educational organisation which has since made Saxony one of the best educated countries in the world. It was a saying of his own day that "in Gotha the peasants are cleverer than the nobility of other places."

The year following his accession (that is, in the year 1641) Ernest despatched a commission of enquiry into the various parts of his dominions for the purpose of learning the actual conditions of churches and schools, and the immediate result of this enquiry was to concentrate the Duke's attention on the educational requirements of his people. His first step was to secure for the rectorship of the Gotha Gymnasium a scholar and schoolmaster of tried ability, Andreas Reyher, who forthwith took an active part in the reforms then being initiated; the intimacy thus begun was continued till Reyher's death in 1673, two years before his patron's decease. Between them, the Duke and the schoolmaster drew up a memorandum on the kind of instruction most desirable for the boys and girls of the humblest rank in the villages and towns of the duchy, a memorandum which was quickly converted into a book, the celebrated *Schulmethodus* of 1642.

This work states the outline of a complete "folks'" school organisation, whose substantial agreement with the ideas, principles, and practice of Comenius's *Great Didactic* suggests that the two collaborators had made the acquaintance of the earlier work, a thing possible enough, since we know that Comenius began a Latin version of his book as early as 1638, though no version in that language previous to that of 1657 is now known to exist. Moreover, the Saxons could by no means have forgotten the recent sojourn of Ratke amongst them, and it is conceivable that in the changes introduced by Ernest we have the fruit of one or two suggestions made by that unlucky adventurer. In any case, the *Schulmethodus* prescribes compulsory schooling under penalties, makes regulations for the conduct of elementary schools, and lays down their curriculum.

After the completion of the fifth year all children, girls as well as boys, become subject to the school law which ordains that they shall go to school, there to remain till they can pass an examination, held annually, in the studies of the third, or highest class of the school. Attendance is exacted for six hours daily, except on Wednesdays and Saturdays, which are half-holidays : the penalty for absence is fixed at one to six groschen *per hour*. The curriculum may be inferred from that of the highest class, which is as follows : Religion; arithmetic, including the four rules, orally and written, the rule of three, fractions; in the mother-tongue, reading, writing, dictation. The reading lessons are to afford opportunities for acquiring useful knowledge, as, for example, information concerning minerals, trees, animals, weather signs; the magistracy, law, justice, taxation; rules for home-life. The teaching is also to include some elementary geometry, and, of course, vocal music; teachers are required to keep a record of each child's native abilities, defects and acquirements, while parents are reminded that it is their duty to pay the small school-fee cheerfully, to keep their children regularly at school, and help them with their home tasks.

All this reminds one of the Vernacular School as described in the *Great Didactic*; yet another idea of Comenius was worked out by Duke Ernest and Andreas Reyher by the preparation of a series of "School-books for Teachers and Children," some seven in all, intended to help in the teaching of reading, summing, and religion.

The system thus sketched was soon brought into operation, and State-provision secured a minimum salary, lodging, firing and food-stuff for the schoolmasters employed. In 1645 Duke Ernest set going a fund for the widows and orphans of pastors and schoolmasters, and in his will recommended his successors to institute a training college for teachers—testimony at once to his enduring zeal for the instruction of his people, and to the difficulty he experienced in carrying out his enlightened policy.

So complete a fulfilment of Comenius's aspirations as Duke Ernest made possible in Gotha is sought in vain elsewhere during the seventeenth century; but the Moravian thinker was by no means of small influence in German school-rooms during his lifetime. Reyher introduced his elementary Latin books into the Gotha Gymnasium, and the School Ordinances of several German States make reference to the same text-books. The Magdeburg Ordinances of 1658 are full of the principles and opinions of the author of the *Great Didactic*, and mention is made of his writings in the seventeenth-century school syllabuses of German cities from the Bavarian highlands to the Baltic coast[1].

[1] Paulsen, I. 473.

CHAPTER VI.

THE LONG PARLIAMENT. SAMUEL HARTLIB AND EDUCATION.

The resolution of the House of Commons proposing the employment of Church property for "the advancement of Learning and Piety," the resolution which perhaps brought Comenius to our shores, is the first of a series of indications that the Long Parliament was bent upon organising public education. From the time when the Commons became supreme to the close of Oliver Cromwell's Protectorate we hear of educational projects in the House, some of which received effect in legislation. The very year of the King's death is noteworthy in respect of its educational enactments, no less than three important measures then becoming law.

Not every one of these Acts was purely philanthropic, as may be inferred from that concerning Wales. During the months preceding January, 1649, it had become clear that men were far from unanimously approving the Parliamentary government or the proceedings of the Parliamentary army. Local risings against these authorities were suspected to be imminent in many quarters: in some, and notably in Wales, they actually took place. The Welsh insurrection, after causing much anxiety to the Committee of both Houses[1] throughout

[1] The "Derby House Committee"; see *Cal. State Papers*, Domestic Series, 1648-9.

the summer of 1648, was put down by Cromwell himself
in mid-July, preparatory to his discomfiture of the Scottish
invaders a month later. How serious this Welsh rising was
thought to be may be gathered from the following letter of
May 13 from the Committee to the Lord General [Fairfax].
"It hath pleased God to give a very great and happy success
to the Parliament's forces in South Wales against those rebels,
in a very seasonable time, when the malignants were grown
very high, and, upon the expectation of a contrary event,
had the boldness to threaten destruction to all who had been
faithful to the Parliament. The long-continuing of that party
together has given great encouragement to others in many
places of the kingdom, and therefore it will be very necessary
to make such a thorough and effectual prosecution of this
most happy victory that all the remainders of it may be rooted
up in that place, and the country quieted and left safe for well
affected and peaceable men, and all other places be deterred
from making the like attempt to interrupt and trouble the peace
of the kingdom. We therefore desire your Lordship to give
order for the most vigorous prosecution and effectual improvement of this victory for settling the peace of the kingdom[1]."

Royalist Wales, with its unwillingness to adopt the Parliamentary point of view in things ecclesiastical, must be induced
to change its opinions: Lieutenant-General Cromwell's "eight
thousand good horse and foot" of 1648 are to be followed by
the preachers and schoolmasters of 1649. On Feb. 22 in that
year the House passed an "Act for the Better Propagation
and Preaching of the Gospel in Wales," which appointed
Commissioners empowered to arrest "delinquent" and "malig-
nant" clergymen and schoolmasters, and to certify preachers
and teachers whom they should "adjudge to be most for the
advancement of the Gospel, or for the keeping of Schools, and
education of Children." The preachers and schoolmasters

[1] *Cal. State Papers*, Dom. 1648–9, p. 66.

appointed by the Commissioners were to be maintained out of the profits of ecclesiastical livings in the hands of Parliament, agreeably to the principle of the Resolution of 1641, "provided that the yearly maintenance of a Minister do not exceed one hundred pounds, and the yearly maintenance of a Schoolmaster exceed not forty pounds[1]."

The two other educational Acts of 1649 are much less open to suspicion of the *arrière pensée* than is the Act described, though allowance must of course, as always, be made for the circumstances amidst which legislation took place. Each of these two measures occupies a special position in the history of the relations of the English State to Education, the one being the first proposal to make a Parliamentary grant for general educational purposes, and more particularly for Universities, the other being a direct though inexpensive encouragement by the State of the device of voluntary contributions for the maintenance of a system of schools. The earlier of these two Acts set aside and vested in trustees the first-fruits and tenths which, since Henry the Eighth's time, had belonged to the Crown, and whose annual value in 1649 was set at about £20,000. From this source of income the trustees were "to pay yearly all such Salaries, Stipends, Allowances and Provisions, as have been limited or appointed for preaching the Gospel, Preaching Ministers, or Schoolmasters or others in England or Wales, settled or confirmed by Ordinance or Order of Parliament." These payments were not to exceed £18,000 per annum, since the remaining £2000 was ear-marked for the better maintenance of the Heads of Colleges in Oxford and Cambridge. The principle of the Parliamentary subvention is involved in the proviso that, if the first-fruits and tenths failed to reach £20,000, the deficit should be made up from some other part of the current revenue. It may be safely assumed

[1] See Mr de Montmorency's *State Intervention in English Education*, pp. 100–104 and 133–135, for interesting details of the Long Parliament's educational enactments.

7—2

that of this State grant for "the advancement of Piety and Learning," as the phrase ran, piety, personified by the preachers, was meant to get the greater share.

The third Act of 1649 is at once a recognition that Education is a matter of general concern in a community, and an acknowledgment of responsibility towards a subject people. Parliament had been informed that by the exertions of the colonists many of the American Indians had received the Gospel, and were in need of further instruction. It proceeded, accordingly, to found a body of "Commissioners of the United Colonies of New England," who were to co-operate with a similar body in those colonies in propagating the Gospel amongst the natives, "and also for maintaining of Schools and Nurseries of Learning, for the better education of the Children of the Natives." The initial capital was to be raised by voluntary contributions throughout England and Wales, the ministers, churchwardens, overseers and others being authorised to make house-to-house visitations for the purpose[1].

With these three Acts of 1649 the educational *legislation* of the Long Parliament ceased. But the solicitude for educational reform which caused certain of its members to invite Comenius to London outlived the duration of the assembly itself, as a collection of stray references will show. For example: Samuel Hartlib had published, most probably during this same year, 1649, a little book written by his associate, John Dury, and called *The Reformed School*[2]." In accordance with his custom, Hartlib introduces the work with a preface, in the course of which he says, "To propagate [God's] salvation with my poor talents, and to stir up others to contribute their help thereunto, is the utmost aim which I have in the Agency for Learning: wherein the goodness of the Parliament hath owned me. And although towards the busi-

---

[1] De Montmorency, *op. cit.* p. 133.

[2] It bears no date; a supplement to it is dated 1650. The B. M. Catalogue is marked "1649?"

ness itself, nothing hath been further done then to name me
for it (*which for the time hath made my burdens somewhat heavier*)
yet because my genius doth leade me this way," etc.... "Having
then, upon a motion made by some, made myself Instru-
mentall to draw forth from others these following Directions,
towards the Reforming of Schools, and the Advancement of
Piety and Learning, I thought it expedient," etc. A man of
diverse interests, Hartlib's projects nevertheless always tended
towards his pet scheme, the institution of a Public Intelligence
Office, a sort of spiritual clearing-house which should collect
in this country and abroad information respecting progress in
Divinity, Science, Invention, Industry, and School Reform,
subsèquently arranging its treasures for the common benefit
of the contributory States. This *Office of Public Address*, as
its deviser at one time called it, was never realised in its
fulness, indeed it seems never to have got beyond the shadowy
condition of the "Agency for Learning" named above : nor
was it planned at any one moment on so comprehensive a
scale as to include all the branches of enquiry just enumerated.
But as Divinity, or Education, or Natural Science was upper-
most in Hartlib's thoughts at the moment, so he then and
there to that end destined his projected Intelligence Department.

In 1648 he had tried, apparently without success, to enlist
sympathy with the educational ideas of Dr Cyprian Kinner,
a sometime colleague of Comenius. The foregoing passage
from the preface to Dury's *Reformed School* leads one to
suppose that Hartlib had soon after convinced either the
House of Commons, or some of its members, of the utility of
a Bureau of Educational Information, and that his own name
had been brought forward as that of a suitable "Director of
Special Inquiries and Reports," may we say ? Such an actualisation of his cherished idea would put Hartlib on his mettle ;
he involved himself in more labour than ever, and failing
Comenius and Kinner, the book of his friend Dury is offered

as a contribution to the " Reforming of Schools and the Advancement of Piety and Learning."

There happens to be confirmation of the supposition that Hartlib and Parliament were co-operating at this time in favour of education. On the 7th of September, 1650, the Council of State had a busy day, as we learn from its proceedings recorded in the *Calendar of State Papers*[1]. News had come out of Scotland of a great victory gained by Cromwell at Dunbar on September 3rd, and " Parliament not now sitting " the Council issued instructions that " this success of the army against the Scots " should be made widely known, and as widely acknowledged in public services of thanksgiving. There followed much consideration of matters naval and military, with orders to be despatched thereupon. Nevertheless, amidst this martial exultation and warlike debate, opportunity was made for business which is summed up in two brief, kindly lines of the record : "13. When the propositions for reforming schools are presented, Council will give them all possible furtherance." It does not seem far-fetched to connect these words with " the Agency for Learning," and the activity of Hartlib, Dury, and their sympathisers.

In any case the benevolent words close the story of the Long Parliament's good intentions respecting education. On the 20th of April the victor of Dunbar summarily ended the existence of that legislative body, or, at least, suspended its animation : from June to December of that year the Little Parliament, otherwise Barebones' Parliament, maintained a precarious life in the face of the army officers, who usurped the executive functions of Government. Still, even this anxious, short-lived assembly did not wholly neglect the example set by its prede· cessor, as is proved by certain passages in the Journals of the House of Commons, under date July, 1653. Thus, we read, on the 20th of that month : " Resolved that a Committee be

---

[1] Domestic Series, Sept. 7, 1650.

appointed for advancement of Learning[1]. *Ordered*, That the Committee that brought in this Report for Committees, do name a Committee for this purpose: and to present it to the House."

The importance which should be attached to this Resolution may be gathered from the circumstances under which it was passed, and from the means taken on the following day to give it effect. It was adopted at the suggestion of a Committee which had under consideration the best means by which the House could deal with public business, and for that purpose the creation of special committees was advised. Beside that for the Advancement of Learning, there were to be Committees for Ireland, Law, Scotland, Army, Treasury, Petitions, Trade, the Poor, and Commission of the Peace, Public Debt, Prisons, all matters of first-rate public concern. The record runs for the next day (Thursday, July 21), "Sir William Roberts, from the Committee, the Names of Members of the House to be of the Committee for Advancement of Learning, and receiving all Propositions tending thereunto." Here follow 14 names, and 4 subsequently added by the whole House. This Committee of 18 included several men then in the front rank of public life, five at least of them being members of the Council of State, either at that moment or later in the year. The name amongst them most familiar to-day is that of Sir Anthony Ashley Cooper, afterwards the first Earl of Shaftesbury, the friend and patron of John Locke. Science was represented in the persons of Dr Jonathan Goddard, Warden of Merton, afterwards (1655) to become Gresham Professor of Physic, and of Colonel Blunt, a famous mechanical inventor and one of the early Fellows of the Royal Society. The passage last cited from the Commons' Journal, after setting forth the 18 names, continues, "Who are to meet in the Duchy Chamber this Afternoon,

[1] It is perhaps worth remarking that "Piety" has dropped out of the formula.

at Two of the Clock." So far the Journals: the irrepressible Hartlib allows us to make a guess at the occupation in part of a corresponding Committee in the first Protectorate Parliament of 1654. In that year Hartlib dedicated to the Speaker (Rous) a quarto whose title-page conveyed a broad hint: the work consists chiefly of the views on language-teaching held by the three persons named. "A True and Readie Way to Learne the Latine Tongue. Attested by Three Excellently Learned and approved Authors of Three Nations: Eilhardus Lubinus, a German: Mr Richard Carew, of Anthony in Cornwall: the French Lord of Montaigne. Presented to the Impartiall, both Publick and Private Considerations of those that seek the Advancement of Learning in these Nations. By Samuel Hartlib, Esq.[1]"

The tract is a manifesto on behalf of Comenius's ideas on the teaching of Latin: Hartlib opens with a preface in which are the following passages. " Indeed it is easier to see a mote or a web in another man's eye, then to take it out, and most men think themselves justified when they have condemned others, whose way is different from that which they have chosen. And although this seems to be in all other matters the Ordinary Practice: yet in the Wayes of Education, and the Reformation of Schools (the deepest foundation of all other good settlement both in Church and Commonwealth) it hath not been followed hitherto. But my honoured Friend Mr John Amos Comenius, and some other Fellow-labourers and Correspondents in this Work with myself, have studied to make as little alteration as could be, seeking only the best Advantages which upon the Ordinary Foundation of School-teaching could be introduced: and in this Endeavour for a

---

[1] Lubinus had suggested in 1614 the use of pictures in the teaching of languages, and Carew agreed with Montaigne that foreign tongues are best learned conversationally, while grammar should be reserved for " persons who by ripeness of understanding are able to apprehend the reasons thereof."

great many years we have continued, and many wayes attempts have been made to facilitate the course of Universall Learning, and especially the teaching of Learned Tongues." Judging from the oblique reference in the following passage, "the Agency for Learning" is apparently a thing of the past: "But how to Introduce the Way which is here intimated into the Publique Schools of this Commonwealth will be a matter of further deliberation then is fit for me now to enter upon: it may be that the Honourable Committee for the Advancement of Learning will be inclined to reflect upon this matter, and consider the feasableness thereof: and haply something as a Proposal in this kinde may be offered unto them."

With one more allusion we may close the story of State intervention in matters educational during the Parliamentary ascendency and the Protectorate. Though nothing was done at the time, the foundation of a University at Durham was one of the educational projects of 1649, the intention being to employ for the purpose some of the property diverted from the Cathedral clergy. But in 1657 letters patent were issued by the Lord Protector directing the institution of a University at Durham, assigning as its home the houses formerly occupied by the Dean and members of the Chapter, setting aside for its benefit the sum of £900 *per annum* in rent-charges, and granting the University permission to acquire land of the annual value of £6000. These letters patent were, however, never anything more than a memorial to the good-will felt towards education by him who granted, and those who solicited them. They were not immediately translated into fact, and at the Restoration, the Dean and his colleagues of the Chapter resumed possession of their houses and other property, the ghost-like Cromwellian university vanishing in consequence. Nearly two centuries later, a Bishop of Durham with the Dean and Chapter of that city voluntarily devoted a considerable sum out of their corporate incomes to the foundation of a University in that place, and it was one of the earliest acts of Queen Victoria to grant a Royal Charter to the same.

Though his various plans for a State Intelligence Department did not secure effective support, Samuel Hartlib was in his own person just such an Office of Public Address as his project defined. It is not easy to decide what branch of public usefulness most appealed to him; physical science, mechanical invention, the advancement of trade and industry, shared with Protestant reunion and the cause of education in his large-hearted devotion.

The enquiries which these different interests rendered necessary brought him into correspondence with men of all ranks and of different nationalities: though not a man of any great originality himself, he had the merit of discerning sound thinking, and a generosity which made him find his happiest occupation in introducing men of original minds to public attention. Perhaps the thing which lay nearest to his heart was the reunion of Lutherans, Calvinists, and the foreign Reformed Churches generally, an attempt at which constituted his earliest public association with John Dury. But certainly scholastic reform was one of the chief interests of Hartlib's life: though original writing came rarely from his pen, his name, or his initials, were familiar to Londoners through the quarto tracts in which it was his custom to make known the novel schemes of the innovators whom he was continually discovering.

His connection with Comenius in this particular sphere has been reviewed. The state of English politics in 1642 forbade the hope that any serious attention could be given to Comenius's innovations at the moment. The rebuff only turned Hartlib to native reformers, and in the five or six years beginning in 1644 he made himself the occasion for the appearance in print of a remarkable series of tracts dealing with schools and their work. Three of these deserve a closer attention : at this point it will be convenient to state their titles, and return to their contents later. First of the series is the little tract, "Of Education," wherein John Milton, at Hartlib's request, sets forth the idea, long meditated in silence, "of a better education, in extent and comprehension far more large, and yet of time far shorter, and of attainment far more certain, than hath been yet in practice." The date of Milton's tract is June, 1644; three and a half years later (Jan. 1648) a pamphlet of even greater *educational* interest appeared in London, entitled "The Advice of W. P. to Mr. Samuel Hartlib, for the Advancement of some particular Parts of Learning." The writer, then a young man of 24, was to become famous in after years as Sir William Petty, earliest of English students of Economics. Somewhat later than Petty's pamphlet there appeared John Dury's *Reformed School* [1649?] and *The Reformed Librarie Keeper*, "with a supplement to the Reformed School, 1650," both being published with prefaces by Hartlib. We have seen reason to connect these booklets by Dury with the readiness of the Council of State to consider the question of reform in schools.

Besides inducing Milton, Petty, and Dury to state their thoughts on education thus publicly, Hartlib during the period under notice also wrote on his own account, and made at least one more attempt to give currency here to the educational ideas of a foreigner. As to his own work, we have this in a quarto devoted to advocating the erection of that "Office of Public Address," already described. The title is vague, probably with intention; it is of a kind likely to win the eye of many men in 1647: "Considerations tending to the happy accomplishment of England's reformation in Church and State: Humbly presented to the Piety and Wisdome of the High and Honourable Court of Parliament." The significance of this pamphlet in the history of education is in its incidental declaration that the "Magistrate," in other words, Parliament itself, should erect and maintain a system of schools, a repetition, in fact, of Comenius's view as expressed in the *Great Didactic*[1]. "The magistrate," says Hartlib, "should see schools opened, provided with teachers, endowed with maintenance, regulated with constitutions, and he should have instructors and overseers to the observance of good order in this business."

In 1648 Charles was, in effect, the prisoner of the Parliamentary army, and military operations were confined to the suppression of sporadic insurrections against ·the rule of Parliament, and to the defeat of a Scottish invasion. Hartlib seems to have thought the time not unfavourable for once more calling public attention to the ideas of Comenius, or, rather, to a manner of teaching which was in harmony with those ideas. A certain Doctor Kinner, formerly an assistant to Comenius in the preparation of school-books, found himself stranded at Dantzig, and in sore difficulties. He had, or professed to have ideas of his own on education, in which he interested Hartlib, the result being the publication of a small quarto with a big title, in which a not altogether warranted use was made of Comenius's name. "A Continuation of Mr. John Amos Comenius School Endeavours. Or a Summary Delineation of Dr. Cyprian Kinner *Silesian*, his Thoughts concerning Education": etc., etc.

Hartlib, according to his wont, furnished the pamphlet with an introduction, in which he gives some account of Kinner's antecedents. A Silesian by birth, he had studied Law and Physic, taking the Doctor's degree in both faculties, and practising both professions for a livelihood. He had long been interested in the education of children: and on his marriage with a wealthy lady she consented to set apart the sum of 6000 rix-dollars for the advancement of educational ideas[2]. Unhappily for Kinner, his lady, and those who might have profited from their generosity, the Imperial troops

[1] Hartlib in this tract is putting into shape an outline which was the work of Dury. See note to Chapter VII.

[2] "Which sum," says Hartlib, "doth amount to more than 2000 and 600 *li*. sterling."

invaded Silesia : Kinner was despoiled of his property and
was driven from his native land. Hartlib continues the story
thus. "Amongst other places he [Kinner] did passe sometime
of his Exile in Transylvania and Hungaria, where his acquaintance with Master Alstedius, and Master Bisterfeld, and other
Learned men of chief note, and his constant Zeal to promote
the Reformation of Schooling, did cause many upon the report
of their esteeme of his thoughts and endeavours on that
subject, to take especiall notice of him ; and amongst others
M. *Comenius* (who was by the liberality of a private Gentleman
maintained, and set apart to further the same Designe) having
gotten information of him ; and what his inclinations and
abilities were to be helpfull in the work, which he had in
hand, did invite him to come to him in Prussia, that they
might joyne their thoughts and endeavours together for the
advancement of their Common Aimes ; which Doctor *Kinner*
did readily condescend unto, and after a yeare or two, when
by their mutuall communications, and joint labours, they had
ripened severall matters (which will shortly come to light)
Master *Comenius* was called away by the *Moravian-Bohemian*
Church at *Lesno*, where now he is, and Doctor *Kinner* being
taken off fiom his private means of subsistence, and engaged
upon the Object of his publike thoughts, is left alone in
Prussia at *Dantzick*, to depend upon Providence. Whiles
Mr. *Comenius* was with him he had a share in that which was
allowed unto him for his maintenance, but he being now gone,
Doctor *Kinner* is left in a great straight...hee hath engaged
himselfe by a Vow unto God (which is the strongest assurance
he can give of his faithfulness) to dedicate his whole time to
the prosecuting of the Designe, whereof the Summary is
herewith adjoyned ; if God will be pleased to continue, for
a yeare or two, his life, and procure him assistance therein,"
etc.[1] This so-called vow, "sent from Dantzick, the fift of

---

[1] "A Continuation of...Comenius' School Endeavours," etc. The above
is from Hartlib's " Brief Information concerning Doctor Kinner," etc., which
serves as the Introduction.

August, 1648, to Samuel Hartlib," is printed at length; it is a statement, couched in the form of a prayer, of Kinner's purposes, and his inability to fulfil them for want of a patron.

Kinner's own part of the pamphlet is a brief but tedious account of a manner of teaching by means of objects and the vernacular. He says, "The drift of my invention for teaching is, That all Things Necessary to be known may be instilled into Learners without the troublesome getting of things by heart, without the usuall confused multitude of books, and without the ill Custome of Dictations, by the only new help of sensible Objects, and by Talk, and Exercise both serious and by way of sport and pastime, with so much firmnesse (as I believe) that nothing thereof shall easily be forgotten," etc.

The *Delineation* itself was intended as a *ballon d'essai*, to be followed if necessary by an "Elucidarium," or Commentary. The eight or more quarto pages of the *Delineation* give a somewhat confused though would-be systematic account of a plan of teaching, in which object-lessons and the mother-tongue play the chief part. "I shew Naturall Things in the living book of Nature, Things Artificiall in the Shops and Work-houses of their Makers, and both of them in the Re-positories of their figures, and representations which belong to our School, where I shew them either living or carved (yet as neere the life as may be) or at least painted" (*Delineation*, p. 2). These "Things" are to be studied analytically, syn-thetically, and "Syncritically, or by comparing the structure of Things together" (*ibid.* p. 3). Instruction is also given in reading, in writing, "And because Arithmeticall cyphers are numbring words I teach to write and pronounce them also, and to tell the valew of many of them, placed in a certaine order, which we call Numeration" (p. 4). Kinner announces his intention of issuing text-books (Dictionaries, Directories, etc.), which will be especially arrånged in accordance with his plan of instruction.

Obviously, Kinner is but repeating his master, Comenius; we have here only echoes from the *Great Didactic*. There is the same insistence on the part to be played, in early instruction especially, by the organs of sense, and by sensible objects; the employment of the mother-tongue and the preparation of reformed school-books, as well as the use of analogy (so overstrained by the earlier writer) are not Kinner's own. Even Comenius's trivialities reappear, as in the passage on Numeration quoted above.

The pamphlet closes with an invitation which probably met with small response.

"An Advertisement to the Noble and Generous Lovers of Learning.

"If any such (after the favourable perusall of this generall Draught and Information) should be desirous to be more fully informed, concerning either those works of Master *Comenius*, which are to be published, or Doctor *Kinner's* further Undertakings and continuation of them; as also how their assistance and favours may be best conveighed unto the aforesaid Doctors hands, they may please to send or repair to Master Hartlib's House in the great open Court in Dukes-Place, and satisfaction shall be given to all their desires[1]."

The year 1649 was the year of educational activity in Parliament; in the years immediately following Hartlib was showing the comprehensiveness of his interest in education by the issue of three tracts. The first outlined a scheme by which the City Corporation might deal with London pauperism by means of workhouses. "London's Charity inlarged, Stilling the Orphans' Cry," 1650 [April 12], is first and foremost philanthropic: but its author could not omit provision for schooling from these public homes of the poor. It is but a modest schooling which he proposes, but it is discriminating, makes allowance for superior talent, and is altogether much

---

[1] "A Continuation," etc.—last two pages.

more liberal than that proposed for the same kind of institution nearly fifty years later by John Locke[1]. Hartlib writes: "I hope they will take care that poore children may be taught to write and read two houres in a day, so that by the time the Boys come to the age of 12, 14, or 16, they will be able to read and write, fit for Apprentices, but such as are quick witted to make Schollars, or accomptants, or what they delight in, either for Sea or Land." The greater part of their day is to be spent by these pauper children in manual labour; but neither schooling nor recreation is forgotten. Under the latter head Hartlib makes a remark characteristic of his time and not unknown to our own: "In relation to their Recreation: 1. Sometime warlike exercise, which many children take much delight in, this recreation will be commodious to the Commonwealth, by bringing them up, some for the Drum, and Pipe, some for the Trumpet, and all will be skill'd with Warlike terms and postures, which they will not forget, when they come to be men." Hartlib's scheme assumed that each institution would contain 100 children; at the head was to be a steward, with a yearly stipend of £50, in addition to lodging, next in rank coming the schoolmaster, also provided with lodging, with a yearly supply of serge spun by the children sufficient for a suit and cloak, and an annual salary of £20.

This tract, which incidentally touches upon rudimentary education, was followed in 1651 by a proposal for technical instruction which recalls foundations of the later nineteenth century. It appeared in one of the familiar quartos, under the title, " An Essay for Advancement of Husbandry-Learning: or propositions for the erecting a Colledge of Husbandry: and in order thereunto for the taking in of Pupills or Apprentices. And also Friends or Fellowes of the same Colledge or Society." The author asks: " Why may we not conclude

---

[1] "Working Schools," 1697; see Fox Bourne's *Locke*, II. pp. 377 f..

that in the science and trade of Husbandry, which is the mother of all other trades and scientificall Industries, a Collegiall way of Teaching the Art thereof will be of infinite usefulness?" "If the least part of all Industrie is highly improved by Collegiall Institution and Education, how much more may the chief part, and as it were the very root of all wealth, be advanced to perfection by their means?" Hartlib's essay is offered "as a hint of this matter, that it may be further in due time ripened, and with more mature considerations brought to perfection." Meantime, subscriptions are solicited.

These tracts touching primary and technical education belong to the period in his career when he was invested with that "Agency for Learning" to which reference has already been made. About this time also Hartlib prepared "A Memorial for Advancement of Universal Learning," whose subject was higher education. The scheme testified that Hartlib still hoped to share in the foundation of such a "college" of natural science as Comenius, following Francis Bacon, had planned. This college or society was to be called *Antilia*, and a public subscription was proposed to bring it into being. "Mr. John Dury, library keeper of St James's, and Samuel Hartlib, Esq., have accepted the trust of receiving and disposing such sums of money, as well affected persons and lovers of the public good shall be pleased to give[1]."

Nothing seems to have come of this appeal, which is, no doubt, an attempt by Hartlib to do something in his *Agency*. His next considerable performance of an educational kind was in 1654, when the *Agency* was no longer in force: this is the "True and Readie Way to Learne the Latine Tongue," already referred to, in which Hartlib's attitude is more detached than that which an accredited agent of Government would assume.

---

[1] Additional MSS., Br. Mus., ex Leg. J. Ward, No. 6271: see also Dircks, *op. cit.* p. 18.

Notwithstanding his public services Samuel Hartlib was suffered to close his career in great poverty. Of his private fortune, if he had one, no information is forthcoming: he may have brought money with him from Prussia in 1628, or he may have dabbled in commercial speculations during his residence of some forty years in London. He told a correspondent in 1660 that he had spent between three and four hundred pounds yearly out of his own pocket in the public service since his coming to England[1]. It is certain that he was often in sore straits, as the extant records show, and that he received sums of money from time to time at the hands of private and official patrons as a reward for services rendered. Admittedly generous to others, he was careless about his own money affairs. So early as 1636 he is reported as "fallen to decay for being too charitable to poor scholars, and for undertaking the work of schooling and education of children[2]." From time to time his necessities came before the Government, who made, or promised to make, money grants in his favour in return for his public services[3].

As to these last, John Milton says of Hartlib in his preface to the tractate "Of Education," "your aims and actions have won you with me the esteem of a person sent hither by some good providence from a far country to be the occasion and the incitement of great good to this Island. And, as I hear, you have obtain'd the same repute with men of most approved wisdom, and some of highest authority among us. Not to mention the learned correspondence which you hold in foreign parts, and the extraordinary pains and diligence which you

[1] Dircks, *op. cit.* p. 4.

[2] *Cal. State Papers*, 1635–6, Jan. 25. Dury (who had been ordained in Exeter Cathedral a year earlier) commends Hartlib to Sir Thos. Roe, hoping that assistance will be given by the Bishop, who had been indebted to Hartlib for foreign intelligence during the previous two or three years.

[3] *Journals of the House of Commons*, June 25, 1646, March 31, 1647; *Cal. State Papers*, Aug. 17, 1650. These entries talk of "great necessities," "speedy payment."

have us'd in this matter both here, and beyond the Seas." This was written in 1644. The Restoration Parliament had the opportunity of learning what Hartlib's personal material gain had been from the labours which Milton so praised. That assembly was petitioned by Hartlib to grant him money to pay his debts, and to put him "in a capacitie to continue his service to the publick, to advance in his generation the best objects for the use of mankind in all kinds." We do not know what answer was made to the petition, but that document sets forth his services, and his then condition. "The humble petition of Samuel Hartlib, Sen. Sheweth :—

"That your Petitioner, ever since he came into this kingdom, hath set himself apart to serve his generation in the best objects:

"*First*, by erecting a little academie for the education of the gentrie of this nation, to advance pietie, learning, moralitie, and other exercises of industrie, not usual then in common schools.

"*Secondly*, by giving entertainment, and becoming a solicitor for the godly ministers and scholars, who were driven in those days out of the Palatinate, and other Protestant Churches then laid waste[1]. By which means,

"In the *third* place, your Petitioner found an opportunity to maintaine a religious, learned, and charitable correspondence with the chief of note in forraine parts; which, for the space of thirty years and upwards, he hath managed for the good of this nation, as well in civill as in ecclesiastical concernments (as is well known to the leading men of all parties) etc....... Now, your Petitioner having continued in this course of life for the space of thirty years and upwards (without partiality, serving all publick and ingenious spirits indifferently) and in these great and strange revolutions being destitute of support to continue

---

[1] Possibly a reference to the consequences of Wallenstein's successes, 1626-1629. This would give "thirty years and upwards."

this kinde of negotiation; and in his old and sickly age to maintaine himself and his family : for the relief of which, and his agency, he hath been forced to contract debts, which in the end will sinke him except some favourable aspect be shewed unto your Petitioner from your Honours, as the patrons of pietie and learning.

"May it therefore please your Honours," etc.[1]

But the nadir of Hartlib's fortunes seems to have been reached when the Restoration swept away what he must have come to regard as the settled order of things. Pepys, under date July 10, 1660, has a whimsical allusion to his own and his wife's presence at the wedding of Nan Hartlib (Samuel's sister), "which was kept at Goring House with very great state, cost, and noble company." In the following November Hartlib was constrained to approach Lord Herbert with the request that he would join certain other peers "to make up such assistance, as may save your and their most devoted servant from utter perishing, 'till some other means of public love and encouragement may be (if it may be) determined." "I suppose your honour is not ignorant of the votes that passed concerning gifts, pensions, debts, allowed or contracted for by the former powers, that all of them are made void by this Parliament. Also that no motion is to be made concerning money matters 'till the debts of the army and navy be first satisfied.   Both these votes fall most heavily upon your Honour's tormented servant ; so that he hath nothing to expect of all his arrears which (amounting to seven hundred pounds) would have fully freed him from all his debts, and given him a present comfortable subsistence, nor of his yearly pension settled upon him by the first Parliament, consisting of Lords and Commons[2].   I have nothing therefore left to keep me alive, with two relations more, a daughter and a nephew,

---

[1] Dircks, *op. cit.* p. 32.
[2] Query, 1657-8?

who is attending my sick condition[1]." It was probably at the time when this letter was written that Hartlib addressed to Parliament the petition already quoted and whose result is not known. There was no reason to include him amongst the proscribed, yet, on the other hand, his public associations had been of a kind which did not recommend him under the new order, nor was that order disposed to favour the projects, or some of them, with which he had been most closely concerned. However, Hartlib did not long survive the Restoration of May, 1660; he died in the following March and was buried in St Martin's-in-the-Fields, London, March 12, 166$\frac{1}{2}$[2].

[1] Nov. 22, 1660. Dircks, p. 30, quoting White Kennet's "Register."
[2] G. H. Turnbull, *Samuel Hartlib*, 1920, p. 72.

CHAPTER VII.

TWO LETTERS TO HARTLIB; MILTON AND PETTY.

THE publication in June, 1644, of an anonymous eight-page tract, "Of Education," the work of John Milton, was in some respects one of the most notable consequences of Samuel Hartlib's desire to forward a reform in schools. While the tract did not greatly advance either the theory or the art of teaching, it was an addition to English literature in a field where English writers of the first rank have very seldom been seen. Milton's purpose in penning it was, as he himself says, to set forth a general view of that which he had often expressed in conversation with Mr Hartlib concerning education, a matter which is "one of the greatest and noblest designs that can be thought on, and for the want whereof this Nation perishes." The time of its publication was June 5, 1644, within less than a month of the battle of Marston Moor (July 2), and while men were anxiously awaiting, some the fall, others the relief of York, where a Parliamentary army had been shut up since the middle of April. The ultimate end of the Parliament's military operations in general appeared doubtful to many of its friends; though courage and other soldierly qualities were very far from lacking in the subordinates, defective organisation too often marked the work of the central authority and of the higher ranks of officers, so that not even Cromwell's genius could be expected to make up for their deficiencies[1]. While Parliament thus had reason to distrust the education and training which its more aristocratic adherents had received, the Universities had shown their hostility to the Parliamentary cause in a manner calculated to bring about reprisals when opportunity offered. On the 22nd of January in this same year, 1644, Oxford had received King Charles and his Parliament, and on the same day orders had been issued by the Parliament at Westminster for the "reform" of Milton's own University of Cambridge. "Reform" in this sense meant the removal of such as were disaffected towards the powers at Westminster, and especially of those who refused to take the Covenant. A little later 12 heads of Houses and 181 Fellows or others attached to the Colleges of Cambridge were driven forth from the University; at Queens' not a single member of the old foundation was left[2].

Notwithstanding its brevity and somewhat casual origin, the tractate "Of Education" is distinguished by a wealth of high thoughts expressed with the nobility of utterance which came so readily to its author when fired by his subject. The plea for an instruction based upon a properly trained sense-experience was many times repeated from Comenius onward through Pestalozzi to our own day; but who amongst its many advocates pleaded so eloquently as Milton? "The end of learning is to repair the ruines of our first Parents by regaining to know God aright, and out of that knowledge to love him, to imitate him, to be like him, as we may the nearest, by possessing our souls of true vertue, which being united to the heavenly grace of faith makes up the highest perfection. But because our understanding cannot in this body found itself but on sensible things, nor arrive so clearly to the knowledge of God and things invisible, as by orderly conning over the visible and inferior creature, the same method is necessarily to be follow'd in all discreet teaching." Again, concerning the moral

[1] Gardiner, *History of the Civil War*, vol. ii. p. 65.

[2] Gardiner, *op. cit.* vol. i. p. 302.

instruction of the youngest boys we read. "Here the main skill and groundwork will be, to temper them such Lectures and Explanations upon every opportunity, as may lead and draw them in willing obedience, enflam'd with the study [*studium*, zeal] of Learning, and the admiration of Vertue; stirr'd up with high hopes of living to be brave men, and worthy Patriots, dear to God, and famous to all ages." Even the commonplace exercises of the fencing school, or the quiet moments of rest before a meal, are lifted into a loftier region and transfigured by the noble rhetoric of the tract. "The exercise which I commend first, is the exact use of their Weapon,... this will keep them healthy, nimble, strong, and well in breath, is also the likeliest means to make them grow large and tall, and to inspire them with a gallant and fearless courage, which being temper'd with seasonable Lectures and Precepts to them of true Fortitude and Patience, will turn into a native and heroick valour, and make them *hate the cowardise of doing wrong.*" So, before meat, the boys are to be "re-creating and composing their travail'd spirits with the solemn and divine harmonies of Musick heard or learnt; either while the skilful organist plies his grave and fancied descant, in lofty fugues, or the whole Symphony with artful and unimaginable touches adorn and grace the well-studied chords of some choice composer, sometimes the Lute, or soft Organ stop waiting on elegant Voices either to Religious, martial, or civil Ditties; which if wise men and Prophets be not extreamly out, have a great power over dispositions and manners, to smooth and make them gentle from rustick harshness and distemper'd passions."

Its place in the history of education apart, the great and permanent value of the tractate consists especially in the ardour and moral glow with which it invests its topic, making the little essay a perennial source of inspiration to the educator. Many are the books which offer guidance and warning to the teacher; the number of those which bring him fire from off the altar

is few   They are books of the first rank; and Milton's
memorandum to Hartlib is amongst them.

It is, therefore, a book for all time; yet it is also distinctly
a book of its own age, written with a clear vision for the failures
and needs of England in the mid-seventeenth century. Schools
and Universities as Milton saw them were alike wanting in
intellectual seriousness; both spent too much time in mere
holiday-making, and the hours that were given to work were
largely time misspent, because formal studies were in honour
everywhere, and few cared for positive knowledge. The schoolboy spent "seven or eight years in scraping together so much
miserable Latine and Greek, as might be learnt otherwise easily
and delightfully in one year." Leaving school and going up
to the University, the youth is again prematurely thrust into
studies almost purely formal, "I deem [it to be an old errour
of Universities......that in stead of beginning with Arts most
easie, and those be such as are most obvious to the sence, they
present their young unmatriculated Novices at first coming
with the most intellective abstractions of Logick and Meta-
physicks." Where schoolboys and undergraduates might hope
to gather knowledge worth their trouble, they are commonly
put off with an "asinine feast of sowthistles and brambles."
Divines, mercenary or ignorantly zealous, fee-hunting, petti-
fogging lawyers, slavish statesmen, idle men of pleasure are
"the fruits of misspending our prime youth at the Schools and
Universities as we do, either in learning meer words or such
things chiefly as were better unlearnt."

These charges may, perhaps, be discounted as the common-
places of the satirist in all ages; yet they recur again and again
in books dealing with cotemporary education from Francis
Bacon to John Locke, and they are associated in Milton's
tractate with allusions to the failures in war and statecraft,
which were evident in the England of 1644. The noble statement of "the end of Learning" which occurs near the beginning of the tractate is replaced later by another, which

shows the nature of the thoughts surging through the writer's mind, and the book's power of universal inspiration always excepted, these may be said to set the key of the composition. "I call therefore a compleat and generous Education that which fits a man to perform justly, skilfully and magnanimously all the offices both private and publick of Peace and War." These are the ends which Milton sets before himself in planning an education for the sons and grandsons of the men whose failures in Peace and War he glances at as the fruits of an ill-directed education, whereby "this Nation perishes."

The newer generations must "know the beginning, end, and reasons of Political Societies; that they may not in a dangerous fit of the Commonwealth be such poor, shaken, uncertain Reeds, of such a tottering Conscience, as many of our great Counsellors have lately shewn themselves, but stedfast pillars of the State." Above all they were to be capable commanders in time of war. As Milton wrote, more than one Parliamentary general was giving men reason to doubt his capacity, the foreign-bred Prince Rupert was flashing triumphantly along his career, Marston Moor was still in the future, and Cromwell's New Model was an organisation yet to take shape. Hence, in a measure, the quasi-military character of Milton's Academy of young nobles and gentlemen, and the time and care which it bestows upon military science and navigation, so that its pupils "may as it were out of a long War come forth renowned and perfect Commanders in the service of their Country. They would not then, if they were trusted with fair and hopeful armies, suffer them for want of just and wise discipline to shed away from about them like sick feathers, though they be never so oft suppli'd [that is, they would not repeat the conduct of the Parliamentary commander, Essex]: they would not suffer their empty and unrecrutible Colonels of twenty men in a Company to quaff out, or convey into secret hoards, the wages of a delusive list, and a miserable remnant; yet in the meanwhile to be overmaster'd with a score or two of drunkards, the only souldery left about them, or else to comply with all rapines and violences. No certainly, if they knew ought of that knowledge that belongs to good men or good Governours, they would not suffer these things." Again, the note of the moment strikes our ear with a similar bitterness when it is recommended that the pupils of the Academy shall learn "the Institution of Physick : that they may know the tempers, the humours, the seasons, and how to manage a crudity : which he who can wisely and timely do is not only a great Physitian to himself and to his friends, but also may, at some time or other, save an Army by this frugal and expenseless means only; and not let the healthy and stout bodies of young men rot away under him for want of this · discipline ; which is a great pity, and," says Milton, no doubt with Essex in the mind of himself and his readers, "no less a shame to the commander." While these few pages "Of Education " addressed to Hartlib rank among the great inspiring classics of Education, they are also as "actual" as a magazine article of to-day discussing the shortcomings of national training and the consequent national peril or disaster.

The tractate is of its own day also in a sense more general, and especially with respect to the principles that determine the curriculum which it so confidently lays down. Here Milton applies to education the teaching of the *Advancement of Learning*. The current practice at school and University is contemptuously summed up in a line, "pure trifling at Grammar and Sophistry." "Language is but the instrument conveying to us things usefull to be known. And though a Linguist should pride himself to have all the Tongues that Babel cleft the world into, yet, if he have not studied the solid things in them as well as the Words and Lexicons, he were nothing so much to be esteem'd a learned man, as any Yeoman or Tradesman competently wise in his Mother Dialect only." This point of view once established, the writer goes on to range himself with all the seventeenth-century innovators who called

for a school-course framed expressly to bestow a fund of positive knowledge. From Comenius to Locke these innovators
make particular application to the school of the thesis which
Bacon maintained with reference to the general increase of
knowledge : that is, mental gymnastic and the art of expression
must make way for a comprehension of the objects and forces
of the material world, for a knowledge which would tend to
"the relief of man's estate," as Bacon put it. The needs of
the time, and the failure of many whose education had been
on other lines, served to intensify this conviction in Milton's
mind, and, as a consequence, his tractate sets forth a training
which in its higher stages is made directly preparatory to the
boy's future calling as soldier, statesman, or other participant
in the more responsible walks of public life.

The encyclopaedic round of studies by which this training
was to be given is as distinctly of its time as is the principle on
which the training itself was based. It makes a truly astonish-
ing catalogue, when we reflect that it is all to be completed
by the twenty-first year of the scholar's age. On the side of
Science and Technology there are Mathematics, Natural
Philosophy, Physiography, Astronomy, Geography, Natural
History, Anatomy, Biology, Medicine, Fortification, Engineering, Agriculture, Architecture, Navigation. What may be called
the disinterested pursuit of the Humanities forms but a small
part of the design, since Ethics, Economy (in the Greek sense),
Politics, and Law are followed with express reference to the
future specific duties of the individual as Governor, Member of
Parliament, General, or other prominent officer of State. Still,
some seven languages other than the mother-tongue, and five
of them not modern vernaculars, are studied by the pupils, and
the nine years' course closes with a scientific theory of Rhetoric.
How could it be seriously supposed that so many branches of
Learning, with systematic Divinity added, could be acquired in
so brief a time by scholars so young? The answer lies in a
belief which, again, is characteristic of the age, and which may

be concentrated in one word, "Method." Bacon had given this belief expression in more than one passage of the *Novum Organum*[1]; it was transferred to the region of pedagogy by Comenius, whose robust faith is implied in the uncompromising sub-title of the *Great Didactic*, "the universal system of teaching everybody everything." Milton shared this trust in method, though, indeed, he did not hold that method levels all capacities; of his own scheme he rightly says, "this is not a Bow for every man to shoot in that counts himself a teacher." But, unlike Comenius, he does not tell us, except in the most general or merely allusive way, what his method is; the tractate is definitely asserted to be the statement of "that voluntary *Idea*, which hath long in silence presented itself" to the writer, "of a better Education, in extent and comprehension far more large, and yet of time far shorter, and of attainment far more certain, then hath been yet in practice."

It is hypercritical to complain that, by ignoring education given earlier than the twelfth year, Milton falls far below Comenius's standard. He explains that, for brevity's sake, he omits "beginning as some have done from the Cradle, which yet might be wòrth many considerations." It is precisely during these early years of schooling that methods count for so much, and the absence of any discussion by Milton of the right procedure when dealing with young children renders it less easy to compare the principles of Method held by the two men. Yet we are not entirely destitute of the means of gauging Milton's ideas on this important matter, and what he himself tells us is fairly conclusive evidence that he and Comenius were poles asunder in their conception of Method. It is true that Milton sees the purpose of learning, mediately at least, to be the attainment of real knowledge, knowledge of Things, of *Res,* Science, as we should now say, and not culture or gymnastic. Further, he lays it down that " our understanding

---

[1] *E.g.* Bk. I. Aph. lxi., Aph. cxxii.

cannot in this body found itself but on sensible things," and
that the right method of knowledge is, therefore, "the orderly
conning over the visible and inferior creature." Such also is
the opinion of Comenius; but when we note in what manner
Milton proposes to give effect to his principles, the difference
between the two men is well-nigh as great as it can be. After
inveighing against the misuse of Authority in the intellectual
sphere, the Moravian reformer thus expresses himself in the
Great Didactic: "The method of all the Arts shows that the
schools contrive to teach pupils to judge by the eyes of others,
and to be wise by proxy. They do not teach pupils to discover
springs and thence to lead off various streams; they show them
streams drawn from Authors, and bid them return to the
well-head by following these secondary channels...... Hardly
anyone teaches Physics by ocular demonstration and experiments, but all by recitation of the texts of Aristotle, or of some
other.... It comes in short to this: Men ought to be taught,
as far as possible, to be wise, not out of books, but from the
heavens and earth, from oaks and beeches; that is, to know
and scrutinise Things themselves, not the observations and
testimony of others concerning Things[1]."

Contrast the method which Milton sketches in the tractate:
knowledge is but seldom acquired in the first-hand fashion
which Comenius so insists upon. Agriculture is studied by
Milton's pupils, not upon a farm, but in the books of ancient
Latin writers, supplemented by tours of observation which
are both casual and occupied with many other things. The
scholar may "*read* any compendious method of Natural
Philosophy"—precisely Comenius's complaint against the then
current practice; similarly, "the institution of Physick" may
be "*read* to them out of some not tedious writer." The pupils
do not, it would seem, themselves hunt, fish, keep gardens or
sheep, and so on: they hear of the "helpful experiences" of
others who do these things.

[1] *Did. Magn.* ch. xviii. 25, 28.

Tried by the touchstone of Method, the tractate belongs to
a different epoch than that of Comenius and those English
friends like Hartlib, who in the mid-seventeenth century were
labouring so zealously for the reform of school-teaching.

Nevertheless, its adverse criticism of cotemporary educational practice, its insistence on modern studies, and its
particular suggestions for the amendment of secondary and
University curricula, make this brief memorandum to Hartlib
one more instance of those demands for reform which are the
feature of pedagogic history in its day. But it missed becoming
a factor in the subsequent development of opinion which led
to the establishment of a groundwork of educational theory.
Milton's "soul was like a star, and dwelt apart," as Wordsworth
said, and he brought a certain aloofness into a piece of work
such as the tractate, intended though it was to serve some of
the immediate purposes of a modern magazine article, or letter
to the *Times*. We see this, and at the same time begin to
perceive why the tractate failed to inspire a pedagogic following,
in the often-quoted reference to Comenius, with whose ideas
Milton was in some respects in full sympathy. The name and
projects of the Moravian were well known to Londoners in
1644, yet Milton, when addressing a man who was notoriously
associated in English minds with Comenius, refers in a tone
almost of contempt to the reformer. "To search what many
modern *Janua's* and *Didactics* more than ever I shall read,
have projected, my inclination leads me not." This lofty dis-
missal of the claims of the foreigner and theorist, and the
preference extended to personal experience, are scarcely atoned
for by the passing acknowledgment of the benefits the essayist
has received from "old renowned Authors"; whether or not,
the consequence has been that, apart from the effect here and
there on individual educators of the stimulus furnished by its
high level of thought, the tractate "Of Education" is a
negligible quantity in the history of pedagogy[1].

[1] For further remarks on Milton's educational work see Chapter X. below.

Hartlib probably received Milton's memorandum, "Of Education," with mixed feelings, there being in it both strictures and recommendations from which he was bound to dissent. On the other hand, he must have extended a whole-hearted welcome to a letter which he put into print, with the date January 8, 164$\frac{7}{8}$, under the title "The Advice of W. P. to Mr Samuel Hartlib, for the Advancement of some particular Parts of Learning." The "W. P." of this letter was William Petty, in whom Hartlib could not fail to recognise a mind in full sympathy with the aims of the New Philosophy, with a just understanding of the method by which the new learning was to be attained, and, what was perhaps most attractive to Hartlib, of a cosmopolitan breadth which could consider patiently suggestions concerning educational reform from Comenius or from any other foreigner.

At that time a comparatively unknown man of five-and-twenty, Petty was to win renown in diverse fields before his career closed. His contemporaries grew familiar with him, first as Dr Petty, one of the chiefs of the medical service of Cromwell's Irish army, and, later, as a mathematician who conducted in Ireland one of the most accurate and complete surveys made up to that date. As a mechanical inventor he approached our own age sufficiently to devise, amongst many other things, "a wheel to ride upon." His scientific attainments and interests gave him a place amongst the original members of the Royal Society, on the occasion of whose incorporation in 1662 he received knighthood. To-day he is best remembered as one of the earliest students of vital statistics and a founder of the modern science of Political Economy.

Before the letter to Hartlib was made public, Petty's chequered life had given promise of the manner of man he was to become. As a child, his greatest amusement was to watch the doings "of smyths, watchmakers, carpenters, joiners, etc."; and it was said that "at twelve years old he could have

worked at any of these trades[1]." He went to sea early, and
left it to become a student in the Jesuit College at Caen;
later, he served for a time in the Royal Navy. On the outbreak of the Civil War he went abroad, first studying medicine
at Leyden, and afterwards joining Hobbes and the other
English refugees in Paris who formed part of the group of
philosophers, mathematicians, and men of science associated
with Father Mersenne, the intimate friend and correspondent
of Descartes.

Petty returned to England in 1646 to busy himself in his
father's trade of cloth-making and in devising improved processes of manufacture. An invention of an "Instrument of
small Bulke and price" for the rapid and easy multiplication of
copies of letters, etc., brought him some notoriety, and Hartlib,
who dearly loved an inventor, was perhaps attracted to Petty
by the stir which this "Pentograph" was making. Nor was the
attraction a momentary one, since eighteen months later Hartlib
writes to Robert Boyle, "My endeavours are now, how Mr Petty
may be set apart or encouraged for the advancement of experimental and mechanical knowledge in Gresham College at
London[2]." But Petty in this same year, 1649, resumed his
medical studies, this time at Oxford, and was fairly launched
upon his career.

The *Advice of W. P.* is a small quarto of 26 pages, with
another referring to the multiplying apparatus, the pentograph,
and a short preface addressed "To his honoured friend, Master
Samuel Hartlib." This preface is noteworthy for the precise
significance which it attaches to the word *Real*, a significance
roughly paralleled by the German use. Petty says that he has
"had many flying thoughts, concerning the Advancement of
Reall Learning in generall, but particularly of the Education
of Youth, Mathematicks, Mechanicks, Physick, and concerning

[1] Quoted from Aubrey in the *Dict. Nat. Biography* article on Petty,
from which this account of him is derived.

[2] Dircks, *Hartlib*, p. 20.

A.   9

the History of Art and Nature," and he believes that his letter to Hartlib "can please only those few, that are Reall Friends to the Designe of Realities, not those who are tickled only with Rhetoricall Prefaces, Transitions and Epilogues, and charmed with fine Allusions and Metaphors (all of which I do not condemn)." He hopes that his recent invention of "the Art of Double Writing" will prove so generally and permanently useful that it will provide sufficient money to set going those plans for the public good which the inventor and his friends had formed.

The *Advice* itself falls into four parts, dealing with different aspects of the common theme, the advancement of learning. The first part (pp. 1–3) recommends the institution of Hartlib's cherished project of a General Intelligence Department, the "Office of Publick Addresse," whose officers shall search all existing records of inventions with the purpose of compiling a catalogue, making reference to such records easy. The material so arranged will make plain where invention is most wanted, and capable men are thereupon to be set to work in the quarters thus discovered, assisted by a knowledge, gained through the catalogue, of what has already been done in any given field. The idea thus includes the endowment of research, and the compilation of bibliographies, whose absolute necessity is one of the convictions of the modern student in all branches of knowledge.

The third division of the letter (pp. 7–17) is the longest of the four: it helps us to imagine how Petty's corps of researchers would proceed to their own especial work. The general scheme is that of Solomon's House as depicted in Bacon's *New Atlantis*. Most prominent amongst the various departments, though not most exhaustively described, is the "Gymnasium Mechanicum or Colledge of Tradesmen for the Advancement of all Mechanicall Arts and Manufactures." The Nosocomium Academicum (an academic infirmary or hospital) is an institution for the pursuit of pure science; here are a botanic garden, a collection of domestic and wild animals, living and dead, a museum, a library, an astronomical observatory, picture gallery, geographical collections, in short "an Abstract of the whole world. So that a man conversant within those walls would certainly prove a greater Schollar, then the Walking Libraries so called, although he could neither write nor read. But if a Child, before he learned to read or write, were made acquainted with all Things and Actions (as he might be in this Colledge) how easily would he understand all good Bookes afterwards, and smell out the fopperies of bad ones" (p. 8). There is a hospital in this academy to advance the science of medicine and surgery, and we are reminded of Petty's profession by the elaboration of this part of the scheme.

In the last division of the letter (pp. 17–26) the writer returns to those studies for "the relief of man's estate" which claimed so great a share in Bacon's thoughts. Through them "even hogs and more indocile beasts shall be taught to labour, when all vile Materials shall be turned to Noble uses, when one man or horse shall do as much as three, and every thing improved to strange advantages. There would not then be so many Fustian and Unworthy Preachers in Divinity, so many petti-foggers in the Law, so many Quack-salvers in Physick, so many Grammaticasters in Country-schools, and so many lazy serving-men in Gentlemens houses, when every man might learn to live otherwise in more plenty and honour" (pp. 22–23).

The strictly educational portion of the letter is the second, extending over three or four pages (pp. 3–7), with casual references elsewhere, all being set down in a fashion which Petty's own phrase, "flying thoughts," very well describes. The writer is no schoolmaster, and therefore offers no advice on the matter of method, his pronouncements on that topic being limited to disapproval of cotemporary plans for teaching reading and foreign languages. On the other hand, we get a clear view of the kind of education which this able young man conceived as most desirable, and an indication of the administrative machinery through which that education might be given. Universal schools naturally formed part of the plan, and it does not seem to be straining Petty's words to add that he would conduct these schools by means of a body of professional teachers specially prepared for their occupation. "The businesse of Education," he says, "should not be (as now) committed to the worst and unworthiest of men, but... be seriously studied and practised by the best and ablest persons." Again, "We cannot but hope that those, whom we have desired should make [education] their trade, will supply [what here remains to be said thereon] and render the Idea thereof much more perfect." In other words schoolmasters should study and improve the theory of their profession.

The universal schools are called by Petty, "*Ergastula Literaria*, Literary work-houses," or workshops, a phrase which is meant to cover a whole theory of Education, and that a revolutionary one. All children above seven years old may frequent these school-workshops, "none being to be excluded by reason of the poverty and inability of their Parents, for hereby it hath come to passe, that many are now holding the Plough, which might have beene made fit to steere the State": to remedy this condition of affairs arrangements in the nature of sizarships and scholarships are proposed for poor, but intelligent and able *children*. (Petty does not once use the words "boy" or "girl" in this connection.)

"Literary work-houses" is Petty's own phrase, but "school-workshops" more nearly describes the novel institutions he is proposing. Literature is virtually absent from their programme, and her humble handmaidens, reading and writing, are not the earliest studies of the children. These, and the learning of languages, says Petty, require an exercise of judgment of which young children are incapable; and the first two are unnecessary so long as the little ones are unacquainted "with the Things they read of, or...before their thoughts are worth the recording" (p. 4). Reading and writing are, therefore, "deferred awhile," and instead an extended course of lessons is given, with the purpose "that the Educands be taught to observe and remember all sensible Objects and Actions, whether they be Naturall or Artificiall, which the Educators must on all occasions expound unto them." When reading is learned in due course, it should be taught "by much more compendious meanes then are in common use, which is a thing certainly very easie and feasible"; and the teaching of writing is to include that of shorthand and the use of the pentograph.

Music may be taught to such as possess a natural aptitude for the art, but every child without exception must learn to draw. "In no case [should] the Art of Drawing and designing be omitted, since the use thereof for expressing the conceptions of the mind, seemes (at least to us) to be little inferiour to that of Writing, and in many cases performeth what by words is impossible" (p. 5). Another compulsory study is Mathematics: "The elements of Arithmetick and Geometry be by all studied, being not onely of great and frequent use in all human Affaires but also sure guides and helps to Reason, and especiall Remedies for a volatile and unstedy mind"—exactly Bacon's prescription[1]. Another mental gymnastic which Petty favours, in suitable cases, is "the Artificiall Memory," that is, Mnemonics, Memory-systems, and so forth.

The study of foreign languages is only for "such as shall have need to learne" them, and the process ought to be "by incomparably more easie ways then are now usuall." Physical training is incumbent upon all: "they use such Exercises whether in work, or for recreation, as tend to the health, agility and strength of their bodies."

Most remarkable of all Petty's suggestions is that "all children, though of the highest ranke, be taught some gentile

---

[1] *De Augmentis*, Bk. VI. cp. 4: *Essays*, "Of Study."

Manufacture in their minority," and he gives a curious list of suitable handicrafts, which includes turning, the making of watches and of mathematical instruments, painting, graving, etching, carving, embossing and molding [modelling], gardening, the making of naval and of architectural models, confectionery, perfuming, dyeing, "Anatomy, making Sceletons and excarnating bowells," etc.—the list should be compared with that given by Locke in application of his precept, " I would have him *learn a trade, a manual trade*: nay two or three, but one more particularly[1]."

These were the studies which caused Petty to name his proposed schools "literary *work-houses*." They were an integral part of his plan which was expressly intended to teach children "as well to doe something towards their living, as to Read and Write." He foresaw that he would meet much opposition, especially from such as felt they belonged to "the highest ranke," or to ranks approaching thereto, and he is, therefore, at pains to give some eight reasons in favour of such instruction. The reasons are not all convincing, but the proposals made its author one of the earliest of that series of writers, which through Locke, Rousseau, Pestalozzi, Froebel, and others, culminates in the successful advocates of manual training in our own time.

One other feature of education as Petty would have it deserves mention, namely, the attempt to understand individual children, and in the light of that understanding, to give each the particular training he or she needed. The writer supplies no details, nothing in fact beyond this paragraph. "That effectuall Courses be taken to try the Abilities of the Bodies and Minds of Children, the strength of their Memory, inclination of their Affections either to Vice or Vertue, and to which of them in particular, and withall to alter what is bad in them, and increase and improve what is good, applying

---

[1] " Some Thoughts concerning Education," secs. 201–209.

all, whether good or bad, to the least Inconveniencie and most Advantage" (p. 5).

The severely utilitarian, not to say money-getting, type of education which Petty is recommending comes out in his description of the books which he would have read in the schools, first of which comes a proposed *Vellus Aureum sive Facultatum Lucriferarum discriptio Magna*, "wherein all the practised wayes of getting a Subsistance and whereby men raise their fortunes, may be at large declared." The advantages to be gained by boys from the perusal of this compilation are set out in two paragraphs, which also convey Petty's opinion of the value of ordinary schooling as it existed in 1648, together with an anticipation of ideas which present-day Englishmen more frequently associate with the name of Froebel than with Petty, Locke, or the Edgeworths. The paragraphs run as follows:

"Boys instead of reading hard Hebrew words in the Bible (where they either trample on, or play with Mysteries) or parratlike repeating heteroclitous nounes, and verbs, might read and hear the History of Faculties expounded, so that before they be bound Apprentices to any trade, they may foreknow the good and bad of it, what will and strength they have to it, and not spend seven years in repenting, and in swimming against the stream of their Inclinations.

"All apprentices by this Book[1] might learn the theory of their Trades before they are bound to a Master, and consequently may be exempted from the Taedium of a seven years bondage, and having spent but about three years with a Master, may spend the other foure in Travelling to learn breeding, and the perfection of their Trades.

"As it would be more profitable to Boyes, to spend ten or twelve years in the study of Things, and of this book of Faculties, then in a rabble of words, so it would be more

---

[1] That is, the *Vellus Aureum*.

easie and pleasant to them, as more suitable to the naturall propensions we observe in them. For we see Children do delight in Drums, Pipes, Fiddels, Guns made of Elder-sticks, and bellowes noses, piped Keys, etc., painting Flags and Ensignes, with Elder-berries and Corn-poppy, making ships with Paper, and setting even Nut-shells a swimming, handling the tooles of workemen as soon as they turn their backs and trying to worke themselves; fishing, fowling, hunting, setting sprenges and traps for birds and other animals, making pictures in their writing-bookes, making Tops, Gigs and Whirligigs, quilting balls, practising divers juggling tricks upon the cards, etc., with a million more besides. And for the Females, they will be making Pyes with Clay, making their Babies clothes and dressing them therewith; they will spit leaves on sticks as if they were roasting meate; they will imitate all the talke and Actions which they observe in their Mother and her gossips, and punctually act the Comedy or the Tragedy (I know not whether to call it) of a Woman's lying-in. By all which it is most evident that children do most naturally delight in things and are most capable of learning them, having quick Sences to receive them, and unpreoccupied memories to retaine them. As for the other things whereunto they are nowadays set, they are altogether unfit for want of judgment, which is but weake in them, and also for want of *Will*, which is sufficiently seene both by what we have said before, by the difficultie of keeping them at Schools, and the punishment they will endure rather then be altogether barred from this pleasure which they take in Things" (p. 24— marked " 12").

We have travelled a long way from Milton's tractate in conning the *Advice of W. P.* Milton might protest that language was merely "the instrument conveying to us things usefull to be known," but himself a scholar before all else, he could not dream of the exclusion from education of the ground-work at least of literary culture. Petty carries Milton's principle to its logical conclusion, and reduces language-study to an optional course for those whose personal needs made it requisite, an heroic recommendation which a schoolmaster like Comenius could not venture to make openly, however implicit it might be in his thought. But differences of curriculum are not the only lines of separation between the *Advice* and the *Tractate*. Milton plans an education beginning at 12, for the benefit of boys belonging to the wealthy classes; Petty's scheme is universal, and applies to girls as well as boys, the instruction beginning five years earlier than Milton contemplates. Milton's Realism is of the verbal sort which Rabelais had advocated a century earlier; Petty's Realism is thoroughgoing and undoubted. Moreover, he anticipates Pestalozzi and Froebel when he insists that instruction must follow the lines indicated by the child's natural propensities for learning, that the child is essentially an active creature, who learns best by *doing*, and that he must be taught in reference to his powers and needs of the moment, and not by ways which respect his future only. The similarity between much of the brief *Advice* and the prolix *Thoughts on Education* of Locke cannot escape the notice of readers.

CHAPTER VIII.

THE "REFORMED SCHOOL" OF JOHN DURY.

THE book called the *Reformed School*, the work of Hartlib's fellow-worker and close friend, John Dury, is one more token of Hartlib's perennial interest in the school, and his desire to widen its aims and improve its methods. The precise date of publication is not known, though 1649 probably fits the facts: a "Supplement to the Reformed School" appeared in 1650.

Born at Edinburgh in 1596, Dury's life of 84 years was a very active one, and though its chief concern lay outside the domain of schooling and of education in the ordinary sense, a brief outline may indicate what manner of man the author of the *Reformed School* was.

Both his father and grandfather had been at odds with the authorities in the Scottish Church and State. The grandfather, a monk who had left his cloister to become a devoted follower of John Knox, suffered imprisonment for his tirades against the Scottish Court. The father was banished for declining to submit to the jurisdiction of the Scottish Council, by which it came about that his son, a boy of ten when the family quitted Scotland, received his education at Sedan and Leyden. In the latter city John Dury's father laboured till his death as minister of the Scots Church.

John Dury himself received ordination at the hands of presbyters in the Reformed Church, and in 1628 he was minister to that English Company of Merchants at Elbing in Prussia in which Hartlib's father and grandfather were so prominently concerned[1]. The friendship of Dury and Hartlib dated from the previous year, and it is possible that about the same time Comenius made the acquaintance of one or other of the two men[2].

It was at Elbing that Dury began what proved to be his life's work, namely the attempt to effect a reconciliation between Lutherans and Calvinists, and to bring them into accord where common advantage was at stake. In spite of his admitted ability and of years of travel from one centre of religious life, or of theological learning, to another, in the face of untold discouragements, poverty and calumny, Dury failed, so far as the disputants themselves were concerned. But towards the end of his days it became evident that his strenuous endeavour to restore unity had had its effect in his own life, bringing him to a point where he ventured to dream of a peace and unity comprehending both Catholic and Protestant[3], a point of view very uncommon in the seventeenth century—to say nothing of any later time.

At first Dury seems to have looked to Gustavus Adolphus and Sweden for the realisation of his desire, and he ventured to address the King on the subject while he was minister at Elbing[4]. In 1630, he left for England "chiefly," says Hartlib[5], "because his Congregation at Elbing was dissolved by reason of the inconveniences which warre had brought upon the Trade in that place." Archbishop Abbot and some

---

[1] *A Briefe Relation, etc.* 1641.

[2] The authority for the first statement is Dury himself in *The Unchanged, Constant and Single-hearted Peace-maker* of 1650. Kvačsala, *Johann Amos Comenius: Sein Leben und seine Schriften*, p. 239, suggests the possibility in connection with a letter in the Sloane MSS.

[3] *Dict. Nat. Biog.* "John Durie."

[4] In 1628, *A Briefe Relation.*

[5] *A Briefe Relation*, p. 2.

of the English bishops and clergy were interested in Dury's project and they furnished him with letters to the Swedish King, who in his turn approved the attempt to reconcile the disciples of Luther and Calvin, a united Protestant Germany being essential to the success of his policy. To the Continent Dury returned with a commission more or less informal to the courts, churches, state assemblies and synods of Germany and of Holland; but the death of Gustavus Adolphus on the field of Lützen in 1632 led to the temporary crippling of the plan for reunion which Oxenstiern, the Swedish Chancellor, unlike his dead master, did not approve, and Dury himself returned to England, burdened heavily with debt.

At home he sought orders in the English Church, and was ordained by the Bishop of Exeter in 1634, passing in that same year to a great evangelical assembly at Frankfurt, taking as his credentials letters from Archbishops Laud and Ussher, from three other bishops and a score of English doctors of divinity. The great defeat of the Swedes at Nördlingen and its disastrous effect on Protestantism in southern Germany put an end to the conference, and Dury returned to England.

In the following year (1635) he was again abroad, where for the next ten years he remained, a short interval in 1641 excepted; Sweden, Denmark, Germany, Holland were the scenes of his labours for ecclesiastical unity, and he attempted to advance the same cause in France and Switzerland by means of letters and memorials. In November, 1643, he was appointed a member of the Assembly of Divines which drew up the Westminster Confession and Catechism, but he did not return to London till November, 1645. From that date to April, 1654, he ·continued in England, and it is to this period that the *Reformed School* belongs. Then followed a three years' sojourn abroad, Amsterdam being his head-quarters, whence he visited the Low Countries, Germany, and the Swiss cantons. He returned to England for the last time in 1657, and at the Restoration, finding himself and his services ignored both by Church and King, he went to Cassel, which became his home till his death twenty years later. From Cassel he periodically sallied forth to different quarters of Germany and Switzerland, but the result is summed up in his own words, "The only fruit which I have reaped by all my toils is that I see the miserable condition of Christianity, and that I have no other comfort than the testimony of my conscience[1]."

The *Reformed School*, the work which more particularly connects Dury with the history of educational opinion, made its public appearance under Hartlib's auspices during the author's comparatively long sojourn in England from 1645 to 1654. In accordance with his usual practice Hartlib presented the book in a preface of his own, from which citations have already been made[2]. From it we learn that some sort of Parliamentary recognition had been bestowed upon Hartlib's projected Public Intelligence Department under the guise of an "Agency for Learning," with Hartlib himself as its chief. In this capacity he had gathered about him a number of friends, amongst whom there grew up the idea of establishing a religious community which would undertake the work of education. Such communities were then flourishing exceedingly in Catholic Europe, but especially in France, and their success may have suggested this projected corporation, though (needless to say) it was not proposed to require any of the monastic vows from the men and women who might feel attracted to a common life with the religious education of youth as the end in view. Of these John Dury is put forward as the spokesman, and the first part of his book is an account of the proposed "Association" or community, and of the manner in which it was thought its ends might best be attained.

[1] *Dict. Nat. Biog.* "John Durie."
[2] p. 100 above.

But before turning to Dury's work a further reference may be permitted to Hartlib's preface. Here he tells us that the reformation of the adult population seemed too hopeless an enterprise for his friends to embark upon, and, consequently, they preferred the more promising material to be found in the children of the time, a choice sanctioned by the action or the thought of philosophic and statesmanlike reformers in all times and places. In one particular, at least, Hartlib and his friends show that Comenius's ideas of a school-system influenced theirs; they proposed not only to institute reformed schools, but also to place these under the care of reformed school-masters, "the training up of Reformed School-masters is one of the chief parts of this Designe......The School master in a well ordered Common-wealth, is no lesse considerable than either the Minister or the Magistrate; because neither the one nor the other will prosper or subsist long without him...... The Authour of this new Model of schooling was intreated to put it to paper, upon a serious motion made to him, and to some Friends of his, by others; for the entertaining and regulating of a Christian Association, whereof all the Members might be serviceable to each other, and to the Publick; therefore he speaks not in his own name alone concerning the Association, but in the name of those, who were jointly called upon to give their assent thereunto, who agreed with him in these Proposals. The Motion is not as yet come to maturitie in the Resolution of those that first made it, and the cause is, of some Conveniences to effect it, and the fears of unsettlement, after that it shall be set upon: and till there be a further ground laid for the prosecuting of this Designe, it is needlesse to give the Directory concerning the Education of Girls," etc.

Dury's work begins with a brief indication of the nature and constitution of the "Association" of persons who, while not being "religious" in the technical sense, are to live a common life according to rule, with the purpose, first, of personal edification, and next, of providing the means by which the Reformed School may be carried on. The school is to afford a reformed education intended to make "good Commonwealths men" apt in husbandry, trade, navigation, administration, in peace and in war. Girls who are "capable of Tongues and Sciences" are also to enjoy the benefits of the Association's labours, but as only a modest beginning is possible at the moment, the account of girls' education is deferred. The school which is designed is a boarding-school for fifty boys in the care of a Governor and three Ushers; its daily routine as compared with that of a similar school of to-day shows longer hours and harder work, or, at least, less opportunity for play. In winter the "aged scholars" are to be awakened at five o'clock, in summer at four; the smaller fry arise an hour later in each case, and all are to be abed at or before nine, the Governors, Ushers and Stewards retiring at ten o'clock. Breakfast "of bread and butter, or some other thing" is at eight o'clock, dinner "precisely at twelve of the clock," supper "precisely at half-an-hour past six of the clock, and before seven taken away." The diet is to be plain and nourishing, "bread and beer of good quality" being allowed *à discrétion* as a staple, in case any should find a particular meal contrary to his taste or power of digestion. Two hours a day are spent in exercise, that is, "in husbandry or manufactures or military employment." The hour from 12.30 is a free time.

The several educational aims of the School are said to be four; they closely resemble "the four things" which Locke afterwards proposed as the aims of his own system of training. Dury states them as, 1. Godliness. 2. Bodily Health. 3. Manners, and "last and least part of true education, proficiencie in Learning,"—an arrangement which reverses Comenius's *Eruditio, Mores Honesti, Pietas.* The general principle which was to guide the establishment throughout is laid down in words which imply that belief in the power of system and method which marked all who drew inspiration from Bacon: the same words also express the conviction which Comenius so repeatedly insisted upon, *Nil invita Minerva.* "The chief rule of the whole work is that nothing be made tedious and grievous to the children, but all the toilsomeness of their business the Governor and Ushers are to take upon themselves; that by diligence and industry all things may be so prepared, methodized and ordered for their apprehension, that this work may unto them be as a delightful recreation by the variety and easiness thereof" (p. 24). This is but an exaggerated statement of a principle which Locke repeated, and which makes up so much of the pedagogy of the eighteenth and nineteenth century thinkers.

The latter and somewhat longer part of Dury's book is, in effect, a discussion of education in general, and not a mere description of a scholastic Utopia. The several parts of the subject with which it deals are the purpose of learning, the sources of knowledge, the capacity of the childish mind with reference to those sources, the curriculum as consequent upon the foregoing, the methods of teaching and of moral training. The last-named topic occurs early in the discussion, but it does not occupy a predominant place therein: the noteworthy thing about it is, the declaration that to be successful, moral training must be addressed to individual children, taking the disposition of each into account.

Beginning with a section which repeats the ordinary indictment of School and University at the time, that they occupied themselves with "Words" to the neglect of "Things," and consequently offered knowledge merely superficial, Dury states his own conception of the purpose of learning, which is in brief the Baconian "relief of man's estate." He deduces from this that the learning which effects this purpose is the only true learning, that students must at the outset be made aware of the special purpose of their particular science and its relation to the end of learning in general, and, lastly, that "sciences must be taught orderly," with respect to the mutual subordination of their several ends, and with respect to the learner's capacity—that is, logic and psychology both have a share in determining the order of learning.

The means by which knowledge is acquired, says Dury, are three in number. First, the employment of the organs of sense, the eye, the ear, and so on; secondly, Tradition; and thirdly, Reason, the mind's reflection upon that which is received through the Senses and from Tradition. He elaborates this in a passage which sets forth the same hierarchy of "Faculties" that is to be found in Comenius, associating therewith a conception of mental development which requires in his theory of instruction a corresponding auxiliary order of studies.

"From the subordination of these Means to one another, and their properties to advance us into Learning, we shall gather these following Rules of teaching Arts and Sciences :

"1. The Arts or Sciences which may be received by meer Sense should not be taught any other way ; for it is no wisdome to make work to ourselves.

"2. Whatsoever in any Art or Science can be made obvious unto Sense, is first to be made use of, as a Precognition unto that which is to be delivered by way of Traditionall or Rationall precept.

"3. As in Nature Sense is the servant of Imagination ; Imagination of Memory ; Memory of Reason ; so in teaching Arts and Sciences we must set these Faculties a work in their Order towards their proper Objects in everything, which is to be taught : whence this will follow, that as the Faculties of Man's soul naturally perfect each other by their mutual subordination ; so the Arts which perfect those Faculties should be gradually suggested ; and the objects wherewith the Faculties are to be conversant according to the Rules of Art should be offered in that order, which is answerable to their proper ends and uses and not otherwise. As Children's

Faculties break forth in them, by degrees to be vigorous with their years, and the growth of their bodies, so they are to be filled with Objects whereof they are capable, and plyed with Arts ; whence followeth that while children are not capable of the Acts of Reasoning ; the Method of filling their Senses and Imaginations with outward Objects should be plyed. Nor is their Memory at this time to be charged further with any Objects than their Imagination rightly ordered and fixed doth of itself impress the same upon them."

" Moreover hence followeth, that no Generall Rules are to be given unto any, concerning anything either to be known or practised according to the Rule of any Art or Science : till Sense, Imagination, and Memory have received their Impressions concerning that whereunto the Rule is to be applyed ; and so farre as those faculties are stored with matters of observation, so farre Rules may be given to direct the mind in the use of the same and no further. Lastly hence followeth, That the Arts or Science which flow not immediately from particular and sensuall objects, but tend immediately to direct the universall Acts of Reasoning, must be taught after the rest ; because their Use is to Regulat that, which is to make Use of all the Rest, viz., the Rationall faculty ; therefore, it is a very absurd and preposterous course to teach Logick and Metaphysics before or with other Humane Sciences, which depend more upon Sense and Imagination then Reasoning."

Dury's consideration of the allied topics of curriculum and method is of a see-saw kind which does not complete one before trenching upon the other ; but both arise naturally from a third topic, which the writer calls " Children's Naturall Capacities." The reformed education of which he treats acquires its name not only from the use of a different method and the extension of school-studies ; deeper than these is the conviction that instruction must be conditioned not solely by the will of the instructor, but also by the nature of the mind to be instructed, with the added suggestion that, in the past, the instructor's own ideals had been often opposed to the "natural capacities" of the young. Dury is, in short, insisting upon that reference to the child, which, appearing before him in Comenius, was later in Locke and Rousseau to begin a reform in school practice that is only now taking effect. Reflecting upon what is due to the natural capacities of children, Dury deduces a number of important principles of didactics. Amongst these are the following : That the learner's co-operation must be secured, servile constraint being removed, and nothing being taught till the time is seasonable, that is, till the child's capacities are fit to cope with it—platitudes, certainly, but all the same, truths often distinctively styled Froebelian, and, in any case, truths not infrequently denied in practice. There is a similar anticipation of Herbart, when Dury insists that all studies, while following the principle of sequence, must unite in leading the pupil to achieve the true end of learning, and that due connection should be maintained between different branches of learning.

Accepting Sense, Tradition and Reason as the sources of knowledge, and holding that the last is a source but partially open to children and young scholars, Dury divides branches of learning into two great groups. First, " profitable Arts and Sciences," that is, " all matters of knowledge which direct man to the right use of all Creatures, and the ordering of his owne Faculties about them." Secondly, the Tongues which are most useful to enlarge the knowledge thereof, namely, Latin, Greek, Hebrew, and the Oriental affinities of the last. But in prescribing these ancient languages he is not urged by the literary motive, by the desire for culture, or by scorn of the " useful." Quite the contrary : " Tongues are no further finally usefull then to enlarge Traditionall Learning : and without their subordination unto Arts and Sciences, they are worth nothing towards the advancement of our happiness. The Immediate Use of Tongues is only to Understand what others say to us, according to their custome of speaking ; and to expresse our minds unto them significantly according to our custome."

Dury thereupon deduces certain general rules relating to the order of studies and to method.

The first, if adopted, would have revolutionised the schools of the time. It is the proposal to teach "Arts and Sciences" in the mother-tongue from the first, postponing the study of languages to a second stage. "Words" and "Things" are to be taught in association, rules and form are to follow, not precede examples and matter ; more especially, the knowledge of language is to advance "Reall Truths in Science." "The teaching of words is no further Usefull then the things signified therby are familiar to the Imagination, and that the teaching of Rules before the Materiall Sense of the words is known, or before the formall coherence of things which their construction is to represent in a Sentence, can be apprehended, is wholly preposterous and unprofitable to the Memory.

"So farre as children are capable of Traditionall knowledge : so farre in every degree of Science they may be taught the Tongues which serve for that Use ; but till they be fitted for the one, the other is Useless to them.

"Whatsoever in the teaching of Tongues doth not tend to make them a help unto Traditionall knowledge, by the manifestation of Reall Truths in Sciences, is superfluous, and not to be insisted on, especially towards Children, whence followeth that the Curious study of Criticismes, and observation of Styles in Authors, and of straines of wit, which speak nothing of Reality in Sciences, are to be left to such as delight in vanityes more then in Truths."

These general rules being laid down, Dury states a curriculum in considerable detail, into all points of which it is not possible to follow him here. The period of tutelage extends to the twentieth year, the whole being divided into four parts, the first from birth to the age of four or five, the second to eight or nine, the third to 13 or 14, the fourth completing the period to 19 or 20. Like Comenius and Petty, Dury spares thought for the little ones who are too young for the formal sort of schooling which begins at the age of eight or nine.

Practically nothing is said of the first four or five years, but when these are completed, the child is to enter "a peculiar school," "a Nursery not farre from the place of the Society," having teachers distinct from those of the school proper, whose Governor, however, is to visit the Nursery and note what care is given to the manners, habits, and dispositions of the children. Dury hopes that *schoolmasters* may be specially trained for these infant schools. The studies and other occupations are those which Comenius proposed for the "School of Infancy." The children are to learn to speak the mother-tongue distinctly, to read it readily, intelligibly, naturally, to write it legibly, to draw lines and figures with ruler and compasses, and freehand. They must learn the signification of the numerals, and by observation and trial make estimate of quantity by means of eye, ear, and hand. They are to learn the names and shapes of objects, and "to make circumstantiall descriptions thereof by word of mouth, and painting in black and white." Finally, the desire for omniscience, which is very rarely absent from the seventeenth-century writers, suggests that the nurselings shall get by heart a statement in outline (a very attenuated outline, no doubt) of the history and geography of the world, with a somewhat closer attention to the national history.

Schooling of the formal order begins at eight or nine. From that time to 13 or 14 the boy is engaged in ordering, classifying, and extending the kind of knowledge which he has previously acquired, and in that way preparing for the traditional and rational studies which are to occupy him in the last stage. He continues his object-lessons and drawing, and adds, amongst others, the following branches: an outline of geography, of astronomy, geometry, mensuration, surveying, "the practical parts of mathematics "; and in arithmetic, beside the Four Rules, he learns the Reduction of Fractions, the Rule of Proportions (the Golden Rule), "and no further." Latin, Greek, and later, Hebrew, are all begun between 8–9 and 13–14; these languages are learned from Comenius's *Janua*.

The last stage, from 13–14 to 19–20, is filled with a round of studies too long to repeat; nor is it necessary to repeat it, as it is Milton's course over again, with few exceptions. After the first year, "their speech shall be wholly Latin." Nevertheless, these Latin-speaking lads are students of science who are now encouraged to make researches, and to apply themselves to a special branch of work.

"In the third course of this period, that is, in the two last years thereof, all the Sciences belonging to the period shall be taught practically, that is, they shall be exercised in the practice of all that which they have been taught, in the whole former course of their education : and they shall be put upon the occasions of making Use of their skill in every Science for their own and others advantage, and the improvement of the wayes of learning : and here as their Genius shall lead them, they shall be left a little larger scope to follow it ; either in wayes of Action, or of Theorie, or of Utterance ; in the first year of this course they should be exercised and put upon the practice of all ; but in the last year, according as their Faculty should be found most eminent (with some few Directions and Manuductions to Improve it) they should be suffered to apply it to the subject which amongst all the Sciences they should like best to exercise themselves in. And in the latter end of this year, that is, in the last quarter thereof, having received such Directions for the future Government of their life as will be found necessary to order it Judiciously and Prudently ; they may be dismissed to take some Public Service in hand ; or follow some private Calling which the Commonwealth doth stand in need of."

Dury now returns to Method, and in a couple of his tiny

pages[1] lays down directions which remind one of the "Formal Steps" of the Herbartian, except that Dury's steps are those of a single *lesson*. The intention of the Association was to train teachers, and the three ushers are assumed to be in the stage of studentship. In beginning any one branch of knowledge, the Governor or Headmaster shall "teach the first lesson of every kind himself in the presence of his Ushers, that they may observe his way"—that is, he shall give a demonstration lesson. The following lesson, given by an usher in the presence of the governor is what was known in training colleges as a criticism lesson.

The children's attitude is described as "affectionat towards the task which is to be offered unto them, that is, attentive and greedy to receive it." This desirable frame of mind is induced by making the children "sensible of the End, wherefore it is taught them." Dury's lesson, lasting an hour, is divided into two parts equal as to time, and called respectively the Proposing and the Entertaining. The Proposing begins by stating the aim, analysing the subject-matter of the lesson, then synthesizing it, which, formally at least, is the function of the opening steps in the Herbartian procedure—as, indeed, it is in every completed piece of good teaching. The whole having been analysed, and the parts united again in a whole, that whole is reviewed in the light of what synthesis has revealed. Then comes a recapitulation, or summary. The Proposing may be compared with the first four of the "Five Formal Steps," and the Entertaining is, in effect, the Fifth Step, since it is a practical application of, or exercise in what has been learned in the preceding half-hour. "The way of enterteining that which shall be thus proposed is partly in the Scholars by themselves, partly in them together with their Ushers. By themselves they shall entertain the things which have been taught them, by the exercises of writing, of painting, or drawing figures, of compen-

---

[1] *The Reformed School* measures 2⅝" by 4¾".

diating, and of methodizing, as they shall from time to time be directed : for the fixing of their thoughts upon that which they shall have received : and by the reading, and understanding, and translating of their *Janua's*, or of their Authors from one Tongue to another, according to the way which shall be shewed them[1] " (pp. 72–73).

The very complete curriculum detailed by Dury, and the character of that curriculum in its highest development, which included specialising and research, made some readers object that he aimed at the suppression of the universities. Milton had actually made that proposal, his Academy being designed to give every sort of instruction, Law and Medicine, the only exceptions, being relegated to special professional colleges.

Dury answered his critics in a "Supplement to the Reformed School subordinate to Colleges in Universities," published in 1650 in the *Reformed Librarie-Keeper*. He protests that it was not at all his intention to "make Colleges and Universities useless." Schools have one purpose : Universities another, and he goes on to say what he conceives these to be. The passages in which he describes the purpose of a University and the function of its professors are in accord with much that is being written in magazines and spoken from platforms and elsewhere at this hour ; and as the same passages also make clear John Dury's point of view concerning public education in general and the Reformed School in particular, they are here quoted *in extenso*.

"The true and proper end of Schooling is to teach and Exercise Children and Youths in the Grounds of all Learning

[1] The *locale* of the Reformed School is a country-house sufficiently near town to allow the observation of the artificial as well as the natural. Each usher is to have his own class-room, with desks for 20 pupils. In addition there is a "gallery" or hall filled with very varied collections of objects, instruments, pictures, diagrams, maps, etc. It may be of interest to note that besides pens, penknives, compasses and rulers, the boys also use "a pen or stick with black-lead" and a slate.

and Virtues, so far as either their capacitie in that age will
suffer them to com, or is requisite to apprehend the principles
of useful matters, by which they may bee able to exercise
themselves in everie good employment afterwards by themselves, and as the Proverb is, *sine Cortice natare.* The true
and proper end of Colleges should bee to bring together into
one Societie such as are able thus to Exercise themselves in
anie or all kind of Studies, that by their Mutual Association,
Communication, and Assistance in Reading, Meditating, and
conferring about profitable matters, they may not onely perfit
their own Abilities, but advance the superstructure of all
Learning to that perfection, which by such means is attainable.
And the true and proper end of Universities should bee to
publish unto the World the Matters, which formerly have not
been published ; to discover the Errors and hurtfulness of
things mistaken for Truths : and to supplie the defects and
desiderata, which may bee serviceable to all sorts of Professions.

"Now according to those aimes and ends, I suppose it may
bee inferred that none should bee dismissed out of the Schools,
till they are able to make use of all sorts of Books, and direct
themselves profitably in everie cours of Studie or Action,
whereunto their *Genius* shall lead them ; and that none should
bee admitted into anie Colleges, but such as will join with
others, to elaborate som profitable Tasks, for the Advancement and facilitating of superstructures in things already by
som discovered, but not made common unto all: And that
none should bee made Publick Professors in Universities, but
such as have not onely a Publick aim, but som approved
Abilities, to supply som defects and to Elaborate som *desiderata*
of usefull knowledge, or to direct such as are studious, how to
order their thoughts in all matters of search and Meditation,
for the discoverie of things not hitherto founde out by others ;
but which in probabilitie may be found out by rational
searching.

"Thus then I conceiv, that in a well-Reformed Common-

wealth, which is to bee subordinate unto the Kingdom of
Jesus Christ, wherein the Glorie of God, the happiness of the
nature of man : and the Glorious libertie of the Sons of God is
to bee revealed ; all the subjects thereof should in their Youth
bee trained up in som Schools fit for their capacities, and that
over these Schools, som Overseers should bee appointed to
look to the cours of their Education, to see that none should
bee left destitute of som benefit of virtuous breeding, according
to the several kinds of emploiments, whereunto they may bee
found most fit and inclinable, whether it bee to bear som civil
office in the Common-wealth, or to be Mechanically emploied,
to bee bred to teach others humane Sciences, or to bee
emploied in Prophetical Exercises [that is, as preachers].   As
for this School, which at this time I have delineated, it is
proper to such of the Nobilitie, Gentrie, and better sort of
Citizens which are fit to bee made capable to bear offices in
the Common-wealth : the other Schools may be spoken of in
due time, so far as they are distinct from this ; but that which
now I have to suggest is chiefly this, that as out of the Schools
the chois which ought to bee made for Colleges, ought,
Caeteris paribus, onely to bee of such as are most fit to
Advance the Ends of a Collegiall Association ; so out of
Colleges a chois ought to bee made of Professors for the
Universitie onely, of such as are fittest to advance the Ends of
Publick teaching in Universities, which are not to Repeat and
Compendiate that which others have published twentie times
already, over and over again, but to add unto the Common
stock of humane knowledg, that which others have not observed,
to the end that all these degrees of Studies and Exercises of
the minde of man, beeing subordinate unto the Kingdom of
Jesus Christ, the happiness of Man by all Rational and
Spiritual Waies of . improving humane abilities, may bee
advanced unto its perfection in this life so far as may
bee.

"But how far short we com now of all these designs, I need

not to relate unto you ; the Colleges as they are now Constituted, can scarce reach to the half of that which the Schools
might bring us unto ; and the Professors of the Universities
com not up to that, which the Collegiall Associations might
elaborate, if they were rightly directed to set their talents a
work ; and if the publick Spirit of Christian love and ingenuitie
did possess those, that are possessed of publick places in the
Colleges of the Universities[1]."

NOTE.—DURY'S "EXERCITATION OF SCHOOLING."

The *Reformed School* was not its author's earliest contribution to educational discussion. In the Sloane MSS. there
are some pages (said to be in Hartlib's handwriting) belonging
to the year 1646, which show that Dury was then considering
the problem of organised public education. These outline-
notes are headed " Mr Dury's Exercitation of Schooling, 1646,
Mensis (?) 3. Winter. Matters to be elaborated for the
Education of Children[2]": their purport is to the following
effect. A system of publicly supported schools, primary and
secondary, should be set up under the authority of the
Executive (both central and local) and of the " Ministerie,"
that is, the Presbyterian ministers then paramount. The
purpose of these schools is to help children to the *mens sana
in corpore sano*, and otherwise " to set them in a way to become
serviceable unto others, publickly and privately." Three types
of school are contemplated. (1) Common Schools, teaching

---

[1] *A Supplement to the Reformed School*, 1650, pp. 4–7. Compare the
passage in the 1st Book of *The Advancement of Learning*, which declares
that "professors of any science ought to propound to themselves to make
some additions to their science." The respective spheres of School and
University here defined by Dury are those assigned to-day by German
educational writers.

[2] Sloane MSS. (in British Museum), 649, pp. 52, 53.

all "in their mother-tongue the right notions, names, and expressions of things." Children intended for trades and "servile work" will receive all their education in the Common School. (2) Schools teaching Hebrew, Greek, and Latin, whose pupils are intended for the learned professions. (3) Schools preparatory to the public service, civil and military; the young nobles and gentlemen are to be taught modern foreign languages chiefly, "French, Spanish, Italian, etc.," to prepare them for "Commerce," *i.e.* intercourse with people abroad. After the model of Comenius's School of Infancy there is a suggestion that directions be drawn up to assist parents and nurses in the home-training of very young children : in the later *Reformed School* Dury proposes a "Nursery" or Infant School for such children.

It has already been surmised that Hartlib worked up these rough notes in his "Considerations" of 1647. (See p. 107 above.)

CHAPTER IX.

A SUCCESSFUL SCHOOLMASTER: HOOLE.

HARTLIB and Milton, Petty and Dury picture the school-
room as they conceived it should be; the actual school of their
day was quite different in aims and in method. The need for
reform which had seemed so necessary to Comenius at the
beginning of the second quarter of the century was much more
obvious when the third quarter was well advanced ; but consideration of the work of Charles Hoole, a schoolmaster of
repute, shows that those who then ruled in the class-room were
seldom of that opinion.

Born in 1610 at Wakefield, Hoole was educated in the
Grammar School there and at Lincoln College, Oxford ; and,
taking orders at or about the termination of his University
course, he returned to his native county as Master of the Free
School at Rotherham, where he seems to have remained till
1642[1]. In that year he held a Lincolnshire living, which was
sequestrated by Parliament as being in the occupation of a
delinquent clergyman. He removed to London, where he set
up a very successful private school, first " betwixt Goldsmith's
Alley in Red-cross Street, and Mayden Head Alley in Aldersgate Street[2]," and later " in the Tokenhouse Garden in

[1] Testimonial from Thomas Hayne " of the Citie of London's School in
Christ Church" prefixed to Hoole's *An Easy Entrance to the Latin Tongue*
(1649).
[2] Hoole's *Propria quae maribus*, etc. 1650.

Lothbury[1]." In this "private Grammar School," says Anthony à Wood, "the generality of the youth under him were instructed to a miracle." In 1660 Hoole became a Prebendary of Lincoln and Bishop's Chaplain, and was preferred to the Essex Rectory of Stock, where he ended his days[2].

Hoole's success in the class-room is not his sole claim to the attention of the historian of education ; he was also a man very well read in the professional writings of his own day and of earlier times, and an industrious compiler of school-books. These last all dealt with the teaching of Latin, and the earlier of them were attempts to mollify the rigour of Lily's Grammar, chiefly by turning parts of that standard manual into English. Though it must be admitted that a great deal of Hoole's work in this kind fairly deserves the epithet "arid," one book, bristling, as its title implies, with paradigms, " The Terminations and Examples of Declensions and Conjugations for the use of Young Grammarians," survived as a class-book for more than two centuries, being reprinted at Dublin in 1857. But during the last three years (1657–1660) which he spent in the school-room, Hoole produced class-books which seem to show that he was reconsidering the problem of teaching Latin rudiments. Apart from a version of Comenius's *Orbis Pictus* and a treatise on School-keeping to be noticed presently, the school-books in question were intended to help children to use Latin conversationally, after the older fashion. Thus in addition to an English version (1652) of Cordier's *School Colloquies*, Hoole published " A Little Vocabulary, English and Latine," "Sentences for Children, for the first Enterers into Latin " (1658), and the Comedies of Terence with an English translation, " For the use of young Scholars that they may the more readily attain the purity of the Latin Tongue for common discourse " (B.M. copy, 1676). The purpose of the *Vocabulary*,

[1] Hoole's *Common Rudiments of Latine Grammar*, 1650.
[2] See the article " Hoole " in *Dict. Nat. Biog.*; other particulars are also taken from this article and from Hoole's prefaces.

English and Latin, according to its author, is "to teach little ones how to call those things in Latine, which are every way obvious unto them, and whose names they know in English. *And this we may observe to be the first step towards the gaining of any language.*" (The italics are not Hoole's.)

The foregoing were small school-books compiled for scholars : Hoole's *magnum opus* was *A New Discovery of the old Art of Teaching Schoole*, a treatise which formed a sort of legacy to schoolmasters from the writer, when he ceased to belong to their profession in 1660. The substance of the book had been with its author for nearly a quarter of a century, its practical parts having been in actual use at Rotherham, and these improved by "fourteen years trial by diligent practice in London" (title-page). In scope, in plan, and in the opinions enunciated, this treatise "published for the general profit, especially of young School-masters" is very like Brinsley's work of nearly half a century earlier. Both books are, first and foremost, the expression of long experience in the conduct of a school, and of teaching school-children. Both display a knowledge of English and classical works on education, Hoole being lavish in his references to professional writers of the 16th and 17th centuries, and to the doings of other London teachers then living.

The *New Discovery* names some forty or fifty school-masters and educational writers in the course of its 300 odd pages, amongst the best-known being Farnaby, and Busby of Westminster, both then living, Helwig ("Helvici Colloquia"), the sometime admiring colleague of Ratke, Brinsley, Mulcaster, Ascham, and Erasmus. These names are all significant of the older culture; for a different reason, the scanty reference to contemporary English school-reformers is significant also. Hoole makes no mention of Milton, of Hartlib, of Petty; John Dury's name occurs once as the author of the *Reformed School*, and a promoter of public interest in elementary education. "Mr John Comenius" is named more than once, but always as one whose claim to attention is, that he proposes to improve the teaching of school Latin. In brief, Hoole, with all his practical knowledge and great interest in the subject, appears to be unconscious of, or indifferent to the real nature of the reform in education which Comenius was endeavouring to effect, and which men prominent in London life were publicly advocating in this country. It is John Brinsley and the *Advancement of Learning* over again. In spite of all that had been said or written, and of all that had been done to extend the bounds of knowledge since *Ludus Literarius* appeared, and notwithstanding the fact that Hoole had himself recently written an English version of the *Orbis Pictus*, the *New Discovery* remains an exposition of "the old Art," or, as its author approvingly styles it, "the good old waie of teaching by grammar, autors, and exercises[1]."

The book is divided into four parts, the whole work "showing how Children in their playing years may Grammatically attain to a firm groundedness in and exercise of the Latine, Greek and Hebrew Tongues." Its debt to John Brinsley's *Ludus Literarius* is great, and, on the whole, it is inferior and pedantic when compared with the earlier production. The several titles of the four parts give a fairly comprehensive idea of its contents, with the possible exception of the first part. They read as follows :

"*I. The Petty School.* Shewing a way to teach little children to read English with delight and profit. [There is more than this, however.]

"*II. The Usher's* ⸌*Duty*, or a Platform of Teaching Lilies Grammar. [This describes the work of the three lowest forms in a grammar school, whose chief aim is the mastery of "Lilly's Grammar, which is yet constantly made use of in most schools in England, and from which I think it not good for any master to decline" (chap. v. of Part ii.).

---

[1] The third part (*The Master's Method*), ch. ii.

Hoole's experience of this widely-used boy's book is that children proceed in it "very slowly, because it being all in Latin, is hard to be understood, and being somewhat long in learning, boys are apt to forget one end of it before they can come to another" (*ibid.*).]

"*III. The Master's Method*, or the Exercising of Scholars in Grammars, Authors, and Exercises, Greek, Latine, and Hebrew [that is, the work of the three highest forms, who are especially in the care of the Master himself].

"*IV. Scholastick Discipline*, or the Way of ordering a Grammar School, Directing the not experienced how he may profit every particular Scholar, and avoid confusion amongst a multitude."

Of these four parts, or "treatises," as Hoole calls them, the first, though it is evidently penned with Brinsley's book in the writer's mind, is of most interest. The topic is the Petty School, that is, the school preparatory to the Grammar School ; its pupils commence about the age of five, remain two or three years, and occupy themselves chiefly in learning to read, that is, in learning to read English with the understanding and Latin with the lips. The method is the time-honoured one associated with the learning to read in Greek and Latin, namely, the A-B-C-and-syllable plan, for which a phonetically spelt language affords colourable excuse. Here Hoole, like Brinsley before him, and like Locke a generation later, is, of course, merely repeating Quintilian. There is nothing in this to detain us, except, perhaps, the following piece of "child-study" and Hoole's inference therefrom. "One having a son of two and a half old, that could but even go about the house, and utter some few gibberish words in a broken manner, observing him one day above the rest to be busied about shells and sticks and such like toys, which himself had laid together in a chair, and to miss any one that was taken from him he saw not how, and to seek for it about the house, became very desirous to make experiment what that child might presently attain to in point of learning. Thereupon he devised a little wheel, with all the capital Roman letters made upon a paper to wrap round about it, and fitted it to turn in a little round box, which had a hole so made in the side of it, that only one letter might be seen to peep out at once. This he brought to the child, and showed him only the letter O, and told him what it was. The child being overjoyed with his new gambol, catcheth the box out of his father's hand, and runs with it to his playfellow a year younger than himself, and in his broken language tells him there was 'an O, an O.' And when the other asked him where, he said, 'In a hole, in a hole,' and showed it to him; which the lesser child then took such notice of, as to know it again ever after from all the other letters. And thus by playing with the box, and enquiring concerning any letter that appeared strange to him what it was, the child learned all the letters of the alphabet in 11 days, being in this A. B. C. character, and would take pleasure to show them in any book to any of his acquaintance that came next. By this instance, you may see," says Hoole, "what a propensity there is in nature betimes to learning, could but the teachers apply themselves to their young scholars' tenuity; and how by proceeding in a clear and facile method that all may apprehend, every one may benefit more or less by degrees" (chap. ii.).

But the most interesting thing about Hoole's Petty School is, that besides serving as a preparatory course to the work of the Grammar School for those who are subsequently to receive instruction in " the tongues," this school is also a place "wherein children for whom the Latin tongue is thought to be unnecessary, are to be employed after they can read English." Instead of dismissing such as "incapable of learning," the Petty School · is to give them still more practice in reading English, and to add writing and arithmetic to their school work. While the other children are to learn the accidence, these Latin-less youngsters are to " be benefited in reading orthodoxall catechisms and other books that may instruct them in the duties of a Christian, such as the *Practice of Piety, the Practice of Quietness, the Whole Duty of Man;* and ever afterward in other delightful books of English History, as *The History of Queen Elizabeth,* or poetry, as *Herbert's Poems, Quarles' Emblems;* and by this means they will gain such a habit and delight in reading as to make it their chief recreation when liberty is afforded them. And their acquaintance with good books will (by God's blessing) be a means to sweeten their (otherwise) sour natures, that they may live comfortably towards themselves, and amiably converse with other persons" (ch. v.). This ascription to the vernacular literature of value, from the point of view of culture is noteworthy. That letters "soften men's manners, and do not permit them to be brutal" was, of course, a venerable statement perfectly familiar to every student of Lily's *Grammar*; but very few schoolmasters of Hoole's day thought of "letters" and of English as being connected. The fact is, that our worthy pedagogue is in this repeating what he had read in the "Elementarie" (1582) of Mulcaster, who was an enthusiast for the English tongue. Indeed, the idea of Hoole's Petty School as a universal elementary school had already been anticipated by Mulcaster. Hoole would have one such institution, at least, in every town and populous village, to which all could resort, and wherein "all such poor boys" (Mulcaster expressly includes girls: not so Hoole)—"all such poor boys as can conveniently frequent it may be taught gratis" (chap. vi.). Each form is to have its own master, and no master is to teach more than 40 boys together—a *dictum* which it is to be regretted has not yet attained general observance in modern schools of the same standing. In accordance with the usage of his day a writing-master is especially attached to the Petty School, and the whole establishment is under the direction of an inspector, or supervisor, that is, a headmaster who teaches no particular form.

But the *Petty School* is a mere *hors d'œuvre* in the "New

Discovery of the old Art of Teaching Schoole "; the really serious dishes which secure their author's chief care are "the tongues," Latin, Greek, Hebrew. Into the wilderness of detail with which Hoole works this out we need not penetrate : for the curious, the whole book stands reprinted in Barnard's "English Pedagogy[1]." But we may look at a typical point or two here and there. The second part of the book, the *Usher's Duty*, is intended to show how the boys of the three lowest forms are eventually to be made masters of Lily's *Grammar*. As a practical schoolmaster Hoole found himself compelled by circumstances to keep the youngsters to this distasteful task ; but his opinions show that, if he had been a free agent, he would have gone far in the direction of reform in language-teaching as it was understood by Comenius and his fellow-innovators. The passage which follows needs no commentary. "There is a great disproportion betwixt a child's capacity and the *accidence* itself. Children are led most by Sense, and the grammar rules, consisting in general doctrines, are too subtile for them. Children's wits are weak, active and lively, whereas grammar notions are abstractive, dull and lifeless ; boys find no sap nor sweetness in them, because they know not what they mean, and tell them the meaning of the same rule never so often over, their memories are so waterish, that the impression (if any were made in the brain) is quickly gone out again....

"Besides it will clearly appear to any that shall mind the confused order (especially of the verbs) and the perplexity of some rules and examples, that that book was rather made to inform those of riper years, who knew something of Latin before, of the reasons of what they knew, than to direct little ones (as we now do) to use it as a rule about that whereof they are ignorant altogether. It is one thing to learn the Latin tongue, or any other language, and another to learn the grammar as a guide to it, or as a means to attain the reason of it. We see how readily children learn to speak true

[1] See also E. T. Campagnac's reprint, *Hoole, The Art of Teaching Schoole*.

and proper English (and they may also do the same in Latin) by daily use and imitation of others, long before they are able to apprehend a definition of what grammar is, or anything else concerning it." (Part ii. chap. ii.)

From these and the like considerations Hoole lays it down, first, that "a child may have his reading perfect and ready in both the English and Latin tongue, and that he can write a fair hand *before ever he dreams of his grammar,*" and, secondly, that, side by side with the conning of the grammar-book, the boy must speak Latin conversationally, read Latin, write Latin, and use double translation, after the manner described by Ascham and Brinsley. Where the student of Latin is an adult, Hoole recommends, beside the grammar-book, the study of a familiar work translated into Latin (he names St John's Gospel) and the use of translations, recommendations which were endorsed thirty years later by John Locke.

The schoolmaster's aim is to teach boys "languages and oratory and poetry, as well as grammar,": and to these tasks the third part, the *Master's Method*, is given up. In the fourth form boys begin Greek, study rhetoric and style, and write Latin verses. In the form above, they add Greek verses, and translate freely from Latin into Greek and *vice versâ*. In the sixth form, Hebrew is commenced.

There is no mention whatever in the six years' course of mathematics, of modern foreign languages, or of physical science. Bacon had fulminated against "the first distemper of learning, when men study words and not matter"; Comenius reiterated Bacon's advice that men should "grow accustomed to things themselves"; Hartlib was ever devising plans, or inducing others to devise such, by which schoolboys might get some taste of "real knowledge." Hard by Hoole's own house in Lothbury the *savants* had held those Gresham College meetings which culminated in the foundation of the Royal Society two years after the publication of *The New Discovery*. But so far as Hoole's daily labour was affected these things might as well not have been. His concern was to concentrate the attention of his boys on the "tongues," and here we see them at their work : " Now forasmuch as this form (the fifth) is to be employed weekly in making themes and verses, which they can never well do except they be furnished with matter beforehand, I would have them provide a large commonplace book, in which they should write at least those heads which Mr Farnaby hath set down in his *Index Rhetoricus*, and then busy themselves (especially on Tuesdays and Thursdays in the afternoon, after other tasks ended), to collect : 1. Short histories out of Plutarch, Valerius Maximus, Justin, Cæsar, Lucius Florus, Livy, Pliny, Paræus Medulla Historiæ, Aelianus, etc. 2. Apologues and Fables out of Æsop, Phædrus, Ovid, Natalis Comes, etc. 3. Adages out of Adagia Selecta, Erasmi Adagia, Drax's Bibliotheca Scholastica, etc. 4. Hieroglyphics out of Pierius and Caussinus, etc. 5. Emblems and symbols out of Alciat, Beza, Quarles, Reusnerus, Chartarius, etc. 6. Ancient laws and customs out of Diodorus Siculus, Paulus Minutius, Plutarch, etc. 7. Witty sentences out of Golden Grove, Moral Philosophy, Sphinx Philosophica, Wits' Commonwealth, Flores Doctorum, Tully's Sentences, Demosthenis Sententiae, Enchiridion Morale, Stobæus, Ethica Ciceroniana, Gruteri Florilegium. 8. Rhetorical exornations out of Vossius, Farnaby, Butler, etc. 9. Topical places out of Caussinus, Tresmarus, Orator Extemporaneus. 10. Descriptions of things natural and artificial out of Orbis Pictus, Caussinus, Pliny, etc. I may not forget Textor's Officina, Lycosthenes, Erasmi Apophthegmata, Carolina Apophthegmata, and Polyanthea, which together with all that can be got of this nature, should be laid up in the school library for scholars to pick what they can out of, besides what they read in their own authors." (Part iii. c. ii.)

How apposite is Comenius's criticism : " Of a truth, schools hitherto have not striven to train minds as saplings which grow from their own roots ; but, on the contrary, they have taught their scholars to attach to themselves branches plucked down elsewhere, and like Æsop's crow, to dress up in borrowed plumes." (*Didact. Magn.* chap. xviii. 23.)

Here, again, is a suggestion for the Sixth Form, which is full of significance when regarded from the standpoint of even the least subversive of innovators. "Though it be found a thing very rare, and is by some adjudged to be of little use, for schoolboys to make exercises in Hebrew, yet it is no small ornament and commendation of a school (as Westminster School at present can evidence) that scholars are able to make orations and verses in Hebrew, Arabic, or other oriental tongues, to the amazement of most of their hearers, who are angry at their own ignorance, because they know not well what is then said or written." (Part iii. chap. iii.) It does not occur to Hoole that the amazement might have quite a different origin, and one by no means " a commendation of the school."

Hoole's fourth part, Scholastic Discipline, is a treatise on School Management, historically valuable as affording glimpses of the daily life of the class-room at the time. Below the greater or collegiate schools, as Hoole names the public schools, there were two great classes, those that taught grammar only, and those that received " petties " as well as " grammarians." The latter, called Mixed Schools by our author, served under a single teacher for the education of the boys of three or four adjacent villages or hamlets : they taught children to read and write, and made a pretence of teaching Lily's *Grammar.* Their general want of success is ascribed to two causes, first, the master " is overburdened with too many petty scholars," and, secondly, the greed and carelessness of parents, many of whom " will not spare their children to learn, if they can but find them any employment about their domestic or rural affairs, whereby they may save a penny." In more populous places these mixed schools have an usher for the " petties," the master teaching the grammarians only, their respective salaries being £10 and £20 per annum. The difficulty in this kind of school is the frequent change of masters, who "for the most part either weaken their bodies by excessive toil, and so. shorten their days," or quit their school "as soon as they can fit themselves for a more easy profession, or obtain a more profitable place." Still, even these schools occasionally send a boy or two up to the university, though that is usually the achievement of the institution which confines the work both of master and usher to grammar teaching. But since these have few or no scholarships to offer, they suffer from the competition of the great public schools, who take their most promising pupils ; and as the latter schools will not teach rudiments, a type of preparatory establishment where the pupils are boarders has consequently come into existence, with varying degrees of success in different cases. Hoole sums up in this familiar fashion : "Comparing all the schools which we have in England with some that I read of in other countries......we evidently see how many places of education beyond the seas do quite outstrip us."

Many schools began their day at six in the morning, most at seven, winter and summer. "The common time of dismissing scholars from school in the forenoon is 11 every day," and in the afternoon at three on Thursdays, at four on Tuesdays, at five on Mondays, Wednesdays, and Fridays. In London, it was the practice for children to go, at 11 a.m. and 5 p.m., to the writing-school (which might have no connection whatever with the grammar school) ; there they learned to write, to cipher, and to keep accounts. It is noted, as exceptional, that the well-known master, Mr Farnaby, had "a famous penman, Mr Taylor," in daily attendance at his school throughout the year. "The usual way for scholars learning to write at the country grammar schools is to entertain an honest, skilful penman......for about a month or six weeks together, every year, in which time commonly every one may learn to write legibly" ; this man of art generally arrives about May, as "days are then pretty long."

Hoole has something to say of the lighter side of school life, in a chapter (x.) entitled "Of Exclusion and Breaking up School, and of Potations," the last being the name of a feast held yearly "commonly before Shrovetide," the cost being met by the pupils' contributions. "Exclusion" is the practice which used to be familiar not so long ago as "barring-out"; Hoole says that it is "of late discontinued in many schools," and he gives directions which, if carried out, would turn that schoolboy Saturnalia into a procedure highly respectable, but exceedingly dull. "In London and most other places," schools break up a week before Christmas, Easter, and Whitsuntide for a fortnight's holiday, the occasion being marked by a public examination, the delivery of orations, the performance of a Latin or Greek play, or the provision by the master "of some fitting collation to be imparted and distributed by himself to his scholars, who will thankfully take a small gift as a token of more singular favour at his hands than another's."

London, in Hoole's opinion, is the best of all places in England known to him, "for the full improvement of children in their education, because of the variety of objects which daily present themselves to them, or may easily be seen once a year by walking to Mr John Tradescant's or the little houses or gardens where rarities are kept......could parents at home but half so well look to their behaviour as the masters do to their learning at school." The implication here, that a museum should co-operate with Lily's *Grammar* in securing the attainment of a child's education, is one which is rather out of place in a book devoted almost exclusively to "the good old way of teaching by grammar, authors, and exercises." But it should not be forgotten that the "New Discovery" was not a brand new work, when it first appeared in print in 1660; on the contrary, a good deal of it belonged to the time some 23 years earlier, when its author had not long been established in his profession. While the intervening years had confirmed his good opinion of the methods by which he discharged his daily business of teaching Latin, Greek, and Hebrew, they probably also brought occasional questions to his mind concerning the value of the education which could be extracted from that daily business. Thus, while the *New Discovery* is what in the main it is, there are indications in the book, due probably to the reflections of later years, that Hoole was moving towards a wider outlook. There can be no doubt that he was influenced by the school-books, well known throughout Europe when Hoole was writing, which Comenius had prepared. Of these the most popular proved to be the *Orbis Pictus*, the Latin first-book, liberally supplied with pictures, which appeared at Nuremberg in 1658, though a notice of it and its preface are included in the Amsterdam folio of Comenius's didactic works, published in the preceding year. Owing to Hoole's keen interest, English schoolmasters enjoyed the use of one of the earliest versions of this celebrated text-book, which appeared in 1659 in an English translation by Hoole himself[1].

Comenius introduced the *Orbis Pictus* by a preface, whose latent revolutionary ideas were not all suspected by the translator, as may be inferred by comparing the spirit of the "New Discovery of the old Art of Teaching Schoole," with such passages as these : "The ground of this business is, that *sensual objects be rightly presented to the senses*, for fear they may not be received. I say, and say it again aloud, that this last is the foundation of all the rest; because we can neither act nor speak wisely, unless we first rightly understand all the things which are to be done, and whereof we are to speak. Now there is nothing in the understanding which was not before in the sense. And, therefore, to exercise the senses well about the right perceiving the differences of things, will be to lay the grounds for all wisdom, and all wise discourse, and all discreet actions in one's course of life. Which, because it is commonly neglected in schools, and the things that are to be

[1] The preface is dated Jan. 28, 1658 (*i.e.* 1659).

learned are offered to scholars without being understood, or being rightly presented to the senses, it cometh to pass, that the work of teaching and learning goeth heavily onward and affordeth little benefit."

" It is a little book, as you see, of no great bulk, yet a brief of the whole world, and a whole language : full of Pictures, Nomenclatures, and Descriptions of things......Which such Book, and in such a dress may (I hope) serve,

" I.   To entice witty Children to it, that they may not conceit a torment to be in School, but dainty fare.   For it is apparent that Children (even from their Infancy almost) are delighted with Pictures, and willingly please their eye with these sights.   And it will be very well worth the pains to have once brought it to pass, that scarcrows may be taken away out of wisdoms Gardens.

" II.   This same little book will serve *to stir up the Attention, which is to be fastened upon things, and ever to be sharpened more and more ;* which is also a great matter.   For the senses (being the main guids of Childhood, because therein the mind doth not as yet raise up it self to an abstracted contemplation of things) evermore seek their own objects, and if they be away, they grow dull, and wry themselves hither and thither, out of weariness of themselves ; but when their objects are present, they grow merry, wax lively, and willingly suffer themselves to be fastened upon them, till the thing be sufficiently discerned.   This Book, then, will do a good piece of service in taking (especially flickering) Wits and preparing them for deeper studies.

" III.   Whence a third good will follow ; that Children being won hereunto, and drawn over with this way of heeding, may be furnished with the knowledge of the Prime things that are in the World, by sport and merry pastime."

Comenius says that the children are to look at the pictures, and, afterwards, to be examined on what they have seen. Wherever it is possible, they are also to be made to observe the real things of which the pictures are images, and, lastly, they are to draw the pictures, "first, thus to quicken the attention also towards the things; and to observe the proportion of the parts one towards another, and, lastly, to practise the nimbleness of the hand, which is good for many things."

Moreover, every great school should possess its museum, or collection, so that it "would indeed become a school of things obvious to the Senses, and an entrance to the school intellectual."

Here, indeed, is that which promises to put an end to the monopoly of "the good old way of teaching by grammar, authors, and exercises," and to remove such "scarecrows in Wisdom's garden" as Lily's *Grammar*. Young children are to pursue studies which are in harmony with their abilities, and of a kind to appeal to what is most characteristic in their mental life. At bottom, the fitting instruments by which such children receive early instruction are not books at all. It is true, Comenius claimed that his *Orbis Pictus* would also effect much which was expected, sometimes in vain, from schools as they were. Thus, "our little Encyclopædia of things subject to the Senses" might be used not only as a first book in Latin, but also as a help to learning to speak, read and spell the vernacular. These are the virtues which most impress Hoole, though he was too good a schoolmaster not to appreciate Comenius's fundamental position, that the sequence of instruction must be determined by the powers of the learner; it is only when the matter of that instruction is in question that he falls short of what might be expected from him. Hoole's own preface to the *Orbis Pictus* shows this; it also gives us interesting contemporary professional criticism of Comenius's school-books in general.

"The Translator to all judicious and industrious school-masters.

" *Gentlemen,*

"There are few of you (I think) but have seen, and with

great willingness made use of (or at least perused) many of the Books of this well-deserving Author, *Mr John Comenius*, which, for their profitableness to the speedy attainment of a Language, have been Translated in several Countries out of Latine into their own native tongues.

"Now the general verdict (after trial made) that hath passed, touching those formerly extant, is this, that they are indeed of singular use, and very advantageous to those of more discretion (especially to such, as have already got a smattering of Latine) to help their memories to retain what they have scatteringly got here and there, and to furnish them with many words, which (perhaps) they had not formerly read, or so well observed ; but to yong Children (whom we have chiefly to instruct) as those that are ignorant altogether of most things, and words, they prove rather a more toyl and burden, than a delight, and furtherance. For to pack up many words in memory, of things not conceived in the mind, is to fill the head with empty imaginations, and to make the learner more to admire their multitude and variety (and thereby to become discouraged) then to care to treasure them up, in hopes to gain more knowledge of what they meant.

"He hath, therefore, in some of his later works seemed to move retrograde, and striven to come neeier to the reach of tender wits, and in this present Book, he hath (according to my judgment) descended to the very Bottom of what is to be taught, and proceeded (as Nature itself doth) in an orderly way, first to exercise the Senses well by presenting their objects to them and then to fasten upon the Intellect by impressing the first notions of things upon it and linking them one to another by a rational discourse......You, then, that have the care of little Children, do not too much trouble their thoughts and clog their memories with bare Grammar Rudiments, which to them are harsh in getting, and fluid in retaining (because, in-deed, to them they signifie nothing but a more ⌊mere⌋ swimming notion of a general term, which they know not what it meaneth till they comprehend all particulars); but by this or the like Subsidiarie inform them first with some knowledge of things and words wherewith to express them ; and then their rules of speaking will be better understood and firmly kept in mind. Else how should a Child conceive what a Rule meaneth when he neither knoweth what the Latine word importeth, nor what manner of thing it is which is signified to him in his own native language, which is given him thereby to understand the Rule? For Rules, consisting of generalities, are delivered (as I may say) at a third hand, presuming first the things and then the words to be already apprehended touching which they are made. I might indeed enlarge upon this subject, it being *the very basis of our profession to search into the way of children's taking hold by little and little of what we teach them,* that so we may apply ourselves to their reach, but I leave the observation hereof to our own daily exercises, and experience got thereby." (Hoole's English version of the *Orbis Sensualium Pictus,* 1659.)

This was as far as Hoole could go in Comenius's company, and, certainly, the journey was not a short one. To teach so as to secure the willing co-operation of young children, to postpone abstractions, generalities and rules till some first-hand knowledge of the concrete had been acquired, and to apply this principle to instruction in Latin by beginning with the names of familiar objects and conditions, and using these in simple conversational fashion, instead of commencing with the grammar-book—these are principles which rank Hoole as a reforming schoolmaster, and, if they represent his own practice, explain Wood's remark that he instructed youth "to a miracle."

But they are not enough to place the man who held them side by side with Petty, Dury, Hartlib, and others who shared the convictions and aspirations of Comenius, beliefs ánd hopes derived immediately from Francis Bacon, but resting ultimately upon the solid achievements of the men of science and philosophers who gave distinction to more than one country of Europe in the 16th and 17th centuries.

CHAPTER X.

THE COURTLY "ACADEMIES."

It was an integral part of the Comenian educational reform that the school curriculum, restricted almost entirely as it had been to the study, and, more particularly, the grammatical study of the ancient languages, should be widened by the inclusion of the mother-tongue at least among "living" languages, of mathematics, of natural science, of geography, and similar branches of knowledge. Hoole makes it clear that, so far as the ordinary English school of his time was concerned, no steps had then been taken to modernise the school-course. Indeed, with the important exception of the foundations of Ernest the Pious in Saxony, there seemed to be no visible outcome of a permanent kind to the urgent pleading of Comenius and his sympathisers ; in England, the opinions of Dury, Petty, and Hartlib remained opinions, and no more.

The insurmountable obstacle to the general adoption of their reforms was the absence of qualified teachers ; and the lack of these was the natural consequence of a general un-willingness to spend money on schooling. The Church of the Middle Ages had created the tradition of an education to be obtained *gratis* : when statesmen deprived the Church both of the opportunity of teaching and of the wealth which made teaching free to the pupil, they were seldom careful to set up institutions which should continue this branch of the Church's work. In any case, the conviction was rooted that the services of teachers were sufficiently rewarded by emoluments of a very modest kind.

But the call for a reformed curriculum made by the friends of the New Philosophy was reinforced in a quarter where consideration of cost was less deterrent than in the world at large to which Comenius and others appealed. This narrower circle was not only powerful; it was also very much in earnest, and the immediate answers to its demand effected a permanent change in school studies. Bacon's followers complained that the unreformed school did not promote the advancement of knowledge; the other malcontents found fault with it from the standpoints of the soldier, courtier and man of the world. In short, Society had passed beyond the ideals which had served the schools for centuries; the attempt to bring about adjustment to new conditions fills educational history in the seventeenth century and still continues.

The new spirit which thus came to the help of the Baconians was French in origin; though it tended to dilettanteism when the century was old, it was virile enough at the beginning, as Montaigne's pages prove. The school, so he thought, debased the prerogative of Knowledge by neglecting the all-important man of affairs and busying itself with the insignificant scholar and professional man. He tells the Comtesse de Gurson : " Knowledge is a great ornament and a tool of marvellous worth, especially to persons elevated to a degree of fortune such as yours. In truth, Knowledge ever misses its proper employment in hands vile and base ; she is far more proud to lend her aid to the conduct of a campaign, to the government of a people, to the attainment of the friendship of a prince or foreign nation, than to preparing a logical argument, pleading a case, or prescribing pills." (*De l'Institution des Enfants, Essais,* I. 25.) " Let those who seek to form a grammarian or logician, waste their time; we who seek to form neither, but a gentleman, have business elsewhere" (*ibid.*)[1].

Montaigne finds his ideal, or at least his preference, not amongst the cultured Athenians, but amidst the martial Spartans and Turks, and at Rome, "*avant qu'elle feust sçavante*" (I. 24). Here were men in whom character and capacity for action had not been weakened by learning. He asks for a revival of the old knightly arts, for an education in which "even games and exercise will form a good part of study; running, wrestling, music, dancing, hunting, the management of horses and of weapons. I desire that the soul should fashion for itself an outward propriety, tact, and bearing. It is not a soul, it is not a body which we train, but a man, and we must not make two things of him; as Plato says, one must not be trained without the other, but as two horses harnessed to one pole."

The essay On Pedantry (I. cp. 24) is an attack on erudition considered as an end in itself without regard to character, judgment, or ability; the ordinary course of instruction caused books and precepts to usurp in the pupils' minds the place of principles and the exercise of judgment. The discontent with conventional education thus felt by Montaigne, a recluse when public life was turbulent, was shared by many of his order when more peaceful days arrived and, with them, opportunity to enjoy the elegancies of life.

At a time when travel had become familiar to the leisured class and the grand tour constituted the crown of a wealthy man's education, the schools did not concern themselves with modern tongues. They exhibited as little interest in those scientific studies, experiments, and inventions, which were so

---

[1] Compare Locke: "No man can pass for a scholar that is ignorant of the Greek Tongue. But I am not here considering the Education of a profess'd Scholar, but of a Gentleman, to whom Latin and French, as the world now goes, is by everyone acknowledg'd to be necessary." *Thoughts*, § 195.

generally in men's thoughts during the sixteen-hundreds, that it became almost "the mode" to dabble in anatomy, chemistry, or some branch of physics. The schools left the future soldier ignorant of mathematics, as pure science very frequently, and almost always in its practical application to engineering, fortification, and the like; at school and university the future statesman received from the *official* round of studies no express training in jurisprudence, politics, or state-craft generally, regarded as an actual science to be applied, there and then, to life and government. Certain arts, as drawing, painting, music, carving, and other forms of manual skill were highly esteemed as accomplishments throughout European society in the mid-seventeenth century; the schools did nothing to make their attainment easy. The courtier aimed at a high standard of skill in riding, fencing, and dancing; the ordinary round of instruction gave him no help in these, nor in genealogy and heraldry, nor in the more scholastic studies of history and geography. As for the courtier's all-important study of *conduite*, the art of conversation, compliment, bearing, and dress, it was usually supposed that the schools fostered an intolerable pedantry quite incompatible with any such elegancies. The collocation of "scholar and gentleman" was a later and an English conception; for the time we are considering Montaigne represents the common opinion in his antithesis of logician (or grammarian) and man of birth.

Courtly education and scholastic education, therefore, stood apart, and the rift grew wider as the seventeenth century advanced and the court of Louis XIV became the model for all courts. The children of the great and noble ceased to attend school, and received their education from private tutors at home, completing the course, in the case of young men, at special establishments called *academies*, in which the ideals of the courtly education were finally embodied.

The demand for "accomplishments," chiefly of a martial kind, first brought these academies into being in France, where, during the closing years of the sixteenth century, they began as schools of arms and horsemanship (that "maniement des chevaulx et des armes" desired by Montaigne), their directors usually being noblemen or gentlemen of acknowledged standing. Lord Herbert of Cherbury, who was first abroad between the years 1608 and 1616, now and again makes mention in his autobiography of instruction of this kind. Thus, he says, speaking of his host, M. de Montmorency, Constable of France: "He told me also, that if I would learn to ride the great horse, he had a stable there of some fifty, the best and choicest as was thought in France, and that his écuyer, called M. de Disancour, nor indeed inferior to Pluvenel [Louis XIII's chief écuyer] or Labroue, should teach me.... He commanded also his écuyer to keep a table for me, and his pages to attend me, the chief of whom was M. de Mennon, who, proving to be one of the best horsemen in France, keeps now an academy in Paris." Herbert remained some eight months with de Disancour and then went on to Paris, where he "much benefited" himself by the conversation "of that incomparable scholar, Isaac Casaubon"; "besides," he says, "I did apply myself much to know the use of my arms, and to ride the great horse, playing on the lute, and singing according to the rules of the French masters."

John Evelyn, who was in France in 1644, enables us to see a later development of the academy. Speaking of the Palais Cardinal in Paris, he says, "Here also I frequently went to see them ride and exercise the Greate Horse, especially at the Academy of Monsieur du Plessis, and de Veau, whose scholes of that art are frequented by the Nobility; and here also young gentlemen are taught to fence, daunce, play on musiq, and something in fortification and the mathematics. The designe is admirable, some keeping neere an hundred brave horses, all managed to the greate saddle." Five months later Evelyn was at Richelieu, near Tours; he writes: "To this towne belongs an Academy where besides the exercise of the horse, armes, dauncing, etc. all the sciences are taught in the vulgar French by Professors stipendiated by the great Cardinal," etc. Richelieu's foundation dated from 1640; two years earlier Louis XIII had prevailed on the Oratorians to open their *académie* at Juilly, between Paris and Soissons. The curriculum of this *Académie Royale* included some study of Mathematics, Geography, Physics, Heraldry, *French* History, Italian and Spanish; the lowest class was distinctly a class for teaching French[1]. Drawing, music, riding and dancing were also taught.

The part played by these academies in assisting the modernisation of the German school-course has been explained by Professor Paulsen[2], to whose account the present chapter is greatly indebted. The political connections of France and the courts of Protestant Germany, beginning in the middle of the sixteenth century, brought the German princes into close touch with French culture; they sent their sons and their courtiers' sons to France for education, and themselves acquired French manners and French speech. Heidelberg and Cassel were especially under French influence, and at the latter court, Moritz, Landgrave of Hesse, founded his *Collegium Adelphicum Mauritianum* in 1599, for the spread of French culture amongst the Hessian nobility and their peers throughout Germany.

Reconstituted in 1618, this German academy proposed to teach religion, the liberal arts and their useful application, Latin, Greek, and the living Romance tongues. Military studies and exercises formed part of the curriculum, and the pupils learned horsemanship, fencing, and the use of arms generally, while the arts of peace were represented by dancing and music, vocal and instrumental. Moritz himself was a personally distinguished member of that *Fruchtbringende Gesellschaft*

---

[1] Chas. Hamel, *Histoire de l'Abbaye et du Collège de Juilly*, Paris, 1868.

[2] *Geschichte des Gelehrten Unterrichts*. The third book of the first volume deals with the academies.

which Ludwig of Anhalt had founded in 1617 for the advancement of German culture, morals and patriotism[1].

The Collegium Mauritianum, with other German academies of which it was a type, died out during the fierce disorder of the Thirty Years' War; but when the Peace of Westphalia permitted men once more to turn their thoughts to education French culture became the model which was imitated by the German higher classes, an example which others were obliged to follow. French was the language of society and of diplomacy; French literature, French manners, French ideas in arms, government and administration obtained an extraordinary ascendancy in Germany especially.

In education the French influence is more particularly marked by the creation up and down Germany of those *Ritterakademien* which, for a century after 1648, repeated the model of the Collegium Mauritianum and bestowed upon the German nobility the courtly and military education of the French academies. Under the impulse given by Francke and his Pietist friends, and by Leibnitz, these German academies grew rapidly in number during the first half of the eighteenth century. (A list will be found in Paulsen, *op. cit.* vol. i. pp. 506 ff.) Their curricula and the social standing of their pupils made them influential agents in the transformation of the character, aims, and methods of German secondary schools in general, their more immediate effect being to discredit that monopoly of the ancient classics which had previously characterised the school-courses.

The attempt to introduce the French academy into England did not meet with general success, the English parent preferring that his son should learn abroad what the academy could teach; as a consequence, the English public schools and grammar schools missed a stimulating influence which was felt by their like in France and Germany.

Yet there were some notable believers in the "academy"

---

[1] See Chapter II. above.

as part of the machinery of English education.   For example, the very brief session of three weeks which bounds the life of the Short Parliament of 1640 saw the announcement of the project indicated in the following extract from the Lords' Journal of that year.   It was moved by the Earl Marshal (the Earl of Arundel and Surrey), "That the House would consider about the erecting of an Academy, for the breeding and training up of young Noblemen and Gentlemen: which was referred to the Grand Committee for Privileges."   This was on May 4: Parliament incurred the King's displeasure by opposing his design of war on the Scots and was dissolved on May 5.   Of course, nothing came of Surrey's motion.   It was probably at a somewhat later date that Hartlib, as he told the Restoration Parliament, erected "a little academie for the education of the gentrie of this nation, to advance pietie, learning, moralitie, and other exercises of industrie, not usual then in common schools."   Hartlib's school was evidently not an academy of the type which we have been considering, but a secondary school of the kind which Francke introduced into Germany half a century later, a school, that is, whose curriculum bore marks of the influence both of the New Philosophy and of the French courtly education.

The young Englishman who desired to remain at home while studying modern languages, physical science, the fine arts, or martial exercises, had recourse to one of the many private teachers who were to be found in London and at the two Universities.   These men had no direct official connection with any seat of learning, and they have left few traces of their labours, such as survive being found, for the most part, in advertisements, pamphlets, and stray references in biographies. John Milton was one of these private adventurers in the new educational field, and the institution which he sketches in the *Tractate*[1] is in name and effect an "academy" of the kind then familiar in France.

[1] That is, the letter of 1644 to Hartlib, "Of Education," discussed in Chapter VII. above.

Milton was content to put forward his letter to Hartlib as the modest contribution of a thinker who had had the topic in his mind during "many studious and contemplative years"; but he might also have alleged practical experience in conducting an education framed on lines which, in some particulars, were those advocated in the *Tractate* itself. In 1639, while lodging in St Bride's Churchyard, he had undertaken the instruction of his two nephews, Edward and John Phillips, and when he removed, in the following year, to a "pretty garden-house" in Aldersgate Street, these boys accompanied him as house-mates and pupils. To Aldersgate Street he brought his bride, after a month's courtship, in June, 1643; she left him in July, and soon after other pupils joined the Phillipses. The same manner of life was followed in Milton's next domicile in the Barbican, where he remained till the autumn of 1647[1].

"He never set up," says Edward Phillips, "for a public school to teach all the young fry of a parish, but only was willing to impart his learning and knowledge to relations, and the sons of some gentlemen that were his intimate friends[2]." The same authority has left an account of the curriculum laid down by his uncle, and followed by himself and his fellow-pupils between the ages of 10 and 15[3]. Apart from its comprehensiveness, and the number of Greek and Latin authors included which were "scarce ever heard of" in "common Public Schools," this course of study presents many points of difference from the usual practice of the time. Greek and Latin books it contains in plenty, but their presence is to be explained on grounds foreign to literature: such purely literary works as the list contains lay somewhat off the ordinary school track, whilst the larger number of books mentioned are obviously chosen for their scientific, or *quasi*-scientific information, and not for their literary excellences. Agriculture, Natural History, Architecture, Military Science, Astronomy

---

[1] For Milton's work as tutor see Masson's *Life*, vol. iii.
[2] See Masson, *op. cit.* iii. 655.   [3] *Ibid.* p. 253.

and what we now term Physiography are the real studies, of which Latin and Greek are only the medium: similarly Hebrew, Chaldee, and Syriac are studied for the sake of theology or of Biblical knowledge. The principle implied is that laid down in the *Tractate*: "Language is but the Instrument conveying to us things usefull to be known."

In the *Tractate* Milton proposes his academy as an alternative to the customary plan whereby "the *Monsieurs* of *Paris* take our hopefull Youth into their slight and prodigal custodies and send them over back again transform'd into Mimicks, Apes and Kicshoes"; yet even a cursory examination of the *Tractate* shows how nearly the continental "academy" approached his ideal educational institution for wealthy lads and young men. In every city throughout the land Milton would set up an academy of some 130 students (their ages ranging from twelve to twenty-one), with a score or so of attendants, all lodged in a spacious house; the establishment is to be at once school and University, such students as intend to practise law or medicine passing from the academy to a professional post-graduate college. A distinct military bias is given to the whole, between three and four hours daily being devoted to soldierly exercises, in addition to the time spent in the study of military science.

The complete curriculum is arranged under five divisions, there being no marks of time between them. The following is the list of studies.

I. The chief and necessary rules of [Latin] grammar, arithmetic, geometry, Biblical history and divinity.

II. Greek, agriculture, natural philosophy, physiography (the term is, of course, not Milton's), astronomy, geography, natural history, mathematics, fortification, engineering, navigation, architecture, medicine, anatomy, animal and vegetable life.

III. Ethics, economics: Italian.

IV. Politics, law, theology, Church history, Hebrew (begun earlier) with Chaldee and Syriac.

V. Rhetoric, logic.

The proposal to attempt so much in the space of nine years is perhaps the most notable illustration of the belief in method which all the educational innovators at that day cherished: but it scarcely admits of doubt that Milton would have been satisfied with very modest achievements by his pupils in more than one of the branches of knowledge enumerated. Phillips's account of his uncle's practice with reference to "Chaldey and Syrian" is good evidence on this head. Throughout the scheme there is obvious a desire to employ the fruits of the New Philosophy as instruments of education: but, himself no natural philosopher, Milton would have these things learned in the scholarly fashion by books, few, if any, of which were in the mother-tongue. Thus, although he is all for modernising the curriculum, he is poles asunder from Comenius in method, if not in aim.

It is clear that the *Tractate* addresses itself to the special needs of that small, but conspicuously placed social class for whom the French "academies" existed. Consequently, some of the criticism to which it has been subjected is irrelevant: as, for example, that it makes no reference to the education of girls and gives no opinion on the provision of schools for the people at large.

The *Tractate* pictures an ideal: a pamphlet of a little later date shows us what was being tried in an actual "academy" of suburban London during the Commonwealth period[1]. The proprietor of this school at Bethnal Green, Sir Balthazar Gerbier, was a Dutchman who in 1616 sought his fortune in England, entering the service of Buckingham; later, he was knighted by Charles I, whose agent he became, and, therefore, found, it advisable to leave England on the outbreak of the Civil War. After the king's execution he returned from France and set up his academy, which was not long-lived,

---

[1] "A Publique Lecture," etc. 1650.

since Gerbier left for Cayenne on a mining speculation in
1659. He died in England in 1667, having acquired some
fame as a painter and architect[1].

The prefatory note to Gerbier's pamphlet is quoted below
in full, since it testifies to the favour in which the numerous
Parisian academies were held by English parents, and to the
absence in London of such an institution other than Gerbier's
own.

"To the Right Honourable the Lord Mayor, and Aldermen
of the most famous City of London.

"Right Honourable,

Having, during my being conversant with Forreigne
Nations, observed among sundry of their honourable and most
usefull establishments that of publick Academies, wherein
Lovers of all noble Exercises (as well as Arts, Sciences and
Languages) are instructed and improved, without repairing to
other parts, and without giving to other Nations the glory and
the advantages of their Education. I have bin so much the
sooner moved to apply myself to the establishment of such an
Academy for the honour and benefit of this Nation, for that it
wanted such an advantage, and that the same proved to be so
prejudiciall to Sons of honourable Parents, when they are
constrained to travell towards forreigne parts for such improvements, for that they often meet with wicked persons,
who doe endeavour to infuse into them most pernicious
principles to their native Country: but the most deplorable
case of all is, the subversion of their Religion to a worse.
And whereas on such just considerations and motives, I have
been moved to advertise the publique of the advantages offered
by the said Academicall Exercises, and to cause publicke
Gratis Lectures to be read, first at the Academies Summer

[1] *Dictionary of National Biography, sub voce.*

Residency at Bednall Green, and for the Winter Months in this place, where not onely the Fathers of Families, but also the Mothers (mutually interested in the good educations of their Sonnes) could be more frequently informed of its method. As I thought it not strange, that sundry Ladies of Honour, and other Gentlewomen (though their vocation is not the maintaining of Arguments, and Theses in any Universities, Academies or Free-Schooles) would be satisfied by their owne hearing of this Academicall institution; and this moved me also to cause one Lecture to be read concerning all Languages, Arts, Sciences, and noble Exercises which is that now by me presented to you: which may inform you at full of all what is meant herein by me, as you will soone perceive: that it doth not onely concerne the glory, and good of the Nation in generall, but particularly that of this great and famous City, which ought not to yield to any other in the World, and therefore not to be to seeke in the possession of one Academy, when Paris maintaines twelve, besides a number of Universities, and famous Free-Schooles, and that there should not be any more cause no ground for Paris to pretend unto the dignity of a second Athens then London: since such a Metripolitan of this Land abounds in men of knowledge, and Masters of Arts: who cannot chuse but have one and the selfe same ayme and marke: that which is excellent, honourable, just, necessary, and usefull. May all such as are indued with excellent capasities, joyne to the promotement of what is so really meant by me, and may it be so well understood as that Forreigners may henceforth be moved to come from Salamanca in Spaine, from Padua in Italy, and from Paris in France to this Academy, therein to learne what they have hitherto wanted in theirs: and that finding themselves also in a State wherein by the great mercy of God his sacred Word is expounded in godlinesse and truth: those that have been misled by spirits of delusion may turne unto the best, turne unto God I say, and live unto righteousnesse: and that this may be in your dayes, and during your great Government, I shall most fervently pray to God, as one that is sincerely

> Right Honourable,
>
> > Your most humble and addicted Servant,
> >
> > Balthazar Gerbier.

From the Academy,
  this 6 of March,
    1649 " [that is, 16⁴⁹⁄₅₀].

The pamphlet itself sets forth the advantages, and more especially the *uses* of the following studies : Languages (modern, spoken tongues alone are meant), Civility (courtesy), History, Arithmetic, "the keeping of Bookes between Debitor and Creditor," Geometry, Cosmography, Geography.   The students of the Bethnal Green Academy also learn "Naturall experimentall Philosophy," by which is to be understood "several means serving to the enriching of noble and profitable Sciences"; for example, medicine, fruit-preserving, grafting and other experimental improvement of plants, trees, soils.

Mathematics, Fortification, Engraving, Drawing are also included in the course, and amongst bodily exercises Fencing and Riding are specified.   Music and dancing help the pupils to acquire social graces, though Gerbier thought it politic to refer to Miriam and David, and to set up the queer defence of dancing that the art prevents young men "buzzing in maidens' ears that which cannot be heard."

By cosmography Gerbier means a mixture of judicial astrology and astronomy; in the latter science he is a sturdy adherent of the Ptolemaic theory, and in that connection presents us with what is probably a unique figure of speech. God "permits men to be verst in the severall aspects of these celestiall Creatures, that the knowledge hereof may oblige us to seeke him incessantly, chiefly when those aspects do threaten us with his displeasure : As also to render thankes and praises unto him, when their constellations do appear favourable and gracious unto us; which is the saving profit that is to be made by this study, and waving all those fond fancies of mens wits of the time, who by the new perspective glasses of their besotted imaginations frame a new world in the Moone, as the other Hereticks of Copernicus his Sect, and such as seeme to beleeve that the Sun is a fixt Center, and *the World to be like a joynt of meat spitted, which turnes and windes about it.*"

Gerbier's aspiration that foreigners would resort to the academies of London was not gratified: but, some thirty years later, M. Faubert, a refugee on account of his religion, succeeded in erecting in London an academy of the original French type, a school, that is, of arms and horsemanship[1]. Evelyn was interested in the man and in his scheme, and it may have been through him that Faubert secured the patronage of the Royal Society. On August 9, 1682, says the diarist, "The Council of the Royal Society had it recommended to them to be trustees and visitors, or supervisors, of the Academy which Monsieur Faubert did hope to procure to be built by subscription of worthy gentlemen and noblemen, for the education of youth, and to lessen the vast expense the Nation is at yearly by sending children into France to be taught military exercises. We thought good to give him all the encouragement our recommendation could procure." On Dec. 18, 1684, Evelyn, in company with Lord Cornwallis, watched the feats of horsemanship performed by a party of young noblemen in Faubert's "newly railed" exercise-ground.

In Locke's "Some Thoughts concerning Education" (1693) there are traces of the influence which was exercised in the matter of school curriculum both by the New Philosophy and by the ideal of education which the academies embodied. Locke's list of studies abounds in branches of what he called "Real Knowledge." But while his "young gentleman" is advised to read the scientific and mathematical works of Boyle

[1] Foubert's Place, connecting Regent Street and King Street, marks the site, or its neighbourhood.

and Newton, to become familiar with law, civil and common, with rhetoric and the mother-tongue, he is also urged to practise dancing, fencing (or wrestling), and "riding the great horse" (the very *fons et origo* of the French academy). It is further recommended that he should find his recreation in gardening, wood-work, metal-work, the cutting and polishing of lenses and of precious stones—in short, in acquiring manual arts requiring a high degree of skill which commended them to the *virtuoso*[1].

[1] On English writings (1622–1732) devoted to "courtly education" see *Cambridge History of English Literature*, vol. ix. ch. xv. and pp. 569 *f.*

CHAPTER XI.

ELEMENTARY EDUCATION.

WHILE the academies were expressly created and maintained for the benefit of a social class whose numbers were
necessarily small, the thinkers who grounded their educational
theories more especially upon the New Philosophy usually took
a very much wider view. Most of them held that, in some
degree at least, education was a process of general application, not to be refused entirely to any rank in life, however
humble, nor to be restricted simply by reason of wealth or
poverty, of ability or inability, or of sex. Two consequences
in the sphere of practice followed immediately from this
principle, the first being the institution by the State of a
system of universal, compulsory instruction, and the second
the creation of a new type of institution resembling the
"Vernacular School" of Comenius.

Wherever schools existed some of course were, in whole
or part, of the nature of preparatory schools, and their curricula
might, to that extent, be called primary. But their exact
character would depend entirely on the kind of advanced
instruction contemplated in the schools to which these were
introductory. The public elementary school of to-day and the
preparatory school whose pupils pass to Eton or Harrow are
both, in a sense, primary; but their curricula have little in
common. The Vernacular School of Comenius was intended

to be, before all else, what our public elementary school most usually is, namely, a first school which confines its studies to the tools of learning, to the mother-tongue and to branches of knowledge which can be acquired through the mother-tongue without reference to others: the course being determined by the shortness of the school-life of the majority of children following it. The primary school, in this sense, was not a familiar institution in many parts of Europe; its general diffusion throughout any one European country would have been an absolute novelty in the mid-seventeenth century.

A system of true elementary or popular schools implies, in the first place, such a general state of culture as is betokened by much written or printed matter in the native tongue, easily accessible and at small cost. Secondly, such a system cannot precede, but must depend upon a general advance in knowledge and its application to the practical arts of everyday life. Times of great industrial or commercial expansion tend to create machinery for popular instruction, as the histories of the Hansa and of the Netherlands under the Burgundian princes remind us. While men are slow to admit that the mass of mankind can be benefited by, or are capable of, literary or philosophical studies, they are usually ready to believe that the artisan and the labourer become industrially more efficient by means of studies of the more obviously " real " order. They give more or less willingly to the " hand " what they are disposed to deny to the " man."

There was small opportunity during the sixteenth century for the existence of a widespread network of schools addressing themselves exclusively to the mother-tongue and the knowledge then to be acquired through it, and employing the " three Rs " of to-day as their field of exercise. To what purpose could the power to read and write the vernacular be turned so long as the vernacular books which made for culture were few, and all books were costly? The teaching of arithmetic in the schoolroom was a seventeenth-century innovation, at first permitted by authority on grounds of usefulness and encouraged by the claims of "business." "It shall be [the Master's] care, and the Usher's charge," say the statutes of Charterhouse (founded in 1612), "to teach the Scholars to cipher and cast an accompt, *especially those that are less capable of learning*, and fittest to be put to trades."

The general acceptance of the conception of the elementary school as now understood cannot be expected before the beginning of modern science and of vernacular literatures, and the wide diffusion of printing-presses. When we add the usual *vis inertiae* of human institutions, the requisite interval of time before a new want is generally recognised as such, and the special obstacles existing in Europe of the sixteenth and early seventeenth centuries, it is easily understood that the latter was well advanced before popular instruction began to make headway.

During the last twenty years of the seventeenth century, and more especially during the final decade, notable attempts were made independently in France, in Germany, and in Britain to set up universal instruction and to organise schools for the mass of the people. These countries were not, of course, previously destitute of schools to which the children of the people might gain admission; but they were not elementary schools in the sense already defined.

Mr A. F. Leach (*English Schools at the Reformation*, 1546–8) has shown how unwarrantable is the assumption that the existing English system of endowed secondary schools dates from the middle of the sixteenth century. He gives documentary evidence concerning 259 schools of the period 1546–8, these, of course, not exhausting the English schools of the time, since the records are admittedly imperfect; but, connected as they are with 32 English counties and comprising establishments of very varying degrees of efficiency, these 259 schools may be accepted as representative. "Imperfect as the record is," says Mr Leach, "it is enough to establish that the

A.

received notions of the provision for education in England are extremely erroneous, and that the history of many of our schools is much longer than is commonly supposed. As for poor Edward VI, meaning thereby the ruling councillors of his day, he cannot any longer be called the founder of our national system of secondary education. But he, or they, can at least claim the distinction of having had a unique opportunity of reorganising the whole educational system of a nation from top to bottom, without cost to the nation, and of having thrown it away " (*op. cit.* p. 122).

In truth, mediaeval England possessed schools which were, comparatively speaking, numerous, well-frequented, and not confined entirely to great centres of population. Schools were erected, maintained or administered by the cathedrals, monasteries, collegiate churches, and colleges; many schools connected with these foundations had, even then, a long history behind them, some going back to pre-Norman times. Hospitals, the refuges not of the sick alone but of the poor also, frequently associated schools with their work, and those characteristic mediaeval corporations, the gilds (whether distinctively industrial, distinctively religious, or more commonly both), often undertook the maintenance of a school. The teaching of children *gratis* was frequently one of the functions of a chantry priest, and Mr Leach's researches have proved conclusively that, over and over again, the suppression, by the abolition of a chantry, of public recitation of prayers for a deceased founder, meant also the abolition of a school, small or great. Beside all these differently maintained places of education, there were also independent schools, existing simply as such.

Of the 259 schools, particulars of which are given by Mr Leach, there are twenty-two " which may, perhaps, be regarded as Elementary Schools " (p. 91). To prevent ambiguity it would, however, be better to call them Preparatory or Primary Schools, at the same time dissociating them in our minds from the Elementary School of to day, with which they had but little in common. They were open to the poor *gratis*, or in return for a trifling fee, and their pupils were young boys, but in most other respects they differed from the kind of school which the word "Elementary" now suggests. They taught reading, but not the reading of English; the aim of such rudimentary instruction was the reading of Latin, as it continued to be far into the seventeenth century. Some taught their scholars to write; but this was an exceptional concession to utility, or the teaching of an art indispensable to the future man of learning. Until the second half of the seventeenth century, Grammar Schools as a rule expected their youngest pupils to learn to write either in a separate "Writing School" or by taking a special course under a visiting "Writing Master," or from a scrivener, apart from the school itself. In short, the schools called by Mr Leach "elementary," were rather the preparatory stage to, or the lower classes of a course of instruction which we should now recognise as distinctly "secondary." That such schools did not themselves supply the higher instruction was more or less an accident, arising from such circumstances as defect in the schoolmaster, paucity of pupils or the presence in excess of boys whose abilities or means did not justify the teaching of "grammar," that is, the Latin grammar and literature. Pupils of this last kind attended, not to receive a complete secondary school course, as we should now say, but from Hobson's choice—they had but a short time for instruction and there were no other schools. This explains Mr Leach's statement that "the proportion of the population which had opportunity of access to Grammar Schools, and, as we can see, used their opportunities, was very much larger then than now" (p. 97).

The Chantry Certificates and Warrants under the Chantries Act printed by Mr Leach enable one to understand how schools, intended to give secondary education, did not, in practice, rise above the preparatory stage; but passages are too long for quotation here[1]. The whole question of curriculum in such schools is fairly summed up in the certificate relating to Peryn (Falmouth): "This ys a mete place. to establish A learned man to teache *a gramer scole* or to Preache godes Worde, for the people thereaboutes be very Ignorante" (*op. cit.* II. p. 32). The point here to be noted is that the ignorance of the townsfolk is to be fought either by preaching or by establishing a fully equipped *secondary* school.

In England these schools declined in number from the time of Edward VI. On the other hand the idea of the elementary or popular school was not new in Germany, though the actual realisation was imperfect. As far back as the thirteenth and fourteenth centuries the question of such schools had arisen in the wealthy municipalities of northern Germany; and the great cities, with the seats of the powerful commercial Hanseatic league at their head, founded schools both elementary and secondary. The former, commonly known as Writing Schools, taught reading in the mother-tongue and such writing and computation as might be useful in office and warehouse. The need both in Church and State of a well-instructed people was a frequent theme of Martin Luther's, which he pressed upon magistrates and pastors in two well-known discourses of 1524 and 1530. His German Bible and catechism implied a people who could read the vernacular, and it was an integral part of his scheme of things that they should do so. In a measure, the older ecclesiastical foundations of Catholic Germany assisted the design, the ancient parochial schools and country schools of the Church serving to keep alive the tradition of an education widely accessible. But the actual school system a century after Luther's death did not effect much for the education of the people at large, and there was full scope for the innovations and reforms of such princely patrons of public instruction as

[1] See pp. 32, 34, 200, 206, 312, all in Part II., that is, the reproductions of the original documents.

Prince Ludwig of Anhalt-Köthen, who employed Ratke to such small purpose, and Duke Ernest of Saxe-Gotha, whose foundations handed on the teaching of Comenius to the schools of the next generation.

The general circumstances which favoured the establishment of a school course based upon the mother-tongue and suited to the needs of a popular school system have already been stated. Special conditions of the second half of the seventeenth century also co-operated to the same end. The religious schism of the preceding century had been followed by the work of the Jesuits and the improvement of secondary education; in a similar manner, the religious and moral declension which succeeded the period of the wars of religion led to the establishment of popular schools intended to counteract the spiritual destitution of the people. The desire to see such schools erected reached its full effect after 1680; but it had existed from a much earlier time.

On the one side, the popular schools which had arisen in response to Luther's appeal taught religion, chiefly, and the reading of German as auxiliary to religious instruction; on the other, the Catholic Council of Bourges decreed in 1584 that in every parish girls should be taught reading and the Christian religion. Thirty years earlier the city of Rouen had opened classes for poor boys, in order that they might learn "the fear and praise of God, the Creed and the Commandments, their little book, reading, writing and chiefly good behaviour[1]."

The religious impulse was seconded by the procedure then adopted for the education of girls, a business wherein the lead was taken by France. One of the striking facts of ecclesiastical history after the great separation of the sixteenth century is the rapid multiplication of religious communities, of societies of women more particularly. The extraordinary success of the Jesuits encouraged imitators to seek in the education of the

[1] Guibert: *Histoire de S. Jean-B. de la Salle*, p. xxvi.

young the means of checking heresy and defection from the
Roman obedience. The majority of these new communities
were either corporations of teachers, or of persons otherwise
especially interested in children, and the number of such
societies then founded in, or introduced into, France was
considerable, those of women greatly preponderating. Communities of men pledged to educational work devoted their
attention to the established form of instruction, that is, instruction which would now be termed secondary; women were
compelled to think out a new type of schooling suited to the
requirements, or supposed requirements of girls.

It would have been clean contrary to the ideas and practices
of the time to give girls, except in rare cases, the erudite instruction which, it was professed, their brothers all received; it
was not desired to leave them without formal teaching. Those
who gave the matter any real consideration were constrained to
devise a curriculum which should be at once complete in itself
and unlike that which usually ruled in schools for boys.

How they solved the problem may be seen from the plans
laid down for one of the earliest French teaching congregations,
"les Filles de la Congrégation de Notre-Dame," founded by
Pierre Fourier in 1597. These plans also enable us to infer
the part which girls' education played in suggesting a curriculum
suitable not for the few of a learned class but for the many of
the popular school. The ladies of Fourier's foundation were
bound to receive as day-pupils, and without fee, such of the
townsfolk's daughters as presented themselves, who were to be
religiously educated, but not without regard to "that which
concerns this present life and its maintenance." They were to
be taught "reading, writing, arithmetic, sewing and divers
manual arts, honourable and peculiarly suitable for girls, which
will bring some profit to those who learn them and wish to
make use of them." (See Guibert, *op. cit.* xxxi., xxviii.).

In this girls' school we have the teaching of the three
R's and of a handicraft, a modern elementary school curriculum,

in fact; and this at a time when hand-work was unknown in boys' schools, when arithmetic was rarely taught, save as an "extra" to the stupider sort, and when schools generally held themselves superior to the teaching of reading and writing in the mother-tongue.

Solicitude for the education of the French poor was, of course, not confined to the congregations of "religious" which expressly undertook the task of popular instruction. During the fifteen-hundreds that solicitude was frequently reflected in the responsible assemblies of French nobles and clergy: in the seventeenth century some parish priests in the great cities added the management of a charity school to the ordinary duties of their cure. The States-General met four times in all during the troubled sixteenth century and on each occasion the business under consideration related to the questions which then sharply divided Frenchman from Frenchman, and which were felt by Catholic and Huguenot alike to be vital to the existence of the French State. Nevertheless, on three out of these four occasions the nobles pressed for the subvention at the expense of the clergy of schoolmasters in all towns and villages and for the creation of a compulsory school system. On the other hand, in many provincial assemblies of the clergy held after 1550 the question was debated, Who shall appoint the schoolmaster?—the ecclesiastical authorities, as of old, or the nobles and municipalities? It may be objected that both nobles and clergy had ulterior aims, and that in any case the practical outcome of their deliberations was small. Nevertheless, their discussions show that responsible opinion was trending towards a popular school organisation.

There is evidence, too, that in seventeenth-century France men were beginning to feel the need not only for a more widely extended elementary school system, but also for a kind of schooling which established institutions did not supply. That evidence is, in part, the existence of the teaching congregations already referred to; in part, it lies in the long-maintained struggle which was waged between the "Little Schools" within the jurisdiction of the Precentor of Notre-Dame, the *Collèges* of the University of Paris, the schools held by the writing-masters, and others. These were continually competing with each other, the schools of a higher grade including in their classes children who might be expected to be receiving instruction in a school of a grade lower, while the latter invaded the province of the higher school. The unseemly squabbles which ensued were not good for education as an organised service of the State; but the overlapping of curricula gave a prominence hitherto not accorded to certain necessary branches of knowledge or forms of skill.

At the time now under consideration there were two authorities charged with the oversight of secondary education in Paris, both of great antiquity. The elder represented the Cathedral Chapter of the city, the younger was the University, a body then some four and a half centuries old. The first was a survival from the early mediaeval period, when the Cathedral Chapter maintained its own school taught by one of its members, the Scholasticus or Scholarch; when, in later days, other schools were opened in the city and this cathedral official had himself ceased to teach, he remained the channel through which the chapter, or the bishop, conferred the license to teach on would-be schoolmasters, a license without which no one could practise in a school. The institution of a University in a cathedral city set up a divided jurisdiction, and in Paris the Faculty of Arts and the Precentor of Notre-Dame (who represented the chapter as scholarch) came to regard each other as natural enemies, destined to quarrel by their very constitution. In the seventeenth century the feud took the following shape. The University, in its Faculty of Arts, had charge of secondary education, inasmuch as it taught boys above the age of nine; the "Little Schools" established under the authority of the Precentor prepared boys below that age for the University, teaching them reading, writing, reckoning, the rudiments of Latin grammar, Catechism, and singing. The masters and mistresses of these "Little Schools" (whose business was chiefly of a preparatory kind and not strictly analogous to that of the modern teacher in an elementary school) were licensed by the Precentor, whose efforts were directed to shelter them from competition. Paris was divided into different districts, and the Precentor would license but one boys' school and one girls' school in each. But interlopers were both many and various. There were private teachers who taught furtively, who were hunted down, and their schools closed remorselessly when found. There were some of the University teachers in Arts who were ready to teach small boys reading, writing, and reckoning; to their intrusion into the province of the "Little Schools" the Precentor could only reply by an incursion into University territory. The "Little Schools" were encouraged to retain pupils beyond the age of nine and to teach both grammar and rhetoric, that is, two of the seven liberal arts, instead of merely preparing for one. The writing-masters, in turn, began to teach other things than writing, and the Little Schools replied by hanging out the sign of a pen, exhibiting specimens of handwriting, and, generally, professing to teach writing as a separate art, thus usurping the privileges of the writing-masters' gild.

In 1675 the Little Schools of Paris contained upwards of 5000 pupils taught by some 330 masters and mistresses. Ostensibly, the poor were entitled to gratuitous instruction in these schools: as a fact they were excluded. The struggles with the Faculty of Arts led these schools to give a kind of instruction which the poor seldom valued, and the schools themselves being poor, scholars who paid fees were welcomed. The parish clergy found it necessary to set up charity schools to meet the case, and of these the school of St Etienne du Mont as it existed in 1679 may serve as a type. It had places for eighty-four children who were to remain only so long as their parents were unable to pay a fee, and in no case might

they remain more than two years; none was admitted under
the age of eight. They learned to read in Latin and in French,
to write, to do sums, and to say the Catechism; they attended
Mass every morning in their parish church (Guibert, *ut supra*,
p. 170).

Comparison of the courses of instruction professed by the
Little Schools and their competitors shows that the popular
subjects in all were the "three R's," including the teaching
of *reading the mother-tongue*. Whether the schools confessedly
gave a rudimentary instruction to the very poor, or teaching
which partially, at least, prepared for more advanced instruction, public opinion had forced upon them a type of curriculum
which was new in France and elsewhere.

Clearly the people of Paris were feeling their way towards
an organisation of popular schools, and the same is true of
other great centres of population in France. It was a time,
not of duly co-ordinated action on the part of Church, State,
or municipality, but of individual experiment in grappling with
crying needs. Men and women of strong character moved
their neighbours to take part in a great public duty. Such
were M. Démia, a Lyons priest, who set up much administrative machinery and schools for popular education between
1666 and 1679; Adrien Nyel, a Pestalozzi in enthusiasm, who
laboured at Rouen and in Champagne between 1657 and 1685;
Barré and Madame Maillefer in Rouen, Paris and Rheims;
Roland, the benefactor of the last-named city[1].

There is evidence that efforts of a similar tentative kind
were being made in England. Hartlib's suggestions of 1650
for an elementary education suited to pauper children have
been stated in a preceding chapter; in the years that followed
some of these suggestions were realised. Thus, a charity
school for twenty boys was founded at Lambeth in 1661 by
Richard Lawrence; ten years later the vestry of Westminster

[1] For full accounts of these pioneers of popular instruction the reader
should refer to Guibert's *Histoire* already cited.

was paying Mrs Hooper half-a-crown a week "for teaching the parish children," and in 1681 the same vestry considered a petition from "Thomas Jordan praying that he may be settled and continued in the Imployment of instructing the parish Poore Children." In the last instance it would seem that the vestry was merely acting as trustee, or agent, of Dr Busby, of Westminster School, who (himself a sometime recipient of help from the vestry) made a "yearely Gift of Six Pounds" for the instruction of the poor[1]. Thomas Gouge, vicar of St Sepulchre's, London, ejected for non-conformity in 1662, received episcopal sanction in 1672 to attempt the diffusion of religious instruction in South Wales, it being part of his plan to teach children to read and write English as well as to make them familiar with the Catechism; he also printed and widely distributed the Bible, Prayer-Book, and other religious works in Welsh. In 1697 at Westbury-on-Severn sixty-seven boys and girls were being instructed in writing and in reading the Horn-book, Primer, and Testament at the expense of Col. Colchester, one of the five gentlemen who attended the first meeting of the S.P.C.K.[2] To the same year belongs John Locke's memorandum on Poor Law reform, proposing to erect "working schools" in every parish, where pauper children from three to fourteen years of age may be fed and taught "spinning, knitting, or some other part of the woollen manufacture, unless in countries where the place shall furnish some other materials fitter for the employment of such poor children"; the only schooling, if it can be so described, which Locke suggested for these unfortunates was to be got by coming "constantly to church every Sunday, along with their schoolmasters or dames." (Fox Bourne's *Life*, II. 385.)

These sporadic experiments were the precursors of well-organised movements in favour of popular education which

---

[1] See De Montmorency, p. 191.

[2] Allen and McClure: *Two Hundred Years, the History of the Society for Promoting Christian Knowledge*, 1898.

were independently begun and continued in France, Germany and England; their common origin in the deplorable condition oī the poor throughout those countries is attested by the lack of any great sympathy between the French and the other reformers, as well as by the native initiation of both the German and English movements, though these latter were encouraged, each by the knowledge of the other.   Moreover, all three movements were the work of private individuals, the State either not participating, or, in Germany, confining itself to informal patronage and the personal payment of a subscription by the Sovereign.   In England the schools were instituted by a voluntary society; both in France and in Germany they are associated with the life-work of one man and his personal followers.   All three movements were distinctly religious; their authors were moved not alone by the helpless ignorance and immorality of the bulk of the people, but by the indifference to religion which was so common.   At first sight such an indifference may seem a surprising sequel to the religious quarrels of the sixteenth and seventeenth centuries; that it was not peculiar to one party or nation appears to be demonstrated by the fact that in France (where the popular movement was earliest) the reformers were strictly orthodox Roman Catholics, while in Germany they were Pietists (Methodists, as one might say) owing allegiance to Lutheranism, and in England, members of the English Church.   One further point in common may be set down.   Working on independent lines, in some cases it may well be in ignorance of Comenius's proposals, all three realised Comenius's conception of a Vernacular School, that is, a place of instruction not merely preparatory to schools of a higher grade, but a true elementary school as that term is now understood.

    These movements for the establishment of religious "folk-schools" are signs of a consciousness in Western Europe that the spiritual condition of the masses was a grave scandal and danger to all; they are also a true sequel to the enunciation of the educational principles associated with the names of Comenius and the adherents of the New Philosophy, since their general agreement in matters of practice reflects the theoretical pronouncements of the earlier thinkers.

Precedence may here be given to the English movement, although it came last in order of time; it marks a decisive stage in the history of voluntaryism, as it is customary to name a form of administration animated by principles which, in the past, have done so much for English popular education. Its story is largely that of the early years of the Society for the Promotion of Christian Knowledge, whose first meeting took place on March 8, 169$\frac{8}{9}$. Dr Thomas Bray, Rector of Sheldon and Bishop of London's Commissary in Maryland, the moving spirit in the foundation of the Society, had prepared a scheme for the better religious instruction of British subjects in the North American colonies and at home; the new movement was simply the orderly evolution of one of the elements of Dr Bray's proposal.

At this first meeting of the Society the five gentlemen present (of whom Bray was the only clergyman) resolved "that we consider to-morrow morning how to further and promote that good Design of erecting Catecheticall Schools in each Parish in and about London, and that Col. Colchester and Dr Bray give their thoughts how it may be done[1]." The good design matured rapidly, so that by the fifth of October half-a-dozen schools were in active operation and steps had been taken to start others. By the middle of June, 1704, London and Westminster had 54 of these "Charity Schools," educating 1386 boys and 745 girls, and other schools were founded or assisted in different quarters of England and Wales.

At Whitsuntide in that year a service was held and a sermon preached before the assembled children and their patrons, thus beginning an annual festival which lasted till

[1] Minutes of S. P. C. K. in Allen and McClure's *Two Hundred Years*, p. 25.

1877; it was the practice to print the sermon, together with a report for the year of the state of the charity schools in the British dominions. The account which follows is for the most part gathered from the first of these publications, supplemented by those for 1711 and 1713. It may be of interest to quote the title of the earliest of these reports, " A Sermon Preach'd in the Parish-Church of St. Andrew's, Holborn, *June* 8, 1704, Being *Thursday* in *Whitsun-Week*, At the first meeting of the Gentlemen concern'd in Promoting the Charity Schools in and about the Cities of *London* and *Westminster.*

" At which time and place, the several Masters and Mistresses of the said Schools appear'd with the Poor Children under their Care : In Number about *Two Thousand.*

" *Published at the Request of many Persons concern'd in the said Charity.* By Richard Willis, D.D. Dean of Lincoln, London Printed by *J. Downing* for *M. Wotton* at the *Three Daggers* near the *Inner-Temple-Gate* in *Fleet-Street.* 1704."

The chief purpose of the charity schools was the nurture of poor children in the knowledge and practice of the Christian religion as taught in the Church of England ; to instruction in the Catechism was added a " secular " curriculum to be mentioned presently. The gratuitous character of the institutions was jealously guarded. " This School being only designed for the Benefit of such Poor Children, whose Parents or Friends are not able to give them Learning ; the Master shall not receive any Money of the Children's Friends at their Entrance, or Breaking-up, or upon any other Pretence whatsoever ; Nor shall the Master teach any other Children besides the poor Children of this School ; but shall content himself with his Salary, upon Pain of forfeiting his Place."

" The ordinary Charge of a School in London, for 50 Boys Cloathed, comes to about 75 *l. per Ann.,* including the Charge of a School-room, Books and Firing, the Master's Salary and

3 Bands, 1 Cap, 1 Coat, 1 Pair of Stockings and 1 Pair of Shoes given yearly to each Boy." A girls' school in like circumstances is said to cost about sixty pounds a year. These early records show that the "voluntary principle" passed into effect in various ways, though, no doubt, the usual•form was the subscription raised amongst neighbours, or the school maintained at the sole charge of squire, parson, or other local magnate. Thus the Trustees of St Katherine's by the Tower "farm the lamps within their own Parish, and give the Profits thereof to the Schools." Elsewhere, effigies of charity children stood by a poor-box at the door of church or school, to solicit alms; in some places " People pay more than ordinary for teaching their own Children, that the Master and Mistress may teach all the Children of the poor *gratis*, as they agree with them to do." A notable example of such co-operation occurred at " Winlaton in the Bishoprick of Durham," where the " Workmen of an Iron-Work, who are about 4 or 500, allow one Farthing and a half, per shilling per week, which together with their Master's Contribution maintains their Poor, and affords about 17 *l.* per annum, for teaching their children." Parish Clerks sometimes received their appointments on condition of teaching a certain number of children gratis; at "Ewhurst, Surrey," "the Minister hath provided 2 Palls, the one of which is let out for 2*s.* 6*d.* and the other for 1*s.* a Time, for the more decent Funerals of the Dead, and the Money so arising bears a good Part of the Charge of Teaching the poor Children there."

" Payment by Results" is often said to have figured first in English educational administration in 1862, when Robert Lowe's Revised Code appeared; but the honour (or odium) of the invention of this device belongs to some nameless financier of 1711, or thereabouts. "Where there hath not been a competent Number of Children for a School, as also where they could not be conveniently spared at School-Hours, especially in Harvest-time, Agreements have been made with proper Persons to teach the poor Children to Read, Write, and cast Accompts, *by the Great*, that is, to give the Master or Mistress *2s. 6d.* when each Child can *name and distinguish readily all the letters in the Alphabet*, and the like Sum when he can *spell*, and *5s.* more when he can *read well and distinctly, and say the Church-Catechism*, and *15s.* more when he can *write and cast Accompts*."

The successful establishment of these schools in London and Westminster was followed by their rapid extension to the cities and villages of England and Wales; Scotland joined the movement in 1709, "for altho' every Parish in Scotland be obliged to maintain one School-Master, yet it is but in some places that the School-Masters are obliged to teach the Poor *gratis*." "The Zeal which has appear'd of late Years amongst us for promoting the Christian Education of the Children of the poorer sort, has not stopp'd within the Kingdoms of *Great Britain* and *Ireland*, but hath influenced *New England* (where at *Boston* were set up 3 Charity Schools, *An.* 1709) and since the Publication of the last Account of Schools, the *Society for the Propagation of the Gospel in Foreign Parts*, hath allow'd 10 Pounds *per Ann.* to Mr. *William Huddleston*, Master of the Free School at *New York* in *America*, on Condition that the said *William Huddleston* shall transmit Yearly to the said *Society*, a Certificate under the Seal of the Mayor of New York, that he teaches 40 poor Children to read and write, and instructs them in the Principles of the Church of *England*."

The foregoing is from the " Account " for 1711, which also shows that the British supporters of these schools were in sympathetic correspondence with those who were conducting a similar work in Germany, Switzerland, Denmark, ·Holland, Sweden, and even in India, where the S.P.C.K. supported Danish missionaries.

The pupils of the charity schools ranged in age from seven to twelve years and, besides receiving religious instruction, were taught "the three R's." These schools, in fact, founded in England the quite modern notion that the three branches of instruction there included are the necessary elements of every grade of education ; by so doing, they rendered a conspicuous service to those reforms in curriculum which date from the seventeenth century. "As soon as the Boys can read competently well, the Master shall teach them to Write a fair legible Hand, with the Grounds of Arithmetick, to fit them for Services and Apprentiships. *Note.* The Girls learn to read, etc., and generally to knit their Stockings and Gloves ; to mark, sew ; make and mend their Cloaths ; and several learn to Write, and some to spin their Cloaths."

It seems clear from the passage already quoted concerning instruction "by the Great," that not all the pupils succeeded in mastering the three R's ; the great increase of payment (from five shillings to fifteen) which marked the passage from Reading to Arithmetic and Writing argues that a strong incentive was needed if the teacher was to bring his pupil on to the arts of summing and of writing. The choice of curriculum was determined by economic reasons which explain the presence therein both of arithmetic and some form of manual employment ; the latter sometimes developed in directions which seem to show that others besides "charity children" were under instruction. Thus, in 1704, at "Brighthelmeston, Sussex" (*i.e.* Brighton) "50 Boys are taught to read, write, cast Accompts, and the art of Navigation" ; the latter was also taught at Exeter and at Gateshead. The facts help one to surmise how it happened that at Clyst Heydon, Devon, "is an old decay'd Latin School, turned into an *English* Charity School."

The "Accounts" from which the foregoing is abstracted are filled with statistics and other matter of the "dry" kind. They are not, however, destitute of more human interest, as the two following excerpts may show. In the first it will be noticed that the rule of payment "by results" was extended

Λ. 14

much beyond the sphere defined for it by the Revised Code of
1862. At "Oswestry, *Shropshire.* 40 Ch. cloath'd, and taught
by a Mistress to read, and give an Account of Mr. Lewis's
Exposition [of the Church Catechism], and the Abridgment of
the History of the Bible by Heart, besides Mr. *Turner's* Spelling-
book, and the Catechism broke into short Questions. And when
any Ch. can perform all this, the Mistress hath a reward of
7*s.* 6*d.* After which the B. are sent to a Master, who teaches
them to write and cypher by the great, for 5*s.* a Head, which
is paid as soon as they have made such Progress as the
Minister judges sufficient for their purpose. But the G. are
taught to spin, knit, and sew, for 10*s.* each. And these Rates
are allowed for their Learning, whether the Time be long or
short. To put them forwards, 20 are set to strive against 20
for Shoes; and the 20 that get most of the Exposition, and
other books by Heart, have shoes. Then there remain 10
against 10, and so on till they are shod all round. A Shift
is hung up in the Sch. for the best Spinner, a Head-dress for
the best Sewer, a Pair of Stockings for the best Knitter, a
Bible for the best Reader, and a Copy-Book for the best
Writer. ("Account," 1713.)

At Tewkesbury is a school for 40 boys. "They of the first
class read the Bible and *Whole Duty of Man,* and after reading,
shut their Books, and cheerfully recollect the Substance of
what they have read. *They are likewise sometimes exercised in
making English Themes and Verse, to try their genius.* And
all they have learned, is rehearsed in a regular manner, at
a publick Examination, to the great Satisfaction of the Sub-
scribers, and others who are then invited to be present."
(*Ibid.*)

The more liberal conceptions of their earlier years did not
abide in the schools during the eighteenth century ; like their
German analogues, they became more and more merely
Catechism schools, and lost their opportunity, in large measure,
as an educating force amongst the bulk of the population.

Many survive to-day, some as public elementary schools for boys and girls, others as secondary schools, for girls chiefly, and a few as charitable foundations on the original lines. Whatever the faults of the Charity Schools in the later seventeen-hundreds, they had established a tradition of popular instruction which was of first-rate importance to the educational labourers of the nineteenth century.

CHAPTER XII.

ST JEAN-BAPTISTE DE LA SALLE.

Of the three movements on behalf of popular education
already mentioned, the earliest had its mainspring in the
career of a French ecclesiastic, Jean-Baptiste de la Salle.
Born at Rheims in 1651, a member of a well-to-do family
of the *noblesse de la robe*, occupant from boyhood of a canon's
stall in the cathedral of his birthplace, de la Salle lived the
first thirty odd years of his life amidst the dignified surroundings
familiar to wealthy clergymen of his time and country. Then
he abandoned family, position, and wealth to consort with a
band of young men engaged in the work of elementary teaching;
these he united in a religious community, founded in 1684 and
subsequently known to the whole world as the Institute of the
Brothers of the Christian Schools. So recently as 1900 Rome
decreed the honours of canonisation to this French educational pioneer who died in 1719. His story and that of his
congregation of schoolmasters have been told by M. Guibert,
of St Sulpice, in a book (*Histoire de S. Jean-Baptiste de la
Salle*, Paris, 1901) which worthily upholds the fame of French
historical scholarship; the statements of fact in this chapter
are made on the authority of that work.

But in the matter of popular education St Jean-Baptiste
had received an impetus from earlier labourers, his friends and
colleagues. Though the Institute rightly ascribes its origin
to the Saint's paternal care, the community was no one-man

organisation, but the outcome of circumstances and of the lessons derived from them by the men and women who at different times were associated with the founder's labours on behalf of popular education. In truth, its most fruitful ideas originated in other minds than his. Its work was not the mere filling in of an *à priori* scheme, but a natural growth, whose extension from time to time was intended to utilise opportunities as they were perceived to be such, or to meet occasions only then recognised as urgent. Its story reveals the existence in the public mind of an appreciative sense of the need for a system of schools quite different from that already established, while it also demonstrates the unreadiness of official agencies to supply what was wanting, even when they did not put obstacles in the way by their support of vested interests. When confined to three French dioceses the Institute evolved a new type of schooling, which, while not losing sight of the wider meaning of education, contrived to make its instruction satisfy some of the particular requirements of artisans, of shopkeepers, and of the humbler ranks of trade and commerce. When the Institute became national instead of diocesan, it still found room for further progress in this direction, and, in effect, became the originator of a kind of school (the Higher Primary School) whose province and most effective organisation are to-day everywhere one of the problems of educational administration.

Those colleagues of M. de la Salle who preceded him in the attempt to establish elementary education found their fields of work in Rouen and Rheims, the former being a city in which the tradition of gratuitous instruction of the poor was thoroughly rooted. In the seventeenth century all the charitable agencies of the city were entrusted to an especially created "Bureau," with its head-quarters in the General Hospital, a kind of combined Almshouse, Infirmary, and Poor School. In 1657 there lived in this hospital a certain Adrien Nyel, whose duty it was to keep the accounts of the

Charitable Fund and to teach the children. Whether he had been a schoolmaster in days preceding his arrival in the Norman capital is uncertain ; but, like Pestalozzi at Stans, Nyel found the task of his life when he entered the General Hospital at Rouen. The extension of schools for the poor, at first under the Charitable Bureau which employed him, and, later, much further a-field, became an absorbing interest against which nothing could compete. He was ever ready to put aside the work of the moment in order to seize any opportunity of opening a new school ; the school once set going, and teachers found to carry it on, he was as eager to discover a fresh field. He shared Pestalozzi's defect of being a bad man of business ; he could create, inspire, but not carry on successfully the prosaic work of administration. He was none the less an excellent teacher of children ; it was noted by admiring colleagues that his mere presence was sufficient to maintain order in the school-room.

Nyel's earliest enterprises were, naturally, confined to Rouen, but his work at the General Hospital did not suffice so active a man, though it suggested a channel for that activity in an addition to the charity schools of the city, four of which he opened between 1661 and 1669. Nyel secured teachers by associating with himself several young men who were boarded and lodged at the hospital in return for their work at one or other of the schools, and for domestic service in the hospital when not teaching. Nyel and his friends ("Brothers" they called themselves) constituted an informal community, united by common interests and duties, but, of course, professing no vows.

Nyel's labours, supported as they were from officially re-cognised sources, were insufficient to cope with the educational needs of a great industrial centre, and it was Rouen that gave an early illustration of "voluntaryism," the provision of popular schools by means of privately raised subscriptions, or of a fund otherwise voluntarily maintained. Schools for girls were opened in working-class quarters by Madame Maillefer, a wealthy widow of Rheims resident in Rouen, and by Father Barré, a Franciscan; later, these two incorporated in a religious community all the mistresses who taught in the schools administered by them.

The zeal, both public and private, displayed in the Norman city was communicated to Madame Maillefer's native place, Rheims (distant some 250 miles), through the person of Nicholas Roland, the director, intimate friend and fellow-canon of de la Salle. In the course of visits to Rouen as Lent preacher, Roland became acquainted with the work for poor girls' education carried on by Madame Maillefer and M. Barré, was greatly struck by it and desired to see the like introduced at home. The lady, naturally interested in a project for the benefit of her birthplace, induced Barré to permit two of their teachers to assist Roland in organising girls' schools in Rheims.

The undertaking rapidly succeeded; the two immigrant Sisters were joined by a body of zealous women numerous enough to permit the formation of a new and independent community, which still exists—or did, till the other day. Within less than seven years from the entry (in 1670) of the two Sisters from Normandy, this Rheims congregation, the Sisters of the Holy Child Jesus, had more than a thousand girls under instruction.

Roland had these schools very much at heart during the few years of life which remained to him. He declared in his will that "he could do nothing more advantageous to the glory of God and the salvation of souls, for the help of the poor unable to get instruction for their children, and for the good of the city which had given him birth, than to contrive that the free-schools should endure for all time." On his death in 1678 he bequeathed a house and 14,000 livres (say, £5250 sterling in money of to-day) for their benefit; he left them as a dying charge to his disciple and *confrère*, M. de la Salle.

Madame Maillefer now began to take thought for the poor boys of Rheims, and in 1679 she persuaded Adrien Nyel to set out for Champagne, taking a boy of fourteen as a helper; they were to erect a charity school in Rheims, their patroness providing them with lodging and a yearly subvention. In all cases of difficulty they were to refer to Canon de la Salle.

The recent experiences of the Canon had not been of the most happy omen for the success of Nyel's enterprise. In his capacity of executor to M. Roland, his dead friend and director, he had endeavoured, and in the end successfully, to place the schools for girls, and their teachers, the Sisters, in a recognised and assured position. To achieve this end it was necessary to secure the patronage of the Archbishop of Rheims, to obtain letters patent from the King, and last but not least, the Municipality had to be convinced that the Sisters and their schools would not add to the charge already laid upon the City funds in respect of religious communities. De la Salle had come successfully through this task, which had occupied about ten months, only a few weeks before Nyel's arrival. The Canon naturally saw lions in the path of Madame Maillefer's emissary. There was the Scholarch, the analogue at Rheims of the argus-eyed Precentor of Notre-Dame at Paris; how would he regard this incursion into his territory? Again, could the Archbishop be induced so soon to use his good offices once more? And how were those tight-fisted *échevins* at the Town Hall to be won over to a scheme lacking a satisfactory endowment?

The solution of these questions was found in the recognised custom which allowed a parish priest to open a charity school for the poor of his own cure. Nyel and his juvenile assistant were soon at work teaching the street-arabs of St Maurice parish to read, to reckon, to behave themselves decently and to acquire some religious knowledge. The improvement consequent on reducing these small vagabonds to order aroused the interest of the city at large in the doings of the two lay teachers; six months after his arrival Nyel had his second school in operation.

M. de la Salle's share in the proceedings had been intermittent, but considerable; he was at the bottom of the plan which utilised the custom of parish charity schools, it was he who made good the additional money required by the increased number of teachers serving under Nyel. That man of energy, in pursuance of schemes for extending schools, was frequently absent from his subordinates, who were not men to be left safely to themselves. The falling-off in the good order of the classes and in the progress of the scholars became noticeable, and the Canon was moved to intervene. He transferred all the teachers to a house which he rented near his home, with the purpose of ensuring the observance of certain rules of life amongst them. Nyel approved the idea, applauded the scheme of "moulding" the teachers, set up a third school in the city and betook himself to Guise, some fifty miles away, since he understood that its magistrates desired to open a charity school.

It would not be in place to set forth here the slow steps by which de la Salle was led to found his Institute; deeply interesting as a study in character, it may be followed at length in M. Guibert's book. Barré, who had tried without success to unite the Parisian charity school masters in a religious community, advised his friend to take the Rheims teachers into his home and there lead the common life. The advice was acted upon—not without penalties. Since the age of twenty-one de la Salle had been the head of his family and the guardian of four brothers and two sisters; the social obligations of his position were well defined in the cathedral city, and the introduction into his home of men of humble rank, with no monastic prestige to counterpoise the disadvantage, brought something like ostracism upon him.

Nyel's energies were now directed to places outside Rheims, and within eight months of the year 1682 schools were set up in four different towns, of which Laon was one. These schools were supported partly by municipal subventions, partly by voluntary contributions; the relation of de la Salle (the recognised head of the enterprise) and the teachers to the undertaking is made clear in the following excerpt from a town-hall register of Rethel-Mazarin, in the French Ardennes, one of the above four places. " M. de la Salle offers to furnish the sum required to purchase a house for lodging the schoolmasters, who, without reward, will instruct the poor children of the town ; provided, however, that another sum is forthcoming for the maintenance of the said school-masters." (Guibert, *op. cit.* p. 84.)

Meantime a stricter regimen had been introduced into the informal Rheims community; in consequence, the teachers complained that "their life was tedious, their [religious] exercises too troublesome, their food too plain, and their liberty too restricted." In the end the society was all but broken up, and its chief had to seek recruits more willing to undergo the rigours which he deemed necessary. Then the Franciscan, Barré, urged him to surrender his official position in the Church, to part with his wealth in favour of the poor, and to found a new religious community.

After long and anxious discussion with kinsfolk who thought him quixotic, de la Salle resigned his canonry in 1683. The autumn of that year saw a bad harvest, which was followed by one of those terrible winters that made dreadful havoc amongst an impoverished, famine-stricken people. At its close, Jean-Baptiste de la Salle had parted with his fortune to the starving poor of Rheims, expending, it is said, a thousand livres daily ; an income of two hundred livres a year (say, seventy-five pounds sterling), the usual salary of the master of a charity school, was all that remained to a man who, for a generation, had enjoyed the wealth and refinement then usual in his rank.

In the spring he recalled to Rheims Adrien Nyel and his colleagues from the distant towns. The whole party, including the men of the cathedral city itself, numbered thirteen; at Ascensiontide they went into retreat at the Carmelite monastery, and there remained till Trinity Sunday. In the intervening fortnight they deliberated upon their future life as a religious corporation, and on Sunday, May 27 (Trinity), 1684, they founded the Institute of the Brothers of the Christian Schools. They left their Rule for future determination in the light of experience; their very name was not decided upon at that moment; they professed but one vow, that of obedience, and even that vow was to bind them for a year only. Forty years were to elapse and their founder himself was to pass away, before royal letters patent and papal bull were to give full authorisation to the Institute.

Nyel was one of the four who did not renew the vow in 1685. His old keenness seems to have disappeared, and he was anxious to return to Rouen, from which he had been absent six years. Back again in the General Hospital, he became Superintendent of the Poor Schools of the city, and in that office he died in May, 1687, at the age of 61, after a strenuous and beneficent public career of some thirty years.

On the day when the Institute of the Brothers of the Christian Schools was founded, M. de la Salle had begun his thirty-fourth year; six years before that day he had received priest's orders and his active participation in educational work on any great scale dated from the same time. The early stages of the Institute's history were two. During the first it was a purely diocesan agency, with its head-quarters in Rheims; this stage closed with the end of the year 1687, three and a half years from the foundation. In the second stage, beginning in February, 1688, the diocesan work continues, but the centre of interest shifts from Rheims to Paris and, more particularly, to the great parish of St Sulpice; from the point of view of the history of the evolution of the popular-school idea this second stage is of great interest.

The first may be rapidly summed up. With the growth of

public appreciation of the community's work, candidates for admission to the Institute increased in number, and boys of fourteen amongst these candidates were so numerous as to warrant the formation of what was called a petty novitiate, where such boys might remain till they passed to work in the schools at the age of 16 or 17. As novices, these boys learned to read and write "perfectly"—a word which would mean much on the lips of their Superior. Frequent requests came from the country clergy for Brothers to teach in their schools, and the attempt to respond evolved a new type of institution, the seminary for country schoolmasters, to which the country clergymen sent their bright lads to be trained for work in the villages. These lads were "instructed in singing, reading, and writing perfectly. They are taught, lodged and boarded gratuitously, and in the end are placed in some country town or village there to serve as clerks. When so placed they have no other relation to the Institute than that of good will. They are however received at times of retreat." This seminary was, in fact, a training college, though not the first in France, since M. Démia had founded one in the diocese of Lyons twelve years before; the German *Seminarium Praeceptorum* founded by Francke in 1696 was twelve years later than de la Salle's seminary.

These three establishments, Institute, Novitiate, and Seminary, contained sixty persons within the first year of the Institute's history. The Brothers themselves followed the example set by their founder in a spirit which nothing could daunt. Out of doors their queer, rustic dress made them the butt of every stupid passer-by : their in-door life is reflected in the popular nickname of "*la petite Trappe*" which designated the Brothers' House in Rheims. Cold, hunger, the hair-shirt, the iron chain and the scourge, the Superior never spared himself; his earliest sons eagerly inflicted a like discipline upon themselves. Yet they also performed the schoolmaster's trying task for six hours every day, teaching large classes con-

sisting of the poorest and roughest boys. The sequel may be
told in the words of an admiring contemporary biographer of
the Saint: "In seven or eight years (1681–88), of the fifteen
brothers who had witnessed the birth of the Institute at Rheims,
at Guise, at Laon, and Rethel, six died prematurely before the
age of thirty, without counting those who quitted the House
in ruined health." Many friends and acquaintances looked
askance at de la Salle's sacrifice of position and wealth, and
some of his censors became active opponents, the Archbishop
of Rheims being of the number. A journey to Paris in the
summer of 1683, undertaken to win over the hostile prelate,
became in due time the occasion of an extension of the
Institute's field of operation. The Archbishop refused to see
M. de la Salle, but the latter found sympathisers in the parish
and seminary of St Sulpice, whither as a lad of nineteen he had
gone to share in the studies and pastoral work of that great
training-school of the French parochial clergy. In those
earlier days the young de la Salle must have become acquainted
with the charity schools which formed one of the many institutions with which the highly organised parish of St Sulpice
had been provided by M. Olier, its saintly priest and founder
of its seminary; and in the ordinary routine of a seminarist's
duties M. de la Salle had, no doubt, perambulated the streets,
bell in hand, to call the children to the catechising which he
and his fellows conducted on Sundays and holidays. Of the
seven charity schools set up in the parish originally, there was
but one survivor in 1683, and its condition was unsatisfactory
to the Curé, M. de la Barmondière, who extracted a promise
from the visitor to send some of his teachers to work in the
school.

At the close of 1687 there were several reasons which made
de la Salle not unwilling to give his Institute, if it might be,
something more than a purely diocesan *status*, and in February,
1688, accompanied by two Brothers, he reached Paris. The
St Sulpice school of 200 boys had virtually broken down, the

priest in charge and his two helpers, a boy of fifteen and a working hosier, being unable to maintain even the outward decency of good order. The hosier formed part of the establishment in order to teach boys knitting and hosiery in the school workshop which the Curé had opened, partly to ensure the up-keep of the school itself, partly to give industrial training, thus anticipating Pestalozzi's experiment at Neuhof by nearly a century. M. de la Barmondière was himself an enthusiastic hand-worker; when director of the seminary, he had been a noted repairer of watches, following his hobby while teaching the seminarists.

The skill of the Brothers from Rheims soon restored the school to order and usefulness, the number of pupils grew, so that in 1690 a second school was opened in the parish, and eight years later the Brothers carried on four schools in Paris, with a thousand pupils, all told. These numbers are altogether exclusive of the still greater numbers in the home dioceses of Rheims and Laon. In Paris, the boys were taught reading, writing, and arithmetic, and—noteworthy additions—drawing and a manual trade. Instruction was, of course, gratuitous; school-books and material were supplied free to most, the parish funds bore the expense also of daily soup, and bread and money were given to the poorest. A staff of visitors regularly went round the schools and a monthly conference was held between these voluntary workers and the teachers. Outside St Sulpice parish the Brothers also conducted a training college for country teachers.

But the most notable educational experiment in which M. de la Salle took part during this period of the Institute's history was the establishment of a school which in aim and method much resembled the modern "Continuation School." It was complained that many lads and young men spent their Sundays in drinking and gambling, and the Curé of St Sulpice took counsel with de la Salle as to measures for providing these youths with a place of resort, where they might pass some of the hours of that day with profit to themselves and without scandal to their neighbours. The result was the institution of a Sunday School, where lads and young men below twenty were admitted to the number of two hundred. These were classified according to their ability and age, and on Sundays and holydays received instruction from the Brothers, some of whom were themselves specially taught the more advanced subjects in order to instruct these young workmen. In the lower classes reading, writing, spelling, and reckoning were taught; the more capable scholars were instructed in drawing, in geometry, and, it is said, in "architecture"—possibly some simple designing applicable to architecture is meant. The school was held for two hours, and Catechism and a sort of sermon from one of the Brothers followed.

This seventeenth-century Sunday School forestalled in a remarkable manner more than one educational institution which is commonly thought of as much later in origin. To say nothing of the Sunday School proper, eighty-one years before Raikes of Gloucester (1780), the school of St Sulpice was first and foremost a "Continuation School" in the modern sense, that is, it gave to lads and young men engaged in wage-earning a course of teaching that was based upon the instruction acquired in their earlier years, through the elementary school, and designed to carry that instruction to a higher stage. The school was also, in a measure, an anticipation of the technical or rather trade school, whose general institution is a noticeable point in the recent educational history of the great cities of our day.

This chapter is not a history of the Institute, or it would tell of the many grievous troubles which fell upon de la Salle and his Brothers from the time of their entry into Paris; as, the defection of Brethren which led to the closing of Sunday School and training college, the period of deep poverty, the virulent opposition, amounting to persecution, from the masters of the "Little Schools" and from the Gild of Writing Masters.

Trouble of this last kind was not peculiar to the sojourn in Paris, though it was most poignant there; the establishment of the Brothers in any town of importance was generally followed by complaints of privileges infringed and of unfair competition. The regularity with which the charge was made that the Brothers accepted *gratis* pupils who could afford to pay, goes to show that their teaching appealed, or was thought to appeal to persons above the poorest class.

The many discouragements and obstacles encountered during the early years in Paris may have tempted de la Salle to regret that he had ever removed his head-quarters from Rheims, his Institute's birthplace and his own; yet it may be surmised that, without the experience in the French capital, the community would not have discovered what varied possibilities for public service were latent in its own organisation. Much was learned from its association with the carefully worked parish of St Sulpice and the able men who directed its affairs; and the close identification of the Institute during its early years with that one Parisian parish was one of the contributory causes to the extension over France of the Brothers of the Christian Schools.   To the seminary of St Sulpice came the young French ecclesiastics distinguished by wealth, birth, and intellectual eminence; in its various parochial agencies the future dignitaries and city clergy learned how a great parish should be administered.   All came in contact there with the Brothers, and noted their success as instructors and civilising agents generally.   Their period of stay in the seminary ended, they departed, and carried the fame of M. de la Salle's community north and south, east and west.   At a later day, whenever the problems of popular education were raised in their presence, their minds inevitably recalled the schools and teachers of St Sulpice, and they turned for help, or at least for advice to M. de la Salle.   For example, in 1699 the parish priests of Chartres petitioned their Bishop (himself an old St Sulpicien) to procure the Institute's presence in their city, alleging that it would prove "a potent assistance in reforming the morals of the people."

The settlement of seven Brothers in Chartres the same year was the beginning of a comparatively rapid extension of the community's sphere of labour. The original work in Champagne and Picardy remained: the Brothers now began to serve in schools established in towns of the Seine Basin, from its upper waters down to Rouen, and in the great towns of eastern France and in the South. While Calais received them in 1700, Marseilles accepted their services six years later. M. de la Salle's last foundation was in Provence in the year 1711; at that time twenty-five schools, stretching in a broad band through eastern and central France, owed their origin, or revival, to him and his community.

The circumstances amidst which these schools were founded were much the same, however different the locality. Though primary schools existed, they were seldom of service to the very poor, whose children were excluded either because they could not pay the fee, or because their presence was an offence to those who were better off. These children grew up in ignorance and vice; and their state became a public scandal. Religious persons, both Catholic and Calvinist, desired to make them and keep them adherents to one creed or the other; nor were those wanting who regarded it as a social duty to be mindful of the morals of these neglected children. Private benevolence was ready to do its part by contributing subscriptions and bequeathing legacies: but the difficulty always was to find teachers. Then, owing to the advice of some ex-Sulpicien, or of some friend of M. de la Salle, or of his work, the Brothers were called in. Thereafter followed in due course the successful administration of gratuitous elementary education, and the opposition of vested interests, ending in a compromise which left the Brothers to do their work much after their own fashion. It goes without saying that the unimpeached

orthodoxy of the Institute facilitated its establishment in an
age and country which vested educational privilege very largely
in the bishops.

At Rouen the two Brothers who conducted a charity
school were so successful, that M. de la Salle was invited to
manage all the boys' schools (four in number) of that kind
which the city possessed. So it came about that, in 1705,
Rouen became the Institute's head-quarters, an old manor-
house, known as St Yon, being prepared for the residence of
de la Salle and his novices.

The establishment of the Novitiate of St Yon occasioned
a new departure in the history of the Institute. A commercial
and industrial city like Rouen numbered amongst its inhabitants a numerous class of persons for whose children no
especially suitable type of school existed. Families of rank
and of wealth, and others whose boys were destined for the
pulpit, the bar, the Court, or the civil service, were served
by the Jesuit schools or by the " *Collèges* " of the University;
the poorest children were provided with charity schools. But
save for the elementary teaching given in the " Little Schools,"
and by the writing-masters, the children who lay between these
social extremes were without school provision. The men of
the lower middle-class, the shopkeepers and small manu-
facturers of the town, the farmers of the outskirts, all, in fact,
who looked to their sons as their natural successors in business,
required for those sons an education which, while in advance
of that given in the schools for the poor, should be of a type
different from that which prepared the future members of
a learned profession. The local success of the Brothers as
teachers, and the establishment of their head-quarters in St Yon,
naturally led the people of Rouen to think of the Institute
as a fitting agent for meeting this particular demand. Accordingly, M. de la Salle was frequently approached by parents
with the request that he would provide the missing organisation,
in return for the fees which they would be glad to pay. The

novitiate of St Yon shared the poverty of the Institute in general, and the proposal of the parents indicated a new source of revenue; these considerations, added to M. de la Salle's zeal for education as a public service, determined him to grant the parents' petition, and St Yon opened its doors to boarders.

The institution which grew from the boarding-school of St Yon is of historic interest, as exhibiting the germ of the French "Higher Primary School" of to-day and of the German Latin-less *Realschule*, even then drawing towards the birth, under circumstances recounted in the next chapter. At St Yon each class was taught by two form-masters, a writing-master, who taught the mother-tongue, and a ciphering-master, who taught mathematics; Brothers specially qualified gave instruction throughout the school in modern languages, drawing, music, and book-keeping. St Yon grew in popularity, and, under the care of the Institute, the type of school was extended to other parts of France; with the years, the curriculum also came to include more and more "subjects," but these always remained "modern."

The creation of this new kind of school was not the only innovation which sprang from the work at Rouen. The discipline at St Yon was matter for admiration on the part of parents and others who had a personal interest in it, and its success brought petitions from certain families asking the Institute to receive children deemed incorrigible by the usual educational procedure. Each such intractable pupil was put into the keeping of a Brother, who never lost sight of him; he followed much the same course of education as that pursued by the ordinary boarder, except that he was made to realise in a special degree the fact that he was a prisoner who might secure comparative liberty by good conduct.

The successful treatment of these abnormal children would seem to have suggested a reform in the penal system to the President of the Parlement of Normandy. Convinced of the

disastrous effect of prison-life on first offenders, he begged
M. de la Salle to receive such law-breakers of this class as
might be condemned to imprisonment either by the local
Parlement or by the King's Judges. De la Salle was naturally
desirous to please so good a friend of the Institute as the
President, and, setting aside his own scruples, he consented
to take charge of first offenders, thus, in effect, opening a
Reformatory School. The " incorrigibles " who were not
criminal were sent to their homes, and a special building was
put up at St Yon to receive the newest kind of pupil there.
These were of various dispositions and from different social
classes ; their names were known only to the Director and to
the Prefect. Some applied themselves to study, and followed
the courses in geometry, in drawing, in civil and military
engineering ; no great objection seems to have been made to
their joining the ordinary boarders in these courses. Others
learned manual arts, such as carving, carpentry, and lock-
smith's work ; indeed, the various handicrafts were followed
so extensively and so successfully at St Yon, that in 1728 the
Brothers undertook, with the help of the reformatory boys,
to build their own chapel. It is also noteworthy that these
juvenile offenders were all permitted to grow flowers in the
windows of their cells, and to keep caged birds. This French
" reformatory " dates from the period 1709-1715 ; the first
general law founding such schools in Great Britain was passed
in 1854, Massachusetts anticipating it by about six years.

It was in this same house of St Yon that the founder of
the Brothers of the Christian Schools passed away on April 7,
1719, at the age of sixty-eight. In 1900, the year marked by
the canonisation of St Jean-Baptiste de la Salle, his Institute
was giving gratuitous, elementary education to more than
300,000 boys in Europe, Asia, Africa, and America ; the
number of Brothers was over 15,000, and some 4000 novices
and postulants were awaiting admission to the higher grade.

St Jean-Baptiste de la Salle, as an educational pioneer, is

essentially the man of action, the administrator, rather than the elaborator of theories; we are to look for his work in the thing done rather than in the word written, in institutions rather than in books. During the course of his forty years' connection with public education, there were necessarily many occasions on which the Saint was called upon to set his thoughts upon paper, and these thoughts remain, *passim*, in his letters, and in one or two devotional books, as well as in the "Rule" of the Institute. His principal writing of the strictly pedagogical sort is the *Conduct of the Schools*, a document which may be called the "Ratio Studiorum" of the Institute. The non-literary character of M. de la Salle's work for education is strikingly illustrated by the fact, that no *printed* edition of this "Conduct of the Schools" is known to have appeared during its author's life-time. The earliest is that of 1720, the year following de la Salle's death. (Guibert, pp. 200 and 690.)

Yet the book, or at least its beginnings, had been in existence from the earliest years, when the Institute was but a small, diocesan association. At Rheims M. de la Salle had drawn up a set of directions to be observed in the school-room by the Brothers, each of whom had his manuscript copy. The experience gained in Paris rapidly developed the system of which these rules were the expression, and somewhere about 1695 the "Conduct of the Schools" assumed a more complete form. The novices made copies for themselves of this official hand-book of school-management and method, and these they carried away with them to their schools. But the "Conduct" never became stereotyped. In its manuscript state it was revised from time to time; the preface to the printed version of 1720 says, "This Conduct has been collected and arranged by the late M. de la Salle after a very great number of conferences between himself and the senior Brothers of the Institute who were most capable of keeping school, and after an experience of several years' duration." That printed version has been often revised since, as times have changed and educational needs have changed with them; we are, however, only concerned here with the early form of 1720.

The book helps us to picture the school-rooms of the Institute as they were in the seventeenth century, sets before us the order that reigned there, and the course of study pursued. Two conclusions force themselves upon the reader; first, that the great aim of the Institute was the teaching of religion and the inculcation of piety, and second, that M. de la Salle had grasped the situation of the teacher of large classes of poor children. His directions for the management of an oral lesson would commend themselves to most teachers whose task it is to emulate the Brothers by instructing 80 or 100 children together. That the outcome would suggest machinery rather than life is as true to-day as it was two centuries ago; but that is the vice of the situation, not of the teacher, as such.

The "Rule" of the Institute expressly states that the "Christian Schools" were established to teach poor children the mysteries of religion and to enable them to live a good life. The "Conduct of the Schools" accordingly directs that instruction in the Catechism shall be given daily after an effective method, which it describes, and that the practice of pious observances shall be greatly encouraged. Prayer, and the attitude of prayer, are associated with all the hours of the school-day. "There shall always be," it is said, "two or three scholars on their knees, one from each class, who shall tell their beads, one after the other, in a part of the school chosen by the Director or Inspector, and arranged for the purpose."

Many a teacher to-day would be saved not a little suffering, while his power of control would be the stronger, if he acted in the light of rules such as the following: "He" (*i.e.* the teacher) "will particularly keep watch over himself that he speak rarely and very quietly....When he gives an order, he will always do so in a tone moderately pitched....He will not speak to an individual pupil, nor to the general body without considering what he will say, and the necessity of speaking at all. When he does speak, he will do it very gravely, and always in a few words....It will be of little use for the master to set himself to secure silence amongst the scholars, if he does not keep silence himself....His silence more than any other thing will produce good order in the school."

To reduce the number of occasions on which the teacher must break silence, the "Conduct" directs that orders addressed to the whole class, or school, shall be conveyed, not by word of mouth, but by signal. A small piece of apparatus, made of iron (a hand-signal, in fact) was used in the schools for this purpose; a simple code made the signal suffice for all ordinary movements of the scholars in common.

M. de la Salle would have his teachers rely upon the ordinary sanctions of school government. He would use, in the first place, admonition and moral suasion, in dealing with an offender; but in the last resort he was prepared to employ the ferule, the lash, the birch, and perhaps also the "cat" (*le martinet*). These are strong measures, which are now unreservedly condemned by French public opinion; they have been repudiated since by the Institute itself. But M. de la Salle was on a level in this matter with the best opinion of Frenchmen of his own time. Corporal punishment is reserved as an *ultima ratio*, and when administered, it is to be administered in a moderation which the "Conduct" carefully prescribes. The Saint lays it down that "firmness must never degenerate to hard-heartedness"; on the other hand, children must not be suffered to do everything they please, encouraged thereto by a false tenderness.

It has been said that the "Conduct" describes an effective method of instruction in the Catechism; the passages dealing with it are worth repeating, as they are of general application to the oral teaching of children, whatever the subject-matter under consideration. "The master," says the "Conduct," "shall not speak to the scholars as if he were preaching, but he shall interrogate them almost continuously, putting question upon question; and, to make them understand what he is teaching, he shall interrogate several scholars in succession upon the same point....In his questions he shall only employ simple expressions and words that are very easily understood, and, as far as possible, which do not require explanation, and he will make the questions and answers as short as he can.... He will take care to talk very little, but to question much....In every Catechism lesson the master must not fail to inculcate some practical principles....He will take care not to disturb the Catechism by fault-finding or ill-timed correction (of the scholars)." The scholar who is to make answer " shall stand upright and uncovered, make the sign of the cross, putting off his gloves, if he has any, and folding his arms, and shall answer the question put to him in such a manner as to make sense, by repeating the question itself in his reply."

These are directions which speak of experience in dealing with large numbers, taught together as a class, a mode of organising a school which was very uncommon, indeed almost unique outside the Jesuit schools. In the "Christian Schools" a class numbered something near 100 boys, more or less; in one of the Rouen schools in 1705 there appear to have been as many as 150. Each class was in the charge of a Brother and was divided into three sections, comprising the most advanced, the mediocre, and the most backward: when the Brother was engaged with one section only, the remaining sections were set to do work under the surveillance of monitors, who kept order, heard lessons, and helped the Brother in similar ways; but they did not teach.

M. de la Salle adopted yet another innovation, this time one of method, taking Port-Royal as exemplar. The "Little Schools" of Paris, and indeed the whole organisation of primary instruction in the capital, were under the jurisdiction of the Precentor of Notre-Dame. The official code issued under that ecclesiastic's authority was "The Parochial School"

("L'École Paroissiale"); the edition of 1654 directs that "before children are put to reading French they must first know how to read Latin well in all sorts of books," the reason being that "French reading is more difficult to pronounce than Latin reading"—that is, the latter language is more phonetically spelt. This was the common practice, and the reason commonly alleged for its employment. Children were not taught to *understand* Latin in this connection, but merely acquired the power of reading Latin words; and they were made to acquire this power, even though (as in the case of charity-school children) it was not supposed that they would ever learn Latin. The "Conduct of the Schools" takes up the attitude of Port-Royal on this question. "The first book," says this document, "in which the scholars of the Christian Schools shall learn to read shall be filled with all kinds of *French* syllables....The book in which they shall learn to read in Latin is the Psalter; only those shall learn it who know how to read perfectly in French."

This innovation appeared so dangerous, that when the Bishop of Chartres visited in 1702 the "Christian School" recently founded in his cathedral city, he required the Brothers to go back to the old-established practice. In the rather lengthy Memorandum by which M. de la Salle changed the Bishop's mind on this point, he asks, "Of what use can the reading of Latin be to people who will make no employment of it in their life? And, therefore, of what use can it be to the children who frequent the Christian Schools and the Free Schools? Certainly, 'Religious' who say Divine Service in Latin need to know very well how to read it: but out of one hundred girls who attend the Free Schools scarcely one of them is likely to become a chorister in a nunnery. Similarly, of a hundred boys in the Brothers' schools, how many will study the Latin language at a later time? And if there should be some, are they to profit at the expense of the others? Experience teaches that the boys and girls who attend the

Christian Schools do not persevere in their attendance long enough to learn to read Latin well and French also. As soon as they are old enough to work they are withdrawn, or they come no more, having to earn their living. That being so, if we commence by teaching them to read Latin, they go away before they learn to read French or even to read well in Latin itself," for it requires "a great length of time to acquire the latter art." (Guibert, *op. cit.* pp. 315–6.)

The course of study prescribed for the schools of the Institute by the "Conduct" is one which under any circumstances would make a by no means unsatisfactory elementary school programme. It deserves much more than this lukewarm praise when one remembers that the school-life of the pupils was brief, and that Europe at large was then only just awakening to the need for popular education. The boys in the "Christian Schools" were taught to read French, printed and written; those who succeeded in acquiring this art, and remained at school, went on to read the Latin Psalter. Writing, spelling, and composition were included in the study of the mother-tongue; a practical turn was given to this part of the course by teaching the boys to write business forms, such as receipts for payments, promissory notes, proxies, etc. Similarly, they were taught ciphering, not only with pen and paper, but also "*au jet*," that is, the solution of money sums by means of counters, a helpful device so long as France was tormented by a most confusing system of money notation. To the foregoing studies, these schools added drawing and geometry, and religious instruction formed a very marked feature of their programmes, as has already been said.

Forty of the sixty-eight years of life granted to St Jean-Baptiste de la Salle were marked deep by a strenuous devotion to the public good, and that earnest career was the occasion of many and varied institutions rich in advantage to popular education. The work of the Institute revealed some of the educational possibilities inherent in a modern vernacular to the men of an age somewhat too prone to associate solid learning exclusively with the ancient languages: and the novel idea of an elementary school as a place frequented even by the very poor, there to receive instruction in and through the mother-tongue, was consequently well established in France. Moreover, the Brothers demonstrated how such a school could be organised and conducted. The industrial occupations and the "continuation classes" of the St Sulpice schools were early and soon forgotten forecasts of kinds of educational work which have engaged the thoughts of administrators and social reformers in all parts of Europe in our own time; and the remarkable work at St Yon, including as it did the first *École Primaire Supérieure*, the first, or certainly one of the first *Realschulen,* and the first Reformatory, attests the truth that the Institute was governed in its early years by men whose great zeal was matched by unusual foresight.

Yet the founder himself was not an original mind of the first rank: of the many educational experiments associated with his name scarce one was due to his direct initiative. It was his disciple-like friendship with Nicolas Roland which first turned his thoughts to the questions of popular instruction. It was his association with Adrien Nyel, and through him, with the work already accomplished by Nyel himself and by Madame Maillefer at Rouen, as well as that of Barré in the Norman capital and in Paris, which gave birth to de la Salle's idea of a religious congregation, devoted to the gratuitous education of poor boys. To a Superior of St. Sulpice and to a Curé of St Sulpice were due the establishment, under de la Salle's direction, of instruction in manual occupations, the Continuation School and the Trade School. Force of circumstances and the requests of others, rather than St Jean-Baptiste's initiative, gave birth at Rouen to what, using modern language, we may call the Higher Primary School, the Modern School, and the Reformatory respectively.

But while it is not possible to place the founder of the Institute amongst the highest class of original thinkers on education, he has an indisputable claim to stand with those whose actual concrete services to educational administration have been very considerable indeed. Original he may not be; yet his mind was of no common order, as is proved when one considers the readiness with which he accepted· reforms, and the effectiveness with which he put them into practice. It is a debatable point whether such minds (practical in the best sense, because they are accessible to ideas) do not confer greater benefits upon humanity than do the thinkers of a loftier type.

CHAPTER XIII.

A. H. FRANCKE AND THE PIETIST SCHOOLS.

THE French and German educational movements at the close of the seventeenth century were both incited by religious motives, both grew steadily in response to the demands of the moment, and, in so doing, independently evolved schools and school-courses of a new kind. But the German movement depended for initiation and continuance much more than the French upon the efforts of one man, and its operations were by no means confined to popular or elementary instruction. On the other hand, while de la Salle's schools were as widely spread as the limits of Roman Catholicism itself, Francke's own institutions never overstepped the bounds of a single German Protestant city, though their example was felt far and wide. The vigorous survival to our own day of de la Salle's Institute and of Francke's establishments at Halle testifies that these reformers laid broad and solid foundations.

The career of August Hermann Francke[1] was of the outwardly uneventful sort which is usually pursued by the university teacher, the clergyman, and the philanthropist. His migrations were from one seat of learning, or pastoral charge,

---

[1] The authority followed in this chapter is Karl Richter's collection of Francke's pedagogical publications, "A. H. Francke, Schriften über Erziehung und Unterricht," Leipzig, 1872. Francke's own *Historische Nachricht* supplies bibliographical details down to 1697.

to another, and the chief vicissitudes of his life were brought about by that spirit of religious faction which was then so easily aroused in Germany. His greatest triumphs were embodied in the many educational, religious and philanthropic institutions with which he endowed the city wherein more than half his days were spent.

Born at Lübeck in March 166¾, Francke was taken three years later to Gotha, where his father, a capable lawyer, had been appointed to administer the ecclesiastical and scholastic business of that Ernest the Pious whose educational reforms have been described in an earlier chapter. The elder Francke died in 1670, and August's education was carried on privately at home till his thirteenth year, when he entered the Gotha Gymnasium, the theatre of the innovations of Duke Ernest and his collaborator, Andreas Reyher. Both were now dead, but their work remained, and, without doubt, the memory of his one short year in their school played its part in his own plans of twenty years later. His subsequent school and university training were obtained elsewhere; while engaged as a private tutor he took his degree at Leipzig, where he also joined in founding a society to encourage Biblical study. A year later (viz. in 1687) he was studying Scriptural exegesis under Sandhagen at Lüneburg, and here occurred the spiritual experience which he always referred to as his "Awakening," or conversion.

Then followed a sojourn in Hamburg and his earliest association with popular education. Moved by the condition of the poor children of the city, this young man of five-and twenty taught many of them in classes set on foot by himself. "Here," he says, "I not only learned patience, charity, and indulgence, whilst struggling against my own manifest faults, particularly in reproving the children—but it also became increasingly evident to me, how corrupt was the customary mode of instruction, and how highly defective the methods in use for the training of children; and this excited in me, even then, the most ardent wish, that God would graciously grant that I might contribute something to the improvement of the method of instructing and educating the young."

Francke's spiritual life had been a preparation for the change which, begun at the "Awakening" of 1687–8, was finally determined in the course of a two months' visit to Jacob Spener at Dresden in 1689. In popular estimation, Spener was the founder of a Lutheran sect, the "Pietists," whose best known aims associate them with the later English "Methodists": but, indeed, the essential tendencies of the Pietists are to be traced in German thought to a much earlier period than Spener's, back to Arndt's "True Christianity" of 1605, and thence, outside merely German limits, to the mystics and others who, within and without the Catholic Church, thought of the religious life as, above all, an individual intercourse of the soul with its Maker. Pietism was marked by its deep sense of the personal side of religion, its consequent love of pious exercises in private, its abstention from "worldly" pleasure, and the diligent study of the Bible as the revelation of God's will respecting the individual soul; personal, living faith counted for much in its esteem, theological accuracy and acuteness, as merely intellectual powers, counting for little. Later, it was doomed to pass into formalism and decay, but its most influential days were still to come when Spener and Francke met at Dresden. Spener himself had said, "All hope for the future rests upon this: the world will become what the up-growing young now are." Francke's task in Halle was accomplished in the same belief.

Established as a *Privat-dozent* at Leipzig, Francke delivered extra-academical lectures on Biblical subjects which aroused so great an opposition from the local clergy that he quitted the city for good. He was equally unfortunate at Erfurt, where the authorities imagined that he intended to found a new sect, and, in the supposed interests of peace, requested him to leave the place. Into the merits of these differences it is not necessary to enquire; but it is noteworthy that at Leipzig one charge against Francke was that he lectured publicly in German instead of academic Latin, a characteristic innovation first introduced in 1688 by the Leipzig professor and future University colleague of Francke, Christian Thomasius.

On the very day on which the command to quit Erfurt reached him Francke received a letter from the Court of Brandenburg, intimating that his services were required by its new sovereign, the Elector Frederick, the Hohenzollern prince who in 1700 became the first King of Prussia. Frederick was already pursuing the policy which converted Brandenburg into the strongest state of Northern Europe, industrially, commercially, and martially; he was equally alive to the benefits which might accrue to his subjects from the possession of a university of a modern type, and it was in this connection that Francke's services were desired. The "Friedrich University" of Halle was actually founded in 1694, but Francke received his formal appointment to the Chair of Greek and Oriental Languages at the close of 1691, and began his professorial duties at Easter following. With the appointment to the chair went also the pastorate of the Church of St George at Glaucha, a suburb of Halle. The connection thus established endured till his death; but no more need be said of Francke's University career than that from 1698 till June, 1727, when he died, he was Professor of Divinity, and that in 1716–17 he was Pro-rector of the University.

So soon as Francke was well established in his pastoral charge he began that season of extraordinary activity, educational and philanthropic, which gave to Halle a remarkable series of institutions, and assured to Francke himself a very honourable position amongst educational administrators. During this period in his life, which ranges from 1694 to

1712, or 1714, he erected a whole hierarchy of schools, whose scope may be gathered from the following catalogue :

i. *Elementary Schools:*

The Poor-School and the Bürger-schule, 1694–5 ; the Orphanage, 1695.

ii. *Secondary Schools:*

Pädagogium, 1694–5, Latin School, 1697, Girls' High School, 1709.

iii. *Training Courses* for teachers for the above elementary schools (1696) and for the secondary schools (1707).

A dispensary was set up in 1698, a printing-office and book-shop in 1701, and about the same time the beginning of a library and a museum of Art and Natural History. Of the Bible-house for the dissemination of the Scriptures, of the Mission-house for the promotion of missionary work in the East Indies (wherein Francke co-operated with S.P.C.K.), and of the many other enterprises associated with Francke's life in Halle this is not the place to speak.

In surveying these achievements it is difficult to decide whether their most surprising feature is their humble beginning, or their rapid growth and speedy adaptation of means to ends. Unlike de la Salle, Francke had no large private fortune to expend upon his benevolent schemes, and he undertook the responsibilities of married life soon (1694) after his settlement at Halle ; he therefore looked to the public at large to support his many enterprises. The event amply justified his confidence, and though often reduced to sore straits, his schools, orphanage, and the like were, on the whole, satis-factorily supplied with money. He himself ascribed this result to a special providence exercised in favour of the Halle insti-tutions ; it is perhaps not profane to include in that dispensation their founder's own benevolent impulses, unwearied labours, great administrative powers, and business instincts. Francke had lost his father at the age of seven; but Duke Ernest's counsellor and capable man of affairs lived again in the son. The Halle institutions were well advertised, not only in Germany, but throughout Protestant Europe. Agents travelled to make the work known, and to learn what any similar establishments might have to teach, the latter with reference more particularly to orphanages. Francke himself made many journeys into different parts of Germany, and one, at least, into Holland, in the interests of Christianity as conceived by the Pietists, and on behalf of the great work which was being done in his home; he was in correspondence almost from the first with the English Society for Promoting Christian Knowledge. Numerous reports were circulated, not in German alone, but in Dutch, English, and French, which periodically called public attention to the great cost of undertakings whose benefits were not confined to Germany.

In Halle itself the plans for housing all these philanthropic schemes excited active sympathy in all classes, beginning with the Elector Frederick himself, and—*ending* does not seem the most fitting word—let us say, including the chimney-sweeper, Klem, who "bound himself in writing to sweep the chimneys of the Orphanage without charge as long as he lived." The Elector gave building material for the Orphan-house, made two donations of a thousand thalers each, and, as King of Prussia, from the year 1700 conferred privileges on both the Orphanage and Pädagogium.

Far-reaching as these various channels of activity proved to be, their source was a quite humble piece of pastoral work which Francke discharged as part of his duties in his parish of Glaucha. His occupancy of a parsonage brought him into much closer relations with the poor, and a strong and abiding concern for their condition was the consequence. The evil practice of more or less authorised mendicancy then common throughout Europe was established in Halle, where the destitute and those who professed to be destitute had their recognised days and rounds, begging from door to door. They visited Francke's home every Thursday and were relieved as a matter of course, with results not satisfactory to the pastor. Early in 1694 he determined to give them instruction as well as bread ("food for the soul as well as for the body," he told them), and, bringing them all into the house, placed the young on one side and the adults on the other. Before distributing the customary dole he spent a quarter of an hour in catechising the younger beggars, the rest simply listening. The enquiry revealed ignorance which troubled him deeply: "so many people like cattle, without any knowledge of God and divine things"; "so many children on account of the poverty of their parents were neither sent to school nor enjoyed any good up-bringing, but grew up in the most shameful ignorance and in every wickedness, so that with increasing years they are good for naught but theft, robbery, and other evil deeds." Casting about for a remedy, his first expedient was to present a sum weekly to those who had children, so that the payment of a school-fee by them might be the more easily compassed. His money was accepted, but the children were not sent to school, or, if they were sent, made but small improvement Then he himself turned beggar in their behalf, and set up a poor-box in the parsonage. The discovery in this box of a single donation worth something less than two pounds of modern English money aroused him to enthusiasm; he tells us that, "in a joyful outburst of belief," he exclaimed, "*This* is a considerable capital, with which one ought to establish something good; *I will begin a poor school.*" He therefore bought school-books and engaged a poor University student to teach the children for two hours daily in return for a weekly payment of six groschen. The not unusual result followed; possessed of their *new* school-books, some of the children failed to reappear in the "school"—four books were recovered out of twenty-seven.

It was clear that some less casual arrangement was needed.

At Easter, 1695, Francke announced that the Poor School would meet in his own house and under his direct supervision, and an immediate improvement followed. More children attended and the attendance of all was more regular. By Whitsuntide it began to be recognised that others beside the poor might profit from the school, and some citizens approached Francke with the request that he would permit their children to attend on payment of a fee. In the summer the pupils numbered more than fifty, and the school-hours were five daily. The elementary school was thus established.

By harvest-time of this same year the school was too big to find quarters in the parsonage, and Francke shortly afterwards rented rooms in two neighbouring houses, at the same time separating the poor children from those who paid fees, giving to each division an instructor who received 16 groschen weekly, with a free lodging and firing. The division of the children was, in effect, the creation of the *Bürger-schule*, the Higher Grade, or Higher Elementary School, the analogue, in part, of one department of the school which, ten years later (1705), de la Salle opened at St Yon in Rouen.

These two schools were not the only creations by Francke in 1695. His experience with the poorest and most neglected children had in many cases been most discouraging; what little could be accomplished in four or five hours a day was rendered nugatory, or even destroyed by home associations. The plan of taking some children entirely away from these associations quickly ripened, and an opportune legacy of small amount determined his action. Early in October he received his first little orphan, and by the close of the year he had nine in his care. This was the beginning of the famous Halle Orphanage, an institution planned originally not for orphans, but rather for neglected children. From the outset it claimed much of Francke's time and thought, and the rapidity of its advance was notable. Its aims appealed to benevolent people, money was soon forthcoming, and the founder was able to buy the houses in which he previously rented rooms for his two "schools," to build around them, and to erect a house in which the orphans were lodged before Whitsuntide, 1696. Then a further division of the schools was made, the orphans being placed under a third instructor; a little later all three schools (poor school, Bürger-schule, or fee-paying school, and orphan school) were subdivided on the basis of sex. The old difficulty remained in respect of the beggar children. Says Francke, "Some, and those the majority, would rather go without an alms than stay half-a-day in school." He continued the systematic relief of the adult poor; his rules for dispensing alms in his own parish were subsequently adopted by the city of Halle itself.

Busy as Francke was in 1695 with the children of the poor, he was also occupying himself with those at the opposite end of the social scale. At Trinity-tide in that year he took charge of the son of a wealthy widow of noble rank, in order to superintend his education amongst a few boys of the same standing. Within twelve months these pupils increased in number, and lodgings were found for them in adjacent houses. The boys formed a distinct school, taught in several classes and known as the Pädagogium.

Yet one more institution was to see the light in the summer of 1695, namely, the Teachers' Seminary (*Seminarium Praeceptorum*). A sum of about £200 of modern money having been entrusted to him for the good of poor students especially, he distributed small sums weekly to about twenty undergraduates, who, in return, taught in one or other of his establishments. In the following year he altered his practice, and, in lieu of money, opened a "free table," at which an increasing number of students, beginning with twenty-four, met daily. For the most part, these young men were theological students whose daily spell of two hours' teaching was supervised and criticised by the Inspectors, as the heads of the different schools were named. When Francke became Professor of

Divinity, he made systematic practice in the catechising of children a part of the ordinary mode of training the future pastors.

The link thus forged between the University and the schools was not the only mode of juncture between the several parts of Francke's scheme. In 1697 he supplemented his school for wealthy boys, the Pädagogium, by opening a class for poor boys whose parents desired that they might be "bred to learning," and these aspirants to the University were joined by promising lads selected from the Poor School and the Orphanage. Within two years the one class became three, and these were the nucleus of the later "Latin School," so called in contradistinction to the schools for the poor and for citizens' children paying fees, in neither of which was Latin taught. As these secondary schools developed, teachers were trained for service in them by the *Seminarium Selectum Praeceptorum*, instituted in 1707.

So early as 1698 Francke was dreaming of a boarding-school where wealthy girls might add to the modest school-lore and many "accomplishments" which then constituted their round of instruction, "good direction" (if they desired it) in the study of Hebrew and Greek. But that part of his plan remained a dream; *bas bleu* is slow in gaining German approval. The education of such girls began in 1698; its more formal inclusion in the Halle system dated from 1709, but the curriculum contained no novelties, religion, French and arithmetic blending with "the necessary feminine occupations."

The success which marked the Halle institutions from the first was not a source of gratification to every inhabitant of the city, and the religious tenets associated with their founder and his friends ensured them much opposition. The consequent controversies may now be left to slumber in peace; but they cost Francke many troubled hours and no little labour with his pen. The stock charges, as they may be called, of sectarian bitterness are too familiar to require repetition : they were levelled against the Halle Pietists, and required reply. As is usually the case in such things, neither side monopolised the wisdom, charity, humility, or frankness discoverable in the quarrel.

In spite of these attacks, the institutions prospered and steadily increased in magnitude right up to the time of Francke's death, after a long illness, in 1727. At that date there were in the Orphanage 100 boys and 34 girls : the Poor School and the Higher Elementary School (Bürger-schule) numbered 1725 pupils of both sexes; there were 400 boys in the Latin School and 82 in the Pädagogium. In all, 2341 children were being educated by 167 masters and 8 mistresses, not counting the inspectors and overseers, both men and women, who exercised the functions of head-teacher. At the Free Table, 255 students were maintained, and a large number of children received mid-day and evening meals gratuitously.

Francke's only regular treatise on education was issued from the Orphanage press at Halle in 1702, under the title : "*Short and Simple Instruction* how Children are to be guided to true Piety and Christian Wisdom : formerly drawn up for Christian tutors [Informatores], and now by desire printed." The title very well indicates the nature of the book, filled for the most part with directions aimed at religious training ; though such directions do not exclude all others, their pre-dominance is significant of the meaning of the educational movements which closed the seventeenth century at home and abroad. To fail to perceive their distinct religious trend is to miss their meaning and place in the larger life of their time.

In Francke's opinion, the supreme end of education, with which no secondary purpose could be suffered to interfere, was nothing else than the glory of God, to be realised in the heart and conscience of the individual believer. The success, or otherwise, which followed the training, or attempt to train a child must depend on God's grace alone: but the educator might co-operate. The first condition of success (divine grace apart) was that the educator himself "stand fast in the Faith, and be himself one of the Awakened." Right belief Francke took to be a necessary factor of the spiritual condition in which it was desired that the pupil should find himself; and to that end much time and trouble were given to Biblical instruction in all the Pietist schools.

Such general pedagogic interest as the little treatise possesses lies in the advice given on training children to attend, to observe, to reason out cause and effect; the tutor is also directed to make a study of each pupil as an individual. All this is put with the acuteness of one who knows his subject at first hand; but the remarks are not more than ordinarily helpful.

Judged by bulk alone, Francke's most considerable pedagogical writings are the series of Regulations and other memoranda which he drew up for the daily management of the schools. From these pages may be learned the special purposes of the different institutions, the subjects and method of instruction, the character of the government, and the hundred and one things which belong to the business of school-keeping, all set out with an exactness befitting official documents, and with a completeness which helps one to understand how much ot the success a   Halle was attained.

At the base of the system were the slightly varying schools, or classes, known as Poor Schools, Free-Schools, etc., which, while separated on the ground of sex, or of social condition, really formed parts of one whole, the German, Vernacular, or Element ry School. Their curriculum was as follows: First, and first by a long interval, came religion, to be followed by reading and writing: the first occupied, in one shape or another, more than half of the seven hours which made up the day, and most of the remaining time was given to the other two. During the course of a week, arithmetic was taught for four hours to those only who could read, and two hours were spent in vocal music. More or less casually, and as opportunity offered in school or out, instruction was given in the knowledge of common things.

"The chief object in view," said Francke, "is that the children may be instructed above all things in the vital knowledge of God and Christ, and be initiated into the principles of true religion." It was, therefore, thought requisite to spend four hours daily in lessons and exercises of a directly religious kind. When in later years Pietism had lost much of its living power and Francke's generation was succeeded by mere formalists, this injudicious arrangement was one cause of the failure of the average German school as a place of popular education. Instead of schools, they became inefficient Catechism classes and so remained till the close of the eighteenth century.

Bible-reading, Catechism, prayer, participation in public worship and the use of pious exercises necessarily made the staple of this instruction. While there was much learning by heart, "children were not to be permitted," said Francke, "to learn to prattle words without understanding them, by which they are little or rather nothing profited." What was learned by rote was to be understood and its application to life per ceived: and he thought the method of "simple question and answer" the best for these purposes.

Francke's directions respecting lessons in reading and writing reflect the common practice of the time as described in Locke's *Thoughts*. The reading-books are Luther's Catechism and the New Testament: tracing is recommended in the early writing exercises. Arithmetic was begun after the children could read, but reading and writing went together. It is characteristic of Francke's conception of instruction, that he directed that the children should be taught to *apply* their ability with the pen, or in summing, to everyday life. Thus they learned not only to write "compositions" in general, but also formal letters, receipts and bonds; and their sums were to involve calculations in thalers, gulden, pounds, hundred-weights, etc., for the practical reason that "children should see the *use* of arithmetic." The course in the latter subject was intended to make the pupils expert in the "Four Rules" and the rule of three, and, at least, to give them a true conception of the nature of a fraction: the method was "always to begin with examples, and not with the rules as they stand in the book." Both boys and girls learned to sing by note that choral church-music for which Germany has so long been famous.

These five subjects (religion, the three R's and singing) made up the formal programme: occasional instruction was also given on the rudimentary principles of astronomy, physics and geography, together with a little history: in short, much the same subjects as are included in the *Realien, Naturkunde*, and so forth, of the German primary school of the present. Such instruction was largely acquired by way of the reading-book and the teacher's comments thereon: from time to time walks in the open country afforded opportunities for "nature-study," especially of the local plants which the children gathered for the service of Francke's dispensary. The children in the Orphanage learned knitting, the girls adding spinning and needlework, and both sexes, of course, performed house-work.

The government of these elementary schools was milder and more humane than that of most schools at the time; but it was severe, nevertheless. The hours were from 7 to 11, and 2 to 5, in the summer, and in winter two hours less each day—the hours, that is, which are common in Germany and Switzerland to-day. But Francke's pupils had no "pause" of ten to fifteen minutes between the lessons, no holidays, no "afternoons off"; games and music other than church-music were contemned as "mischievous trifling." The teachers were bidden to note the characters and progress of individual scholars, and to keep a record of their observations; and the whole body of scholars was examined as to its intellectual achievements once a quarter, the Easter and Michaelmas functions being public.

In these schools Francke had more nearly realised Luther's project of a Folk's School than had Luther himself, or the men who followed him. The advisability and the possibility of popular education, and the means by which it might be achieved had been demonstrated within the dominions of the strongest ruler in North Germany, a sovereign who desired to spread some at least of the benefits of enlightenment amongst his people. The lesson was well learned; and, though it was in later days not always applied in the wisest manner, it was never quite forgotten. The elementary schools of Halle became a pattern for Prussia first, and afterwards for North Germany in general; and the mark which the Pietists left in the North German schools remained visible when the nineteenth century was well advanced.

In the Pädagogium Francke gave concrete existence to an institution which combined some of the features of Milton's ideal Academy with those of the actual *Ritterakademien* then being founded in different parts of Germany. Boys entered at the age of nine, able at least to read the mother-tongue; those who followed the entire course passed the last year in the *Classis Selecta*, whence they passed direct to the University. The chief objects of attention were religion and Latin; next in importance were Greek, Hebrew, French, and the mother-tongue. After these came certain matters of study, or perhaps one should say, of interest, which were characteristic of secondary instruction as conceived by Francke; these were classified in two groups, "elementary knowledge" (*Disciplinae litterariae*) and the "recreational practices" (the *Rekreationsübungen*).

As in the Elementary Schools, religious instruction occupied the place of honour in the secondary school course. Apart from its recognised place in the time-table, it became in effect the "core" of the curriculum, about which other studies grouped themselves, and in which was their common bond. Thus, Greek and Hebrew were chiefly regarded as instruments of Biblical exegesis, the New Testament in French was one of the text-books for the study of that language, Latin rhetorical compositions frequently treated Biblical subjects, and Biblical weights, measures, and money appeared in the scholars' arithmetical examples.

The aim of instruction in Latin was to enable pupils to speak and write the language with facility, while in Greek it sufficed if they could read the New Testament, or a Greek author, in the original. But the authors read included so many Biblical and exegetic books and minor classics dealing with Morals, that not much time could have been found for literature pure and simple. As a matter of fact, the Pietists shared the prejudice expressed by Comenius and nourished by many educational innovators of the seventeenth century, the prejudice which would see in the classical literature little beside the utterances of sin-darkened pagans. Their preoccupation with religious topics and the subordination of the use of Latin to these, were passed on by the Pietists to the secondary schools of Protestant Germany at large, where they remained to blight the pursuit of literature, till the renaissance of classical study in Germany began at the end of the eighteenth century. One service which Francke performed to the advantage of the German schoolboy was to give him a Latin grammar, not in Latin, but in the mother-tongue, a sensible reform effected at an earlier date both in England and in France. But the official language, as it might be called, of tutors and pupils was Latin.

In the secondary school Francke reinforced the claim advanced by the Academies[1] on behalf of "modern studies." The boys of the Pädagogium learned to speak and write not

[1] See Chapter X.

only the courtly and official French, but also their native German, in whose study they were expected to be assiduous throughout their school career. "German style," or rhetoric was an honoured study; orations, letters and poems were the principal material, and the lads of *Selecta* were trained to turn Latin poetry into German verse.

The modernisation of the German higher schools began in the last quarter of the seventeenth century, though advance was very slow at first; Francke's schools, if they did not absolutely lead, took a foremost place in establishing the changes in curriculum then initiated. The introduction of modern studies was tentative, their intention was undisguisedly utilitarian, and instruction in them was casual and superficial; but they became the means of breaking down the monopoly enjoyed by classical studies, and of admitting to the school-room some of that knowledge which had been accumulated during the preceding century and a half. Francke deemed the older culture defective, so far as the scholars of the Pädagogium were concerned, in that it left its votaries ignorant of the advance in knowledge, and destitute of certain forms of skill which it had become the fashion for gentlemen to acquire. He hoped to avoid these defects by two sets of school studies and exercises, which he called by the not very illuminating names, *Disciplinae litterariae*, and *Rekreationsübungen*—which may be very freely rendered as "elementary knowledge" and "re-creative exercises" respectively.

The forms of "elementary knowledge" were six: calligraphy, geography, history, arithmetic, "mathesis," and German oratory. No scholar was allowed to take up more than one at the same time; he spent one hour daily at his particular "discipline," and completed its course in six months, then passed to the next, and completed the whole in three years. Clearly, the treatment was superficial, and the danger, in some subjects at least, of "dry bones" must have been imminent. For example, history meant universal history, beginning with Adam and ending in seventeenth-century Germany; half of the course was characteristically given up to Biblical history. It is significant that a picture-book played a great part in the lessons, as Locke preached and many French teachers then practised. "Mathesis" included geometry, and some trigonometry and algebra; the practical application of these in surveying and in kindred forms of usefulness was most insisted on.

As the name implies, the recreative exercises were taken during the free time, an hour or two daily, which was enjoyed by the boarders. Not every subject was followed by every pupil; but all the boys were compelled to engage, under a master's direction or oversight, in one or other of the exercises. In suitable weather these included excursions into the open country for the study of animals, herbs, plants, and minerals, or into the city to visit the workshops of artists and other craftsmen. Sometimes the boys studied astronomy or anatomy, two subjects of great interest to educated men of the time, the latter more especially since the investigations of Harvey and Descartes, sometimes *materia medica*, the management of estates, the cultivation of gardens and vineyards and the brewing of beer were subjects for consideration. Of the exercises which filled the time in-doors there were music and such forms of manual skill as drawing, turning, modelling in cardboard and the polishing of lenses. In short, these recreative exercises were fitted to discover and foster the tastes and talents of the future dilettante, society man, or landlord of a great estate.

The curriculum of the Latin School repeated that of the Pädagogium, with the exception of French, and some of the manual arts and "recreations"; the difference in rank and future career of the pupils explains these omissions. The annual tuition-fee was six thalers, which needy pupils were excused in whole, or part, and the "very poor" also shared the indigent university-students' places at the mid-day "free table."

A well-knit correlation between school studies and daily life had been one of the fundamentals of Comenius's pedagogy; Francke, pushing this idea still further, was prepared to give instruction avowedly " utilitarian." That word of suspicion, if not of reproach, may be applied to all his schools in the sense that their curricula were frankly addressed to the future avocations of the pupils. Amongst the many projects which occupied him in 1698 was one of a school where boys who had previously been taught Latin, French, writing, arithmetic, and economy (in the original sense of the word) should not continue formal studies, but be prepared to earn their living as officials about the courts of great people, as clerks, in commerce, or as managers of landed estates. So far as Francke was concerned the project came to nothing, but amongst the teachers of the Pädagogium was a certain J. J., Hecker (1707–1768) who, as a Berlin pastor, in later days introduced into the Prussian capital some of the reforms in education which he had himself learned at Halle. He began by improving the elementary school of his parish and followed this up, in 1747, by establishing the first actual *Realschule*, or, as he called it, the "Economic-Mathematical Real School," which gave instruction in religion, German, Latin, French, writing, arithmetic, drawing, history, geography, good manners, and the most necessary parts of geometry, mechanics, and architecture. To these were added special courses preparatory to different callings.

Though Hecker's was the first *Realschule*, the *name* goes back to 1708, when Christopher Semler, a brother clergyman of Francke's in Halle, opened a "Mathematical and Mechanical Realschule," the scene of some few courses which exhibited and explained sundry instruments, models, machines and implements, as well as natural objects of many kinds[1]. Semler purposed by these courses "to accustom youth to a true Reality," as he said. "Here are no empty *speculationes*, nor useless subtilties, but *ipsissimae res, Dei opera*, and machines

[1] Semler was probably influenced by the teaching of Erhard Weigel, professor of mathematics in Jena.

of daily use[1]." Semler's institute was preceded by the publication of a tract (*Nützliche Vorschläge von Aufrichtung einer mathematischen Handwerkschule bey der Stadt Halle*, 1705), which proposed a school on much the same lines as Hecker's later foundation.

The Halle Pädagogium and Latin School became the model secondary schools for Prussia, and through that aspiring kingdom, for Protestant Germany at large. The force of circumstances made the Institutions at Halle a city set upon a hill, and they extended Francke's ideas also by means of the teachers whom they trained, and the school-books which they published. These forces combined with the now well-established ideals of the Academies to modernise the German secondary school curriculum. Francke's utilitarianism made him a willing advocate of the introduction into the school-room of much of that scientific knowledge which the seventeenth century had acquired; but the alterations which, in effect, he made incumbent upon secondary schools were not all pure gain   The Bible excepted, the Pietists were as arrant obscurantists with reference to literature as the old-fashioned educators of the early sixteenth century had been; indeed, not even that exception can be readily granted, as the conception of the Bible as literature would most probably have shocked them.

For Pietism agreed with Comenius' that the paganism of Greek and Roman literature made both dangerous instruments of Christian education; that the classical writers were "heathen" outweighed most of such merits as Pietism was ready to concede. For the learning of the ancients Pietism had but scant respect, for their distinctive culture none at all. Francke and his friends might agree with Aristotle that the formation of the good citizen is one great end of education, though their assent would scarcely be very cordial; they would deny absolutely Aristotle's further proposition, that a second great object of

[1] For Hecker and Semler, see Paulsen, *Geschichte des gelehrten Unterrichts*, vol. ii. pp. 63–4.

education is to teach the good citizen how to enjoy leisure nobly.

In due time the aloofness of the Pietist from the "worldly" folk around him passed into blank sectarian formalism; when that day arrived, it seemed that the educational impulse derived from Francke was exhausted. The Latin grammar and Luther's Catechism, it has been said, thereupon became the pillars of the German secondary school, where they remained the major objects of concern till the close of the eighteenth century.

The Halle Institutions have passed through many vicissitudes since their founder's death; they are still carrying on their educational work, though with a diminished number of pupils, and in schools organised otherwise than were the original establishments. They now form part of the Prussian system, but their individuality has not suffered absorption; and it is pleasant to know that these monuments of an educational pioneer are still capable of undertaking pioneer work. So recently as 1890 there was opened a new Higher Elementary School for boys (*Bürger-knaben-schule*), and the plan adopted at Halle during the past 25 years for the training of secondary school teachers has had considerable influence upon the Prussian practice directed to the same end. Since the Prussian *Seminar* is winning acceptance in most German states, the influence of Halle in this particular is not confined to the Prussian kingdom.

CHAPTER XIV.

CONCLUSION.

IF it were the purpose of this book to tell the story of seventeenth-century education as a whole, French thinkers and teachers would justly require much more space than has been accorded to them. Indeed, there are standpoints in education (of which practice is not the least conspicuous) from which that period may be regarded as peculiarly French. The "pedagogy of good sense" which has been claimed for France as distinctively her own, was fully enunciated in its essentials in the pages of Montaigne, whence the reformers who instituted the various types of the *Académie* might draw direction for their aims and justification for their innovations. While the pedants of his time were trying to resuscitate the mere shell of Roman and Greek civilisation, Montaigne had made the spirit of the ancient world at home in a modern body; to use his own simile, the bee had passed from flower to flower, taking its profit from each, and in the end elaborating a honey which was its own, however diverse the sources of supply. The ancient spirit, thus modernised and Gallicised, was a potent force in French education from the seventeenth century onwards.

The free criticism of use and wont in all departments of human activity, which came so readily to the New Philosophy, had its French exponent in one who was not a New Philosopher of Bacon's school. It is a circumstance neither casual nor indifferent that Descartes's *Discourse on Method* (1637) first appeared in its author's native language and not in Latin, the customary tongue of philosophy and higher learning, which Francis Bacon preferred to employ on similar occasions. Descartes's choice marks a realisation of the fact that one, at least, of the vernacular languages of Europe had reached a relatively fixed and ordered structure, fitting it to be the channel of communication for men debating questions of the greatest human interest. The fact itself becomes conscious in French education, which henceforth unites a keen appreciation of the mother-tongue as an educational instrument with a strong conviction that education without Literature is impossible.

But the new spirit of course met with opposition. Their footing in France at last made good, and favoured by the greatly increased power which accrued to the French Crown in the sixteen-hundreds, the Jesuits constituted themselves the guardians of established ideas and champions of the principle of Authority against all comers. Institutions of a contrary tendency were marked for attack and destroyed when opportunity served. In pursuance of this policy of aggression, the Jesuit society was especially obnoxious to two bodies of French teachers whose labours have conferred distinction upon the educational history of their country. Both were infected, as a Jesuit might have said, with Cartesianism; for the earlier toleration of the philosophy of the sometime Jesuit pupil at La Flèche failed, as the Jesuits perceived how inimical to their own pretensions and the principles for which they themselves stood would be the adoption of that philosophy outside circles strictly academical.

Of the two bodies of teachers in question, the elder, the Oratorians, had engaged in general educational work rather as a consequence of calls from without than in obedience to the wish of their founder, the saintly de Bérulle, whose earliest intention was to found a seminary for priests and nothing more. But the insistence of Louis XIII made them the educators of many of the youthful nobility, and in that office they were amongst the first to give a wider and more scholastic scope to the *Académie*, originally but a school of horsemanship and knightly accomplishments. Their *Académie Royale* (a title conferred by Louis XIII) of Juilly became a model, exhibiting the possibilities of a school curriculum which added such modern studies as geography, *French* history and living languages to Latin and Greek, while giving attention also to studies of peculiar interest to the future statesman, diplomatist, and courtier.

For the first half-century of their community's existence the Oratorians were Cartesian; then the persistent attacks of the Jesuits were successful, the Oratory "purged itself," and its *rôle* of educational innovator suffered eclipse. The Society of Jesus did not succeed in the same way in its struggle with the Gentlemen of Port-Royal. The deep agitation which gathered about the Jansenist controversy is an indication that. Port-Royal touched the roots of the national life, and there is evidence pointing to the same conclusion in the names of the influential men and women who were associated as members, penitents, or sympathisers with the Solitaries, in the bitterness of the quarrel between Jesuit and Port-Royalist, in its violent episodes and melodramatic close at Port-Royal des Champs, wherein the Jesuits were but the seeming victors. It is, therefore, unnecessary to say that the "Little Schools" of Port-Royal were influential outside their own walls.

The whole bent of the educational practice of the Gentlemen was determined not by the cosmopolitan New Philosophy but by the national Cartesianism; there is little, if any, trace in their school courses of an influence springing from the contemporary progress in natural science. With them science meant, especially, mathematics, the study which Descartes had so very materially advanced. The effect of the same great Frenchman's ideas is seen in Arnauld's *New Elements of Geometry* (1660–7) and in the famous Port-Royal *Logic* (1662), the application of Descartes's *Discourse* by Arnauld and Nicole.

Port-Royal education, as an intellectual discipline, was humanist; indeed, when compared with the over-attention paid by cotemporary schools to the *minutiae* of scholarship, it might be called a genuine humanism, bent on steeping the minds of its pupils in the matter of the ancient literatures rather than elaborating their formal rhetorical side, not focussing attention on the grammatical structure, the means, to the exclusion of the literary content, the end. " Reason, not Routine " is the device happily chosen by one of themselves[1] to describe the leading principle of Port-Royal instruction ; men of such a temper were prepared to recognise that true human culture is to be acquired through all great literature, modern as well as ancient. Above all, French received its due meed of honour at their hands as the natural instrument of education for French boys. Long before de la Salle, the Solitaries began the teaching of reading, not in Latin but in the mother-tongue. Their pupils learned to write French prose as carefully as others were taught to make Latin versions. Their Latin grammar-book was in *French*, displacing the long-established Latin book of Despautère; they read French translations of classic authors freely, and " history " at Port-Royal included the history of France. The distinct literary bias and the sense of the value of the mother-tongue which have been prominent marks of French secondary education down to the present day have been greatly due to the example and, perhaps, even more to the popular text-books of the Gentlemen of Port-Royal.

The men whose work has been surveyed in the preceding chapters debated, in many cases to a satisfactory conclusion, the leading questions of educational administration, of method

[1] Guyot, *Preface to Cicero's Letters*, 1668.

and curriculum; subsequent scholastic history has been very
largely the filling in of the outlines which they drew.

"The education of a man's own children is not wholly to
be committed or trusted to himself," and, therefore, free schools
must be erected and properly maintained. The magistrates
are to "animadvert and punish him that sends not his sons
within the ninth year of their age to some one of the schools
of a tribe, there to be kept and taught, if he be able at his own
charges; and if he be not able, gratis, till they arrive at the
age of fifteen years." These are extracts from the statutes of
the Commonwealth, not of England, but of *Oceana*, James
Harrington's ideal State of 1656. But the spirit of these
statutes was already animating men of English blood and birth.
In 1650 the General Court of Connecticut decided that every
settlement of fifty families should maintain a schoolmaster to
teach reading and writing, and that every town numbering one
hundred families, or householders "shall sett up a Grammer
Schoole, the masters thereof being able to instruct youths so
farr as they may be fitted for the University." Parents or
guardians who neglected the education of their charges were
liable to be deprived of the children, whom the magistrates
were authorised to place with masters who would ensure their
orderly bringing up (De Montmorency, *op. cit.* pp. 137 ff.).
Massachusetts was earlier still in dealing with educational
administration; the institution of the first "Latin School"
within the present United States of America was decided upon
at Boston in 1635, and six years later the Salem town's-meeting
debated the opening of a Common School.

The conception of a system of schools, passing upwards in
orderly gradation from the teaching of the rudiments to the
studies of the University, set forth in the *Great Didactic* and
repeated by thinkers through the century, was realised before
the century closed in the Halle Institutions. A widely extended
organisation of schools for the people was a fundamental
conception with Comenius, and, as the century advanced,

the idea was repeated with ever-growing conviction. It was actually realised, though on a small scale, as one of the reforms by which Ernest the Pious benefited his people; it was firmly grounded by de la Salle, Francke, and the founders of the Society for Promoting Christian Knowledge.

The establishment of the elementary school with its three-fold course of reading in the vernacular, writing and summing, gave a prominence to those arts which they had never enjoyed in schools of earlier origin. The utility of instruction in the three R's was much appreciated outside school-room walls, and when the popular school course was rooted, schools of all grades found it necessary to pay those studies some attention. In so far as this was done the elementary school had a share in modernising the studies of the schools above it, though the change did not in all quarters come about speedily. An illuminating anecdote told by Lord John Russell, who was a boy of eleven in the Under School at Westminster in 1803, shows this very well. He says: " We were not taught writing or arithmetic, and we used to go on the half-holidays to a writing-master in Great Dean's Yard to learn these necessary arts. I remember employing one of the hours intended for this purpose in going to see a fight between young Belcher and another famous pugilist....So little, however, had I learned of arithmetic, that when my father gave me two sums to add together, one of which contained a farthing, and the other a halfpenny, I was obliged to ask him what those odd signs meant." (Sir Spencer Walpole's *Life of Lord John Russell*, vol. i. p. 10.)

The suggestions of the innovators were nowhere more fruitful than in the province of Method, and this, less on account of particular rules and prescriptions than by reason of general outlook. Indeed, as their psychology shows, the innovators were scarcely able to deal successfully with parti-cular points of method save in an empirical manner. Their general position was, that method in the class-room must be

determined, first and last, by the mental capacity of the children
to be instructed. As matter of enunciation, this proposition
has probably never been denied; as matter of fact, school
room practice has frequently tried to ignore it, as the pages
of Brinsley and Hoole show—not to cite more modern instances. For example, the burden of the seventeenth-century
innovators is, Matter before Form; but the natural man turned
schoolmaster seems prone to the converse. Then he taught
grammar before speech; at a later day he taught rudimentary
science from books. The adoption of the innovators' point
of view in this respect, and of its logical consequences, means
the acceptance of what is best in later ideas about school
method, from Rousseau to Herbart.

Francis Bacon had urged the philosophers *ipsis consuescere
rebus*, to make themselves familiar at first hand with that about
which they philosophised. Transferring the lesson to the class-
room, Comenius called on the schoolmaster to bring the
studies of children into the closest possible connection with
their ordinary, everyday life and concerns. This was the idea
underlying the *Janua Linguarum* and the *Orbis Pictus*: but
it was from the first an essential part of his theory of instruction.
It was impossible to give it effect and at the same time
maintain the kind of curriculum and teaching which was
familiar to Charles Hoole and other practitioners of the "good
old waie"; room must be found for matters in which the
seventeenth-century man was deeply interested, but concerning
which the ancient studies were either silent or spoke in the
most general terms. The scholar, Milton, and the utilitarian,
Petty, agree in regarding an enlargement of the traditional
school course as vital; the French "Académies" were the first
considerable attempt to realise the newer type of instruction,
and from them the reform passed to the German *Ritterakademien* and thence to German secondary education in general.
Francke employed the modern curriculum as fully as it could
then be employed; traces of it are not absent even from the

more elementary instruction with which de la Salle occupied himself.

The acquisition of a fund of positive knowledge closely related to the interests and needs of daily life meant, first of all, due attention to the mother-tongue as one instrument through which that knowledge might be acquired. It was the perception of this fact which suggested one of the few living ideas due to Ratke, and from his day onwards it was a mark of the seventeenth-century reformer in education that he claimed an important place in the school-room for the scholars' native language. No men equalled the Solitaries of Port-Royal in the success with which they taught the mother-tongue, while most of the innovators fell immeasurably short of them in recognising the legitimate place of letters in all education.

But language-teaching alone was incapable of working all the change in the school-room which the innovators desired to see; from Comenius onwards all ask for the inclusion amongst educative studies of some branch or branches of science, of mathematics and of its applications to the work of the soldier, engineer, and architect. The practical administrators like Francke, de la Salle, and the forgotten men who founded the Académies included such studies in their programmes; once embodied in the actual practice of schools and colleges, they remained to contest with varying fortune the exclusive claims of Latin and Greek.

The advance in knowledge first made men dissatisfied with the narrow range of a curriculum which, in effect, confined most schoolboys to studies preparatory to literature, and secondly helped to convince them of the inelasticity of that curriculum and its consequent failure to appeal to all minds. The desire to provide a course of a wider range and capable of this more general appeal, combined with the characteristic trust in the power of method, encouraged a certain superficiality in this part of the innovators' designs. Thus, Milton's practice as described by Phillips would appear to have sacrificed not a little of that thoroughness which has always been one of the chief merits of a scholarly education. Locke betrays evidence of the same defect, consistently enough with his usual attitude towards intellectual discipline during boyhood. His pronouncements on "Natural Philosophy" as a factor in education are instructive on this head; he thinks enough is done if the young gentleman gains an acquaintance with "the terms and ways of talking" of the different "sects" of natural philosophers, these being things which it is "necessary for a gentleman in this learned age to look into...*to fit himself for conversation*" (*Thoughts*, sec. 193). Natural Philosophy (Science, as we should now say) is regarded by Locke, as it was by the Universities and other official educational authorities of his time, as a mere appendix to philosophy, an opinion which reminds us at once of the inchoate condition of scientific study and of the failure of the authorities to recognise, or at least to appreciate, the value of what had been commenced.

Notwithstanding the restricted range of the school course, it was felt that the proportion of scholars who successfully achieved it was very small. The innovators ascribed this failure to the besetting sin of the school-room, which was the persistent teaching of the formal before the material. Grammatical rules, as forms of language, shared with all general propositions the nature of a summary; therefore, the argument ran, begin with the grammatical summary and you have a short cut to the knowledge of Latin. The innovators, amongst whom the originating minds in this connection were Montaigne, Ratke, and Comenius, proposed to begin the study of Latin either conversationally, that is, as actual talk (Montaigne), or as a mother teaches her child the vernacular, associating word and thing (Comenius), or by the conning of authors and of translations (Ratke). By making formal grammar a later study, by employing induction as the instrument of mastery over the forms of speech, and by the association of foreign word, not with native word, but directly with the object of thought, these seventeenth-century teachers anticipated in principle those reforms in language teaching now so widely known as the Direct Method, or (regardless of the irony of things) the *New* Method.

The most conspicuous failure of the reformers was their inability to see the humanising power which resides in sound literature. A certain ascetic severity and indifference *on principle* to the claims of all beauty other than that of the religious life, is, in part, the explanation. But an intensity of religious conviction leading to a narrowness of sympathy was also responsible. In the eyes of the bigot, the loftiest of the ancient writers was but a sin-darkened heathen, whose utterances were often soul-destroying and always suspect. This temper had no more sincere and thoroughgoing exemplar than St Cyran, the virtual founder of the Port-Royal community of men. Going one day into a room where the boys were reading Virgil, he pointed to a picture of the master and said, " Do you see this poet? He is damned, yes, damned; he passed judgment on himself in the very writing of these beautiful lines, because he wrote them in his vanity to please the men of this world; but you, for your part, must sanctify yourselves in learning these verses, since you must learn them to please God, and to enable you to serve the Church." That point of view could not be maintained in a body which included a Pascal, a Lemaître, and an Arnauld.

In pondering the still debated question of Classical Literature *v.* Modern Studies, it is helpful to remember that two distinguishable ideals have historically directed the mode of employing Latin and Greek as educational instruments. On the one hand are the earlier Italian humanists and their intellectual child, Erasmus ; on the other, the later sixteenth-century humanists and schoolmasters. The first regarded antiquity as a source of light and guidance, whose spirit must be assimilated by the modern world, and in that way made to serve the very different conditions, political, religious, social,

which had come into being since the older civilisation had
passed away. These men were captivated by the essentials
of the antique life, its urbanity, rationality, intellectual freedom,
sympathy, and breadth; they felt the light, colour, and grace
with which the ancient literatures made such things live again
Greek and Latin letters were not only treasure-houses of knowledge; they were also the depositaries of "a criticism of life,"
and this gave them their peculiar educational value.

The ancient tongues had no serious competitors in the
vernaculars of the Renaissance in any of these respects.
But there was nothing in the mental attitude of the earlier
humanists necessarily inimical to whatever advance in knowledge might be achieved; and their training in literary criticism was bound, in the long run, not merely to compel them
to recognise modern vernacular literature so soon as it existed,
but even to hasten its advent.

In short, the true humanist was not in the nature of things
compelled to be a foe to modern studies. Basing himself on
the principle that literature is a criticism of life, his own claim
to share in the process of education is undeniable; no amount
of knowledge respecting what is called "material nature" can
compensate for ignorance respecting those various human
relationships into which all must enter and for which literature
is eminently fitted to be a propaedeutic. The case stands so,
whatever intelligible function be assigned to education; it is
very obviously so, where that function is conceived of as,
above all, moral.

But it would seem that while literary culture is an indispensable element in a truly human education, room must also
be found for other disciplines addressed more especially to the
ascertainment of truth as it appears in non-human "Nature,"
and expressly intended to help the learner to a mastery of his
physical surroundings. Indeed, the conception of a profitable
instruction to be gained through the ordinary occasions of
daily life amidst physical forces as well as in the face of human

volitions is, at bottom, not without kinship to humanism itself, while the advantages of literary culture cannot at all times and in all places be arrogated to one language, however great.

The formation of a curriculum, therefore, becomes a nice adjustment between the legitimate claims of Letters, Science and certain forms of skill affecting the graces and utilities of life, the adjustment itself being determined by the particular ends to be secured in any one case, or class of cases. The seventeenth-century innovators grounded their pleas for modern studies on a variety of propositions; their strongest grounds of objection to the old curriculum, with its monopoly of teaching often only formally literary, were that it failed to appreciate the deep differences between their own time and the ancient world, and by its exclusiveness outraged that very rationality which was the life-blood of humanism.

The declension from the ideals of the earlier devotees of literary culture to those of the later had been the work of the pedants and their allies in the school-rooms, as we may learn from Hoole's account of the "good old waie." Where the humanist asked for literature, the pedant gave rhetoric or grammar, form for matter. It is, of course, true that there could be no appreciation of a literature precedent to knowledge of the language in which it was written, and the keener the eye, or ear, for nicety of form, the greater the appreciation of the literature. But the vice of the school has ever been to over-value form of all kinds, to press it prematurely on pupils, partly in the hope that the form would be clothed later, partly to avoid "losing time" in the present. Thus, ends disappear in means, Grammar and the like studies usurp the place of Letters, even while the value of Letters is proclaimed to justify the usurpation.

As a study of what is peculiarly the work of the human mind, Grammar may claim to be something more than a means, and the claim may be granted, with a reservation in the school-boy's case. It is not a study which appeals to very many boys; certainly, its appeal is not universal. The innovators saw the same defect in the curriculum as a whole; they refused to believe that only dunces failed to respond to a literary culture confined to Greek or Latin. The present chapter began with a paragraph or two concerning French pedagogy of the period with which this book deals; it may fittingly end with an allusion to certain French administrative changes of the other day, since these are intended to secure that variety and elasticity without which a curriculum fails to make a general appeal.

The *Plan d'Études* of 1902 arranges the seven years' secondary school course in two divisions, of four years and three years respectively. The first division is subdivided into two branches. Of these the first, as to curriculum, is mainly, but not exclusively classical, Latin being obligatory, Greek optional; the second branch is chiefly, though not entirely scientific, Latin, however, forming no part of it. Power is reserved to transfer a pupil from one branch to another, if necessary, and the scheme makes such a transfer possible without any serious break in the continuity of studies. The second division, occupying the last three years of the whole course, permits no such interchange between branch and branch. Of these there are four, designated by the first four letters of the alphabet. The A course is constituted by Latin, Greek, and their ancillary studies; B course contains Latin and Science; C course, Latin and Modern Languages; D course, Science and Modern Languages.

When a nation so long nurtured in the classical tradition as France remodels its programmes in this free-handed fashion, the indication seems to be that the struggle of Classics *v.* Science is drawing to a close. On the lines of the *Plan d'Études* a workable compromise seems feasible between the too great comprehensiveness of the courses devised by the seventeenth-century innovators and the narrowness and inelasticity of the curriculum against which they contended.

PUBLICATIONS REFERRED TO IN
THE TEXT.

This list has been compiled to facilitate reference to the works quoted or referred to at any length in the body of the book. It is not meant to be an exhaustive statement of authorities; such books as the various biographical dictionaries, calendars of State Papers, parliamentary "Journals" and the like "sources" are not included.

An Account of Charity Schools in Great Britain and Ireland, etc. Tenth edition. London. Printed and sold by Joseph Downing, 1713. Also the 12th (1713) and 13th (1714) editions. See WILLIS below.

ALLEN, W. O. B., and MCCLURE, E. *Two Hundred Years: The History of the Society for Promoting Christian Knowledge.* London, 1898.

ANCHORAN, J. A. *Porta linguarum trilinguis reserata: the Gate of Tongues Unlocked.* Second edition. London, 1633. (English version of Comenius's *Janua.*)

Ditto. Edition of 1637 with a vocabulary by W. Saltonstall.

BACON, FRANCIS. *The Physical and Metaphysical Works of Lord Bacon* (sic). Bohn's Scientific Library. London, 1858. Contains translations of the *Novum Organum* and the *De Augmentis Scientiarum.*

BACON, FRANCIS. *The Advancement of Learning. The Works of Francis Bacon*, etc., collected and edited by Spedding, Ellis and Heath. Vol. IV. London, 1857.

BACON, FRANCIS. *New Atlantis.* Spedding's *Works of Francis Bacon*, as above. .Vol. III.

BOURNE, H. R. FOX. *The Life of John Locke.* London, 1876. 2 vols.

BRINSLEY, JOHN. *Ludus Literarius or the Grammar Schoole.* Shewing how to proceede from the first entrance into learning to the highest perfection required in the Grammar Schooles *etc.* London, 1612. E. T. Campagnac, editor. Liverpool, 1917.

CADET, F. *L'Éducation à Port-Royal.* Paris, 1887.

CARRÉ, J. *Les Pédagogues de Port-Royal.* Paris, 1887.

CHURCH, R. W. *Bacon* ("English Men of Letters" Series). London, 1886.

COMENIUS, J. A. *Opera Didactica Omnia*, etc. Amstelod. 1657. (The Amsterdam Folio.)

COMENIUS, J. A. *Janua Linguarum Reserata.* Sixth edition. Translated by Horn and Robotham. 1643. See ANCHORAN above.

COMENIUS, J. A. *Conatuum Comenianorum Praeludia.* Oxford, 1637. Edited by Hartlib.

COMENIUS, J. A. *Pansophiae Prodromus.* London, 1639. Latin preface by Hartlib.

COMENIUS, J. A. *A Reformation of Schooles designed in two excellent treatises*, etc. London, 1642. Translated by Hartlib.

DIRCKS, H. *A Biographical Memoir of Samuel Hartlib.* London, 1865.

DURY, J. *The Reformed School.* Printed by R. D. for Richard Wodnothe at the Star under S. Peter's Church in Corn-hill [*n. d.*]. Introduction by Hartlib.

DURY, J. *The Reformed Librarie Keeper* with a Supplement to the Reformed School subordinate to Colleges in Universities. London, 1650.

DURY, J. *Mr Dury's Exercitation of Schooling* (manuscript), 1646. In Sloane MSS. 649, pp. 52–3.

DURY, J. (with HARTLIB). *A briefe Relation* of that which hath lately been attempted to procure Ecclesiasticall Peace among Protestants. London, 1641.

DURY, J. (with HARTLIB). *The Unchanged Constant and Single-hearted Peacemaker*, etc. London, 1650.
See J. D. below.

GERBIER, B. *A Publique Lecture* On all the Languages, Arts, Sciences, and Noble Exercises, which are taught in Sʳ Balthazar Gerbier's Academy....Printed at London for Robert Ibbitson, dwelling in Smithfield near Hosier Lane. 1650.

GUIBERT, J. *Histoire de S. Jean-Baptiste de la Salle.* Paris, 1901.

HAMEL, C. *Histoire de l'Abbaye et du Collège de Juilly.* Paris, 1868.

HARTLIB, S. *A Description of the famous Kingdom of Macaria*, etc. London, 1641. Fuller quotation from title on p. 91 above.

HARTLIB, S. *London's Charity Inlarged*, Stilling the Orphan's Cry. London, 1650.

HARTLIB, S. *A Continuation of Mr John Amos Comenius's School Endeavours.* Or a Summary Delineation of Dr Cyprian Kinner *Silesian* his Thoughts concerning Education : etc. London, 1648?

HARTLIB, S. *The Reformed Spiritual Husbandman* (with an humble memorandum concerning Chelsy Colledge, etc.). London, 1652.

HARTLIB, S. *A True and Readie Way to learne the Latine Tongue.* Attested by Three Excellently Learned and ap-proved Authors of Three Nations : Eilhardus Lubinus, a German ; Mr Richard Carew, of Anthony in Cornwall ; the French Lord of Montaigne, *etc.* London, 1654. Fuller quotation from title on p. 104 above.
See also COMENIUS, DURY above.

HERBERT OF CHERBURY, LORD. *The Autobiography of Edward, Lord Herbert of Cherbury.* With introduction, etc., by Sidney L. Lee. London, 1886.

HOOLE, C. *A New Discovery of the Old Art of Teaching Schoole*, etc. In Barnard's *English Pedagogy*, 2nd series, 2nd edition. Hartford, Conn., 1876. Also, E. T. Campagnac, editor. Liverpool, 1913.

HOOLE, C. *J. A. Comenii Orbis Sensualium Pictus.* London, 1659 (Hoole's transl.).

HOOLE, C. *An Easy Entrance to the Latin Tongue*...with *a vocabularie of common words*, etc. London, 1649.

A.   18

HOOLE, C. *Propria quae maribus etc. Englished and explayned.* 1650.

HOOLE, C. *The common rudiments of Latine Grammar.* 1659.

HOOLE, C. *Terminationes et Exempla declinationum et conjugationum: in usum grammaticastrorum.* 1650.

HOOLE, C. *Vocabularium parvum Anglo-Latinum,* etc. 1657.

HOOLE, C. *Sentences for Children* (Culman's work translated by Hoole). 1658.

HOOLE, C. *P. Terentii comoediae VI Anglo-Latinae.* 1676.

HOOLE, C. *M. Corderius's school-colloquies.* 1657.

HOOLE, C. *Catonis disticha de moribus,* etc. 1659.

J. D. [Wm Prynne?]. *The Time Serving Proteus and Ambidexter Divine.* 1650. (Dury is meant: the *Unchanged Constant,* etc. above is by way of reply.)

KEATINGE, M. W. *The Great Didactic.* London, 1896 (but the citations from the *Didactica Magna* in the text are direct translations from the Amsterdam folio).

KRAUSE, G. *Wolfgang Ratichius...im Lichte seiner und der Zeitgenossen Briefe,* u.s.w. Leipzig, 1872.

KVAČSALA, J. *J. A. Comenius, sein Leben und seine Schriften.* Three parts. Vienna, 1892.

LAURIE, S. S. *John Amos Comenius,* etc. Cambridge, 1887.

LEACH, A. F. *English Schools at the Reformation,* 1546–8. London, 1896.

LOCKE, J. *Some Thoughts concerning Education* in *John Locke's Educational Writings,* ed. J. W. Adamson. London, 1912.

MASSON, D. *The Life of John Milton,* etc. 6 vols. Vol. III. 1873.

MILTON, JOHN. *Of Education.* Mr Oscar Browning's reprint. Cambridge, 1895.

MONTAIGNE, M. DE. *Essais.* Edited by J. V. Leclerc. Paris, 1836? 2 vols.

MONTMORENCY, J. E. G. DE. *State Intervention in English Education.* Cambridge, 1902.

PAULSEN, F. *Geschichte des Gelehrten Unterrichts auf den Deutschen Schulen u. Universitäten,* etc. Leipzig, 1896. 2 vols.

W. P. [Wm Petty]. *The Advice of W. P. to Mr S. Hartlib for the advancement of some particular parts of learning.* London, 1648.

QUICK, R. H. *Essays on Educational Reformers.* London, 1890.

RAUMER, K. VON. *Geschichte der Pädagogik.* 4 vols. Gütersloh, 1877.

RICHTER, KARL. *A. H. Francke, Schriften über Erziehung und Unterricht.* Leipzig, 1872.

SPERBER, E. Pädagogische *Lesestücke* aus den wichtigsten Schriften der pädagogischen Classiker. 4 parts. Gütersloh, 1877–9.

Part I contains the text of Ratke's *Memorial* and its *Elucidation*, Ratke's contribution to the *Methodus nova quadruplex M. Joh. Rhenii, N. Frischlini, Ratichii*, etc., and a statement for Prince Ludwig of the basal principles of Ratke's *Didactica*.

The foregoing are reprints from Niemeyer's *Osterprogramm*, Halle, 1842. Part I also contains Duke Ernest's *Schulmethodus* of 1648, reprinted from Vormbaum, *Evangelical School Regulations*, 1860, etc.

VAUGHAN, ROBERT. *The Protectorate of Oliver Cromwell.* 1838.

WILLIS, R. *A Sermon Preach'd in the Parish Church of St Andrews, Holborn*, etc., by Richard Willis, D.D., Dean of Lincoln. London, 1704. (Full title, p. 206 above.)

Appended is the first of the Annual *Accounts of Charity Schools*, etc. See *An Account*, etc., above.

INDEX.

For EU product safety concerns, contact us at Calle de José Abascal, 56-1°,
28003 Madrid, Spain or eugpsr@cambridge.org.

www.ingramcontent.com/pod-product-compliance
Ingram Content Group UK Ltd.
Pitfield, Milton Keynes, MK11 3LW, UK
UKHW040615240426
470322UK00010B/137